PRAISE FOR

DIARY OF A ROPE SLUT

"I could laud Emily Bingham for her bravery, her wisdom, for choosing herself and her passions no matter the cost. I could try to explain to a mainstream audience how the ropes that bind her are really setting her free. But your time would be better spent lingering over Bingham's own telling, from the ecstasy to the pain, from her mastery of the erotic to the naked honesty that she never shies away from. *Diary of a Rope Slut* breaks all the rules and all the hearts. An original, shameless memoir."

—MO DAVIAU, author of *Every Anxious Wave*

"*Diary of a Rope Slut* is an erotically charged, vulnerable, tangled quest into bondage. Emily Bingham delivers her personal journey into finding her submission, unflinchingly. Illustrating her most earnest beginnings, she humbly reveals her affinity for rope play through an incredible array of intimate, glamorous, and sometimes frightening adventures. An impressive memoir of self-discovery that leaves nothing out. From loves found and lost to dangerously learning the ins and outs of kink-safety and trust, readers will find this a descriptive, intoxicating reflection on sexual curiosity, personal strength, and genuine desire."

—ROSE CARAWAY, writer and host of *The Kiss Me Quick's & The Sexy Librarian* podcasts

Find more by Emily Bingham in these anthologies:

Tonight, She's Yours: Cuckold Fantasies
Dirty Dates: Erotic Fantasies for Couples
Bondage Bites: 69 Super-Short Stories of Love, Lust, and BDSM
Best Bondage Erotica 2015
The Sexy Librarian's Big Book of Erotica
Best Bondage Erotica 2014
Serving Him: Sexy Stories of Submission
Best Bondage Erotica 2011

www.emilyerotica.com

DIARY OF A ROPE SLUT

AN EROTIC MEMOIR

EMILY BINGHAM

Diary of a Rope Slut: An Erotic Memoir
Copyright © 2016 Emily Bingham

All rights reserved. No part of this book may be used or reproduced in any manner whatsoever without permission from the author except in the case of brief quotations in critical articles and reviews.

ISBN-13: 978-0-9973199-0-3
eISBN: 978-0-9973199-1-0

Disclaimer: All stories contained within this book are true as remembered by the author, with the understanding that memory is a fickle mistress and the other parties involved may recall the same events differently. Details have been changed to protect the innocent and guilty alike. Any similarity to persons living or dead are entirely possible, but a lady never names names.

Cover photo © 2009 by JSV Photography
Cover and interior design by HardestWalk
Editing by Susan DeFreitas

To Shebbah, Cleo, and Bailey:
a girl's best friends

If you bring forth what is within you, what you bring forth will save you. If you do not bring forth what is within you, what you do not bring forth will destroy you.
—GNOSTIC GOSPEL OF THOMAS

There's nothing that doesn't happen for a reason; that I endured this really traumatic moment in my life and in doing so got to save someone else's. And I wouldn't change a single thing . . . that's worth it.
—LEE HARRINGTON

CONTENTS

Foreword by Shay Tiziano xi

1 The First 1
2 The Threesome 10
3 The Partner in Crime 19
4 The Tangled Mess 28
5 The Wet Spot 38
6 The Professional 45
7 The Spiritual Enlightenment 58
8 The Game Changer 65
9 The Show Me the Ropes 81
10 The Long Good-Bye 90
11 The Kitten, the Switch & the Vacuum Bed 98
12 The Chair 107
13 The Waterfall 115
14 The Rogue with the Ropes 124
15 The Damsel in Distress 130
16 The Housedress 137
17 The Butterfly 144
18 The Man and His Mustang 152

19	The Guerilla Shoot	160
20	The Unexpected	165
21	The Fuck(ing with Food) Buddy	169
22	The Energy versus Experience	173
23	The Human Mobile	178
24	The Sound and the Flurry	188
25	The Buddha on the Road	195
26	The One That Got Away	202
27	The Disgrace	207
28	The Dive	223
29	The Carrying On	227
30	The Bridge Fetish	232

Epilogue 235
Acknowledgments 239
About the Author 240

FOREWORD

We often grant an almost mythical importance to "firsts." First date, first kiss, first prom, first sexual encounter—and, of course, our first time getting tied up! As I've traveled around the world teaching about kink and bondage, a lot of people have told me about their first time playing with rope. One person, as a kindergartener, copied the action they saw in *Batman & Robin*. Another, as a gangly teenager, restrained their girlfriend to the bed spread eagle the first time they had sex. Another tied up their own cock and balls with shoelaces while they masturbated.

Many of these people talk about discovering the kink community and feeling relief and a sense of belonging. They describe the epiphany of realizing that bondage isn't just something they made up, that there's a whole community of people doing it, teaching it, loving it. That there's a word for this thing that's so a part of their psyche that they thought perhaps they'd invented it. I find that people join the kink community for the same reasons they might join a knitting circle, spin class, or even a church club—we are by nature social creatures, and we crave the sense of camaraderie and sharing that comes with a group based on shared interests.

While first times often stand out indelibly in our memory, they don't define us or dictate the path we will follow. With regards to my own journey in rope, I actually don't remember my first time getting tied up. I played lots of bedroom dominance games—getting physically held down or ordered to stay still were more my speed. There may have been rope involved, once or twice? There certainly were leather cuffs once my partner Stefanos and I started going out into the kink community, but they were mostly decorative, almost just there to check the boxes: Okay, now we are doing an official kink scene. You are wearing a collar—check. We have various leather impact-play implements—check. We have negotiated and established a safeword—check. We restrain you to the cross with leather cuffs—check. *Looking around* Are we doing this right?

What I *do* remember vividly is my first bondage class. I came into the kink community in the early 2000s in Minnesota, and there wasn't much by way of formal education—you were mentored, and you learned from making mistakes (at least Stefanos and I did). We gathered to play and socialize in our friend's basement, and there were four "rules": 1) Here is a mop, 2) Here is a bucket, 3) Here is a shovel, 4) Clean up after yourself.

In 2005, Stefanos and I, hungry for more structured education, traipsed off to a big bondage conference called Shibaricon—just a puddle jump down to Chicago. The first kink class we ever attended was a packed "Bondage 101" taught by Lee Harrington. To this day, when we teach our Remedial Ropes classes, we tell a story from that session (about an unhelpful person sitting near us and how *not* to facilitate learning for newbies). I still have Lee's handout. I think it says something about me that I distinctly remember my first bondage class, but any first times being tied up are a messy blur.

I always love talking to people about their first times in bondage, and I loved reading the formative bondage experiences described in vivid, sometimes sexy, sometimes awkward detail in this book. The childhood experiences, the first relationship with someone who was basically a living display of how bad the author was feeling about herself at the time (I had one of those too), then getting more "properly" (or at least formally) restrained . . . memorable firsts, all of them.

Some firsts are not positive, and I hear those stories too. People tell me about the first time someone didn't listen to their safeword. The first time they got done with a scene and realized it had gone way too far. The time they were injured in rope. Even, tragically, the time they were raped.

This book has those as well, which is part of what sets it apart. We get to see the good, the awkward . . . and the very, *very* bad. That's the real story of being a kinky pervert getting yer rocks off—there are the highs and the hotness, but not without risk and some brutal nadirs.

This is especially true when you consider the broader kink community—finding your way into the local kink groups can feel magical, as there is a natural sense of kinship with these other sexual "outsiders," a sense of freedom and safety that comes from loosening the grip of stigma when we are surrounded by people with whom we feel we can share our deepest desires. However, the kink community is just made up of people, fallible people, who can have the same problems and dysfunctional dynamics as anyone, anywhere. Those flaws are amplified by the amount of trust and power that's implicit in the intimacy of kink and bondage.

The stories I hear in my travels are echoed in the story in the later part of this book, where trauma is heaped on top of trauma as the kink community closes ranks and refuses to believe that there is an abuser in their midst, refuses to address the problem, and silences victims in ways both active and passive. I hope we as a community are getting better at being advocates and creating safer spaces. When I started hosting kink events, I had no understanding that "not taking a side" (a very tempting philosophy, and one I know the author faced when she went public about what happened to her) *was* taking a side—the side of those who abuse and rape and hide behind a manufactured veneer of plausible deniability. The community is much more interconnected than many realize when they first set foot in a local "munch" (a social gathering of kinky people, usually in a restaurant). Though Bingham and I live states apart and have never met, her story reverberated throughout the kink scene and was talked about in my local groups. Her story was an important community "first" and represented a turning point in how safety, consent, and responsibility were viewed in the broader kink scene. Projects like *Diary of a Rope Slut* add to that voice and visibility in a crucial way, hauling the skeletons out of the closet while also embracing the sexy and the fun of "why we do what we do."

First times, however memorable, do not dictate where our explorations will take us. Some first times are fond stories often retold, some should be resigned to the dustbin of forgotten moments, and some may need to be overcome, but *none* should fully define us. We know we are still exploring and stretching ourselves when we are still making mistakes and occasionally falling flat on our faces (hopefully not literally, in the case of bondage), and that's a *good* thing. It means we are not stagnant.

I have three basic criteria when deciding whether I'm on board with trying a given "first" (these are borrowed/modified from my friend Sophia Sky): 1) Is it safe? 2) Is it fun? and 3) Will it make my abs look good? Think about your own intentions. What type of bondage scene do you want to do? How do you want to feel? What makes you hot, or doesn't? What is too unsafe for you, and what risks are you willing to accept? Ask your own questions and develop your own criteria—*Diary of a Rope Slut* can help you do it! I am grateful to this book for providing a window into many bondage firsts and the path that was carved from there, and I look forward to hearing more stories as I continue my own journey through the kink community.

Shay Tiziano
San Francisco, USA
July 2015

DIARY OF A ROPE SLUT

CHAPTER 1
THE FIRST

The first person to really tie me up was a married man I met online.

I was eighteen years old and the Internet was still a novelty. The shy and socially awkward people of the world rejoiced, being able to connect without leaving home or talking face to face with strangers. This was long before OkCupid or the plethora of similar dating sites existed, so in order to hook up with other introverts, I cruised around various chat rooms and message boards looking for someone of interest.

Recently I'd lost my virginity to a nerdy thirty-five-year-old virgin I'd met in perhaps the least erotic locale: a backgammon chat room. In order to meet face to face one weekend, he drove to the small farm town where I grew up.

As a distinctly unpopular kid in high school, in a touch-phobic family, I'd yet to date or otherwise experience physical closeness with another person, so I didn't feel in a position to be particularly picky. I decided to give myself to this man, who turned out to be pale and doughy, with an uneven haircut. The experience lasted all of ten seconds and concluded with him grunting out a climax and rolling over to snore.

It wasn't moral reasoning that had caused me to hold out on sexual exploration; rather, I was waiting for someone to show interest who wasn't from the insular country-music-and-Holstein-cow community I grew up in. Yet a disappointed lacuna nagged at me while watching Mr. Back Gammon sleep on the paper-towel-textured sheets in the musty smell of the room I'd paid for.

His two-thrust contribution to the event couldn't have been less satisfying, especially considering how deeply I'd been looking forward to plunging into the world of sex. I refused to believe this lonely and less than pleasurable first time was all there was to it. There had to be more—not with this man, but somewhere.

So while dating Mr. Back Gammon long-distance, I had been chatting up an older fellow who was himself enduring an equally dull sexual relationship. He was the sort of guy who was charming in a way only someone cheating on his pregnant wife could be. At the time, I didn't care about anything other than the thrill of the conversation and the possibility of hooking up with him, especially when he asked the revolutionary-to-me question, "What have you always wanted to try?"

I had never been asked about my longings, so I didn't know what to ask for, only that in my rare opportunities for masturbatory privacy, my mind wandered toward images of bondage, always involving rope. I had been asking friends to tie me up with jump ropes on the playground since I was four years old, so the idea was obviously deep in my psyche. However, I wasn't sure where the seed of that desire originated. It wasn't an activity depicted in what little porn I had access to, in the stash my father hid under his bed, so I didn't know it was an activity that anyone else in the world enjoyed. I thought I was the only one. And yet, emboldened by the notion that Married Guy and I would never meet, I responded with, "I've always wanted to be tied up."

"Cool," was his response before moving on to other topics, leading me to believe he wasn't interested. My face felt hot with the shame of confessing something so raw, only to have it ignored. Luckily, he was a state away, so he didn't see my disappointment, which did not stop me from flirting or having cybersex with him every night.

"Where's your hand?"

"What are you wearing?"

"Tell me how you'd suck my cock."

He was the director in these fantasies. I simply played along, responding to his questions, hoping that my limited knowledge would nonetheless manage a pleasing response.

Then one evening, a month into our online interaction, he

declared that he would be driving through my town on business. It would be the perfect opportunity to meet and take care of my fantasy. He described what he had in mind in vivid detail, making it clear that not only had he been listening when I'd talked about rope, he was interested in exploring it himself.

I gave him my phone number, still positive he wouldn't follow through. He had a life; there didn't seem to be a reason for him to make time to call, let alone meet. I couldn't imagine what I had to offer.

When the phone rang and he said his name, it wasn't until he repeated himself, adding "from the Internet" as a kenning, that I realized what was happening. I was so shocked that his words sounded like another language. It wasn't until the hum of his voice on the line paused that I realized he'd asked a question.

"Are you ready?"

"Yes?" I tried, not knowing what I was agreeing to and too nervous to ask him to repeat himself.

Married Guy recited cryptic instructions. It took me a moment to realize these were directions to his hotel. He was attempting to add to the mystery by not directly stating where he was staying, instead creating a treasure hunt that would end with me getting tied up by a total stranger.

At the time, I lived with my parents while going to community college and saving money (with the intention of getting away to a better school and a bigger city as soon as possible). So I hid in the laundry alcove of their house, trying to stretch the phone cord far enough that they wouldn't hear this stilted conversation. My hand was shaking with so much nervous energy I could barely write down the directions, let alone casually leave the house, so my mother looked at me like I was crazy as I left to meet "a friend."

I felt like I was watching myself from afar as I got into my car and drove across town, taking the back roads he'd noted in his instructions. I had a vague idea where his hotel was because it was impossible not to in such a small town, yet as his directions led me in circles, I became less sure this was a good idea. I wondered whether he was really in town, if these directions actually led anywhere, or if perhaps he was luring me down a particularly dark road for nefarious purposes.

I laughed when I finally pulled into the parking lot. This wasn't one of the fleabag motels that lined the highway for truckers or afternoon trysts; he was staying at the hotel where only a few months earlier I had attended my senior prom. The juxtaposition was amusing. Somehow, knowing he had rented a nice room made it even more difficult to think about opening my car door. The reality of meeting him terrified me as I sat there, nearly hyperventilating.

In my few other sexual interactions, though I never directed the action, I'd felt like I was the one in control. I decided how far we went, where those partners would touch me, or if we would see one another again. Here, I was asking to have that control taken away. Anything could happen in that room, and I wasn't sure I was ready.

Just before I could talk myself into driving away, an average-looking but attractive man wearing a baseball hat waved at me from the back entrance of the hotel. I guessed he had to be Married Guy, but I couldn't be sure because I'd never seen a picture of him.

All I knew was his first name, that he had a grown-up job, and that he was unhappily married to a wife who'd recently confessed to her own indiscretions. They were staying together for the kid, but he was perhaps understandably eager to explore infidelity himself, as if fooling around with me would make them even. At the time, I didn't know any better than to help him with those urges. I wasn't there to judge, especially not the first person game for partaking in my taboo fantasies.

I turned off my car, stepped into the winter chill, and walked slowly toward the person holding the door open, hoping it was Married Guy. He looked around nervously as I neared him. Then, saying my name as a question, he took my arm to pull me inside. The hotel was sauna-warm, but I felt cold to my core with uncertainty, unable to move any farther forward, or speak.

Holding my hand, he directed me down the long, echoing, and extravagantly carpeted hallway to his room. When he closed the heavy door behind us and latched it, he seemed equally nervous, standing with his back against the door while watching me watch him, not knowing what to do with myself in his room. Finally, we settled on the edge of the bed, shoulder to shoulder and silent. The oddness of the situation taken into consideration, it was surprising how comfortable I felt with him. Married Guy's body close to mine felt pleasant and erotically charged rather than like something I was merely enduring.

Now that our words were no longer on a computer screen, small talk was all we could manage. The conversation didn't matter so much as our proximity to one another, arm to arm, knees drifting closer, looking straight ahead. Social foreplay was a way to kill time, to keep us proper before jumping out of our clothes into what we both knew we were really interested in.

When the lull in conversation became too awkward to ignore, he stood and turned the lights down. Watching him walk toward me, my heart raced, and I gave one final thought to leaving. He loomed, looking down at me for a long moment before leaning in for a kiss, an ardent kiss that was somehow both soft and firm. I wanted to keep kissing him for the rest of the night. I actually liked this guy. This kiss, the shared passion, was everything that was missing from my few other intimate experiences. I could start to see what all the fuss was about.

As we kissed and explored each other, touching without being overtly titillating, I couldn't resist stroking the shiny wedding ring on his finger. The thought of how scandalous our dalliance was kept dancing through my mind: him nearly twenty years older and belonging to someone else. Somehow that made everything more exciting.

It seemed hours later when he got around to undressing me. It wasn't until I took off his shirt that I noticed how slight he was. I felt a bit ungainly, realizing I was twice his weight, and wondered if he would be able to pull off being domineering. When he removed my underwear with one pull, pushed me back on the bed, and told me to stay, it occurred to me that being imposing had more to do with intention than muscle. The look he gave me over his shoulder as he searched through his luggage convinced me to lie still. I waited, naked, goose bumped, and uneasy.

Slowly he unwrapped a coil of cheap, beige clothesline, the only thing he had been able to find that was remotely ropelike in the small-town Walmart. I didn't mind; he was going to tie me up, and that was the important part. But the line seemed to go on forever—it was long and oddly coiled, making it a struggle for him to work with. I simply watched and anticipated, but as the minutes stretched on, I felt strange, lying there motionless. The nervousness returned, and I fidgeted, sensing the same frustration in his body language.

Halfway through the struggle to unwrap the clothesline, he resigned himself to the situation and approached the bed with the tangled mess. He took my right wrist and created a messy loop around it, then attached it to the headboard. Pulling more clothesline free, grunting and tugging at the ball of knots whenever he needed more, he repeated the process on my other wrist, then got to work on my ankles, tying them spread eagle. Not having any scissors to cut the single long piece of rope made this not very elegant or efficient, but it turned out serviceable enough.

Wiggling, I tested my bindings as he stepped back and watched, seeming unsure what to do next. I certainly had no idea—this was as far as my fantasies ever progressed. I was exceedingly curious to see what else he had in mind.

The next thing out of his bag was a white pillar candle. He lit it and crawled onto the bed, straddling my chest, still wearing jeans and a heavy leather belt that rubbed against my skin as he moved above me. After some playful menacing, he slid onto my belly, where he sat and carefully dripped wax onto my chest. It was warm, but I was surprised at how little it hurt.

"Don't worry. I won't leave any marks."

Wide eyed and watching me carefully, he behaved as if he were doing something highly scandalous and painful. When I didn't respond with the expected gasp or moan, he looked deflated, so I played along, squirming and moaning when he poured another bit of wax near my nipple. I smiled and went along with him having his fun; it didn't appeal to me, but he seemed to be enjoying himself.

So far, being tied up was both better than I had expected and somehow disappointing. It wasn't the magical, transformative experience that lived in my head. Then again, realized dreams rarely are. Mostly, I felt ill at ease at the newness of it all. But it was finally happening, and with an attractive man! So I focused on the feel of Married Guy straddling me and the rope biting into my limbs, which created a delightful sense of helplessness as he gazed at me.

Somewhere along the way, one of my hands came untied, but I pretended to be securely bound, not wanting to ruin the moment or make him self-conscious about his bondage skills. After all, it was his first time too. He could have done anything he wanted that night, as long as I was bound while it happened. Though we had talked about doing more, he seemed content to sit back watching me struggle, occasionally touching me in sensual but not overtly sexual ways.

When he began to clean the dried wax from my body, it became obvious he was preparing to untie me. I was a little disheartened at how nearly uneventful the evening had been; that he, playing the role of a perfect gentleman, hadn't taken advantage of his bound captive. My worry was that he didn't find me attractive enough to have sex with me. But I had no language at the time to communicate this concern, so I watched him unloop the rope, not looking forward to leaving him so soon.

Using a dull wine key, he hacked at the impromptu knots in the clothesline, which had tightened during my wiggling, leaving forlorn lengths of unraveled rope on the floor. He promptly hid them, clearly hoping room service wouldn't discover our impromptu rope. I admired the red stripes on my wrists as he tried to apologize for them.

"Don't worry," I told him. "They'll be a good souvenir."

"You sure?"

"Positive."

He smiled, handing me my discarded clothing, and I understood that he didn't want me to stay any longer. This was confusing and disappointing. I'd assumed the rope would lead to the sex we played out virtually most nights. However, experiencing bondage for the first time had been thrilling in and of itself, so I thanked him for everything and hurried to leave. At his door, we promised to meet again sometime soon, though I suspected I would never hear from him.

I was surprised to get a call the next time he was in town. It was the middle of the day, my parents both at work for several more hours, so we flirted with danger by meeting in my living room. And that was as far as we got before undressing, the spark we'd ignited during our first near-chaste meeting exploding, making it impossible for us to wait any longer to consume one another. This time there was no question we would sleep together. He wasted no time getting me naked and placing his hand between my legs to finger me, another first that I found delightful.

Soon he was on top of me, looking at me curiously as if to ask if he could penetrate me, a question I answered by angling my body until he slipped inside me. We fit nicely, him sliding inside me quickly and effortlessly, holding me close to him while thrusting. Our eyes met during the times when he pulled away to watch me, curious about my pleasure. I didn't know that sex could feel this good or last this long. We tangled limbs, switching positions and wrestling across the expanse of the carpet. I didn't know until then that a talented lover would want me to get something out of the experience, would give me pleasure in return, or kiss me endlessly.

Married Guy illustrated what sex could be like when there was a spark. My time with him opened a new world of desire that made the ten-second-long bouts of sex I'd known until then seem ridiculous. Unfortunately, this was before the word *polyamory* came into my vocabulary, before I knew of a way for us to explore one another without him cheating on his wife, whom I rarely gave a thought to.

I messed around with Married Guy a handful of other times

before he disappeared, never to log on to our chat room again. I continued connecting every night, hoping he would reappear, heartsick with the uncertainty of his departure. Then I moved on, distracted by a new body, laughing at myself for thinking Married Guy would become a more permanent fixture in my life.

During that winter we spent keeping each other warm, we never played with power or rope again. He was much more interested in regular, old-fashioned sex—the uncomplicated sex he couldn't get at home. And it was spectacular, each time more powerful than the last. Yet there was always part of me waiting for more rope, unable to ask.

I mistakenly conflated his lack of interest in bondage with my having done something wrong. So I reverted back to thinking of it as a thing to hide. It would be another five years, in another life and another city, before I would get a chance to be bound again.

CHAPTER 2

THE THREESOME

The summer after finishing college, I flailed around, hoping to discover my path in life. I spent my nights sleeping with anyone who offered and my days tutoring inner-city kids at a Christian community center in Milwaukee, where I'd moved, far from my parents and my hometown. To take the edge off the tedium of this unfulfilling double life, I wrote angsty poetry and drank a lot of cheap red wine.

My last relationship had recently ended, and I wasn't skilled at holding on to friends while I was in the frenzy of a new boy. So I was constantly finding myself alone until the next guy came along. This was one of those times. Aside from my numerous one-night stands, I didn't know anyone in town. So when a nearly forgotten friend from a poetry workshop rang my doorbell, I was especially surprised.

Though we'd critiqued each other's poems twice a week, it had taken a traffic accident for us to finally talk. Slippery streets had caused the bus we were riding to slide into oncoming cars. No one was hurt, but neither of us was in the mood to wait for the next public transportation death trap. We decided to walk together, in snowdrifts that were already shin deep, with more snow coming down. That afternoon ended with us flirting and thawing out over tea while huddled around his radiator, but the heat between us, which we politely ignored, was the thing really warming me.

In addition to being neighbors, we both had live-in, long-term relationships that we were trying to break off. Instead of taking the high road, we acted like cowards and started sleeping together while doing the on-again-off-again, break-up-then-get-back-together thing in our respective relationships. It was confusing and sexy because it was emotionally fraught. We were in our twenties and in a liberal arts program; the questionable sexual relationship was practically part of the required extracurricular experience. That winter, I seemed to have either a cock or a pen in my hand at all times. It felt a lot like the sort of thing that happened in the messed-up foreign films the Poet and I watched together.

He became my first muse and my first fuck buddy. Our bodies seemed ideal for each other, and we couldn't stop entangling them every chance we got. The Poet was tall and lanky, with long, unkempt hair, but he felt right, even though his scruffy, unshowered demeanor and blasé attitude was far from what I tended to find attractive.

Since we were pretending to be cavalier and bohemian—and we both needed somewhere to live after officially breaking up with our significant others—we became roommates. He had a friend who was a fellow writer and also needed a place to live. The three of us ended up sharing the bottom of a drafty old Victorian house that fit our starving-artist lifestyle perfectly. The Poet promptly proceeded to get back together with his girlfriend, even as he continued to crawl into my bed at night.

So much for easy and painless.

Soon we stopped fucking—and eventually even talking—during the six very tense months remaining on our lease. Once we weren't under the same roof, I assumed we'd never speak again. Eventually, I heard he'd gone away to Europe without saying good-bye. I started writing even more and fucking around with increasingly shady characters.

The man who showed up at my door over a year later was not the boy who had gone away on a whirlwind tour of all things Joyce, Beckett, and Yeats. This was a new, mature version, which I barely recognized. He had cut his long hair, wore sharp clothes, and had filled out from eating something other than brown rice and lentils. The anger and frustration of our earlier interactions melted away. I rushed to hug him, and the spark between us immediately reopened our sordid and strange relationship.

We began spending a lot of time in bed, cooking meals naked together, taking wandering walks, going on real dates, and perusing bookstores. We took up smoking clove cigarettes to make up for the fact that much of the time we couldn't afford to eat. We would light and share one after sex, the smoke curling around the second-hand-store furniture of our respective apartments, and the smell clung to us much later. This added to the cliché of the poor artist that was important to us then.

One day I noticed he had rope handcuffs hitched to his bed and I gave him a hard time about them. The Poet explained them away as being for the new girl he was seeing. We weren't exclusive, so hearing about her wasn't a problem, but I tried not to act too intrigued, or to give away a mutual interest in rope. Since the Married Guy, the few people I'd asked to play that game with me had laughed it off or shamed me for desiring such things. It was going well with the Poet this time around, so I was afraid to make things weird by opening up about my interest in bondage.

A few weeks later, he invited me to a gallery opening hosted by the artist community he lived in, where I would finally meet his lady friend. This seemed risky, but I was so eager to spend time with him that I agreed, even as I noted his smug grin while showing me her picture.

She was a curvy, retro-bespectacled, pink-haired femme fatale who had done a little porn of the Suicide Girls variety. Calling herself a slut in an empowering way while making no secret of her many lovers, she seemed dangerously appealing. She was the kind of woman I'd dreamed about sleeping with ever since I'd discovered my same-sex desires during Girl Scouts sleepovers, back when I was more interested in kissing the girl in the sleeping bag next to mine than discussing the boys they had crushes on. I'd slept with a number of women in college, but none of them had really appealed to me; they'd just been pleasant experiments.

The three of us met at the center of the college neighborhood we all lived in, plotting our evening. Nervous energy made it impossible to be decisive, so we headed in the direction of the arts district, dressed in our finest: the Poet in a brown corduroy blazer that was inexplicably appealing on him, the Pink-Haired Girl and I in scandalously short dresses and bare legs.

I was wearing a black faux-fur-lined coat with a nipped-in waist that added a dramatic hourglass shape to my then boyish frame. It had become my armor, making me feel sexy and untouchable, though it and my knee-high, four-inch heels weren't anywhere near warm enough for a Wisconsin winter and, as a newly reformed tomboy, I could barely walk in feminine shoes under the best of conditions.

With me as the middle puzzle piece, we walked somewhere to drink. Using my lack of balance as an excuse, I linked arms with the two of them, forcing the notion of a shared intimacy into reality. As the odd woman out, the fuck buddy to her status as girlfriend, I basked in their attention, unsure where the evening would lead but excited to find out. We were young, sexually adventurous, and clearly hitting it off, so anything felt possible.

As they bantered across me, part of me wanted to be jealous of their obvious chemistry, but I was more focused on flirting with them both. The excitement and lust was still there with the Poet, amplified by this new addition. My hand drifted to her ass as we wandered, and the Pink-Haired Girl didn't correct me. Instead, she boldly kissed the side of my face, wiping the red kiss mark off my cheek like a movie siren. My heart did flips.

Giggling and half frozen, we fell into the first appealing restaurant. All we could afford at this French-inspired bistro on the waterfront was one cocktail each, but it was worth the price for the ambiance of dim candlelight and hardwood floors. It was all part of the seduction.

Afterward, emboldened by alcohol, we smoked cigarettes, chain lighting them off of one another's flame in a cancerous kiss that brought our faces close enough to make us smirk. Pink-Haired Girl and I walked with the Poet between us now, a flirtatious posse. It felt arty and Parisian, like for the first time I was having an evening more exciting than the fictions I created in my notebooks.

We dropped into galleries that teemed with well-dressed artists and their friends just long enough to look at a painting, drink tiny plastic glasses of free box wine, and thaw out. When the tide of the room pushed us toward the door, we would hurry back into our coats and stumble to a new art show, where we repeated the process until the wine got scarce, the people aggressive with drink, and the sexual tension so thick it was a fourth presence between us.

Wordlessly, a decision was made, and the Poet guided us toward the artist community where he lived, arms around us both, the closeness more important than the ease of walking. We were silent, the wordplay put on hold as we focused on what came next: navigating from his lobby—where we were all sure to know a handful of people who would want to make small talk—to his bed.

We stepped inside the building and were instantly pulled into the swaying pulse of a crowd of bohemian artists and writers. The gallery-night after-party was loud enough that the door, the floor, and my chest all pounded to the music. The sexy haze of the evening had been replaced by social awkwardness; we were back to the tease, the anticipation, as I watched both of them carry on conversations across the room with the same look in their eyes—searching for the nearest exit, pleading with the universe for an escape. Finally we were in the elevator to the Poet's tiny loft, bringing with us a handful of people lured by the promise of wine and weed. I longed for quiet, and for fewer strange bodies.

There was another bottle of wine in his loft, where we lounged on the dirty floor and couch to drink, smoke, and talk about literature. I was pinned to the spot, riveted by too much wine, until Pink-Haired Girl grasped my hands across the circle of people and pulled me into the bathroom.

My heart was beating so fast that all I could hear was the blood pounding in my head as she closed the door. She forced me against it, pressing her mouth to mine. Her lips tasted like expensive lipstick and cheap wine. Her hands and lips were all over me before I could get my addled brain to catch up. The excitement of her had me just as dizzy as the alcohol.

A pretty girl wanted me! She had her hands under my dress, grasping for flesh, her expert tongue dancing against mine. All I could do was hold up my end of the kiss and reach for her shapely hips. Until this moment, things this hot had only happened in my head. My other intimacies with women had been timid and mechanical. This was entirely different: sexy and requited. I forgot that anything else existed.

We made out in the dark bathroom with the mumble of the party in the background until someone knocked on the door, shocking us out of the moment. Giggling, we rejoined the party with mussed hair and smeared lipstick. It was obvious to everyone what had occurred, which led to teasing and an insistence on details. Pink-Haired Girl demurred, "A lady never tells."

Soon a potent combination of lust and drunkenness emboldened me to act completely unlike myself. I could banter about Calvino and Ferlinghetti anytime, but I would be a fool to let this moment with this girl get away. In full view of everyone, I pulled her onto the Poet's bed and straddled her waist. We became the center of attention as I relieved her of her shirt, allowing her abundant breasts to tumble free and fill my palms. I fondled her chest, licking her exposed skin and kissing her with abandon. We barely noticed the Poet shooing everyone out, lighting candles, and joining us on the bed.

At first he only watched, touching us encouragingly, as we undressed one another in a frenzy that led to exploring every inch of newly exposed skin. But he could only be polite for so long, and soon we were a mess of flesh, hands exploring two different bodies at once. I never knew whose hand or mouth was where, gladly enjoying whatever body part found its way between my lips. Cock, cunt, tit, finger, it didn't matter. It was a dizzying array of pleasure I'd never experienced before.

When the two of them pulled away from me to kiss, I thought the too-good-to-be-true moment had ended and they would ask the third wheel to leave. Instead, Pink-Haired Girl beckoned me to the middle of the bed and slipped my hands into the rope cuffs still secured to the headboard. She smiled and nodded at the Poet.

"That's what you want isn't it, Em? What you've always wanted?" Nodding shyly, I felt melted through, so turned on I no longer had bones. I was a puddle of lust as I tried to determine how the Poet knew my secret and what would happen next. Two wicked faces beamed at me as I lay waiting.

He dragged me down the bed so that my arms were extended above my head, tightening the knot to prevent my escape. Pink-Haired Girl placed her copious cleavage in my face as the Poet pulled my legs to his chest and entered me. I had little say in the matter, and I enjoyed every second.

As he fucked me, she put her nipples in my mouth, telling me how to treat them. "Harder. You can bite. I promise you won't hurt me." Listening to her advocate for her own pleasure was nearly as shocking as the Poet thrusting into me roughly, forcing my face to bounce against her breasts.

Too quickly for my tastes, I was released, and I rubbed the raw rope marks on my wrists, grinning. We switched roles, and I watched as the Poet fucked Pink-Haired Girl while I kissed her. At dawn we were still playing out variations on this theme on an endless loop. I was so raw from the fucking, and so overwhelmed from pleasure, that I passed out, clinging to the edge of the double bed.

The shaking mattress woke me. I was snuggled into Pink-Haired Girl's chest as she and the Poet went at it again. She eventually pushed him away and hurried into the bathroom to lock herself in to sleep in the bathtub, safe from the insatiable Poet. I drifted in and out of consciousness as he continued the endless sexual barrage. It was both arousing and annoying to be used so thoroughly. Mostly I wondered how he had the energy to keep it up so long.

Feeling as if I had only closed my eyes a moment before, I woke to the bright sunlight with the Poet sprawled over me. This made it difficult to sneak out. If only I could gather my clothes from the impressive pile on the floor—I'd hoped to get away for some uninterrupted sleep in my own bed. But just as I was locating my boots, the Poet woke to pull me back in. Before breakfast, he wanted me again, finally coming in a sticky puddle on my stomach.

He lured Pink-Haired Girl out of the bathtub while I cleaned off. Breakfast was grassy tea, strawberries cut with the same unwashed knife as last night's brie and garlic, and French toast smothered in a goopy white cream that too strongly resembled semen to be edible. So I smoked my hunger away, telling myself that things were more glamorous under the lens of darkness, drunkenness, and lust than in the bright morning's hangover.

Having traded the rest of my cloves for bus fare home, I did the walk of shame in my short black dress and heels, getting a lot of attention on the ride to my apartment. On the bus, I pulled up the sleeves of my jacket to look at the red rings burned into my wrists from the cheap plastic rope on the Poet's bed. I fingered the marks to comfort myself amid the leering eyes of the other passengers while replaying the evening in my head.

In the months that followed, Pink-Haired Girl and the Poet continued dating, while she and I became friends. I occasionally slept with the Poet, but the three of us never again shared a room, let alone a bed. It was almost as if that drunken evening had never happened—none of us mentioned it. One day during our strange friendship, Pink-Haired Girl said, almost under her breath, "I think I'm going to tell the Poet that I'm pregnant."

"Are you?" I asked, to be polite and keep up with the story; there was always something dramatic going on in her life. It was hard to keep track of it all. I didn't really want to know, and I definitely didn't want it to be true.

Smiling, she changed the subject. She had a way of steering conversations toward exactly what she wanted to discuss—almost always herself—and far away from everything else, doing it so well I didn't even know I was being manipulated.

Later that week, the Poet and I lay in bed together. I waited for him to mention the words *baby* or *pregnant*, but he didn't. Soon he stopped mentioning Pink-Haired Girl altogether.

"How's it going with her?" I asked, not having heard from her, or heard her name on his lips, in ages.

"Not great. Let's not talk about it."

Instead, we got naked. Sex was the great distraction.

But as if Pink-Haired Girl telepathically knew the Poet had been in my bed, she called the next afternoon with a sob story about needing a new place to live. I offered her the couch for a few nights, an offer she somehow upgraded to sharing my bed, getting me to agree without realizing it.

Cuddling became kissing became groping became her between my legs. With no audience and no one to impress, there was no passion—her tongue was lackluster. I couldn't even pretend excitement, let alone reciprocate. Above all, I was cold and tired, so I rolled onto my side to sleep under the blankets, only to have her sigh all night long, assuring my lack of rest.

She was done with me after that evening. About then I learned that the Pink-Haired Girl was charming when she wanted to be, but when a person no longer served her purpose, she disappeared, an act she played on both the Poet and me, moving without letting us know or answering our calls. The real shame was the divide she created between the Poet and me before leaving town. It wasn't enough to break our hearts and disappear; she had to make sure to sow seeds of distrust between us so we could no longer be friends, let alone intimate.

For a long time, all I had was memories of that one perfect night, and I assumed I would never hear from either of them. Until the Poet appeared at my door again, this time after an absence of ten years. Again we started right where we'd left off, laughing about that night with the distance of many years and new memories between us. Now we keep the flame between us alive in the form of an appropriate, adult passion for words and wine, happily in the same city once again, sharing a connection that doesn't seem likely to end.

CHAPTER 3
THE PARTNER IN CRIME

He said, "Take everything off the coffee table and kneel in front of it. Naked. Don't tell me it's too cold. Light a candle to keep warm. Leave the door unlocked and wait." Before I could quibble, he hung up.

After a long online interaction and a single coffee date, the German and I jumped many steps ahead and leaped into bed, where he'd held me down and violently fucked me, one hand in my hair, the other hurting me in creative ways. The next morning I woke covered in bruises, my entire body sore and purple. I beamed while tracing those bruises, delighted to feel them every time I sat down at work. Since then we'd been meeting whenever possible to explore BDSM, and our encounters had helped me realize that I enjoyed consensual pain almost as much as rope.

This was everything I wanted from a lover: rough sex and bondage in the bedroom contrasted by kindness and an equal partnership outside of it. Also, contrary to what many of the so-called Doms lurking on the Internet thought, sex and kink weren't synonymous. The German understood that bondage didn't equal sex and that beating me didn't mean he'd earned a blow job. It was trust and chemistry that made me eager to sleep with him as well as engage in kinky play.

So I was thrilled to see what sadistic fantasy we'd act out that night. The German's challenging, do-it-or-else tone echoed through my head as I cleaned off the table in my living room. I had the time it would take him to drive to my apartment to talk myself into following his orders. My housemates were gone, but I was unsure of when they'd return.

I unlocked the front door and stood there in my robe, wondering if I could get away with not following this one part of his instructions.

While I waited for him to arrive, I took off the robe, knelt, put it back on, took it off, and repeated this several times. It was difficult to tell whether I was more terrified of getting caught naked by a roommate or the punishment that would result from not following all of the German's orders.

Ultimately, the appeal of allowing myself to be that vulnerable to him won out. So, tossing the robe onto a nearby chair, I got on my knees facing away from the door, breathing meditatively and waiting. As the cold passed between my bare legs, I realized how excited thoughts of him had made me. And yet I couldn't stop thinking—especially when I heard footsteps on the sidewalk leading up to the house—that someone else might come home before he arrived.

The footfalls on the porch got closer and then paused for a moment before the front door opened. Whoever had come in was inches from where I knelt while they locked the door behind them. They dropped something heavy, and I jumped, seconds away from leaping up. Instead, I looked into the lone candle that lit the room, on the table in front of me, reminding myself that I trusted the German and trusted that it was him behind me.

Finished with the door, the person responsible for the footsteps came nearer, standing so close I could hear him breathing and feel his gaze on my naked body. I squeezed my eyes shut, watching the candle flame dance through my eyelids.

I listened to the exhalations of my visitor and heard a rustling that sounded like a coat being removed and then dropped to the floor. The house settled around us, providing no clue about what would happen next, offering only the winter chill that followed my visitor indoors and made me shiver. After what seemed an eternity, he walked closer, and the tension was nearly unbearable as I heard the floor creaking under his footsteps. My heart raced, and I dug my nails into my thighs in an attempt to keep myself still and quiet my anxiety.

When he was close enough that I could feel the cold radiating off him, I realized there was still no way to be positive who had come into my home. I closed my eyes tighter, waiting anxiously. Just before

I was about to go mad from anticipation, this mystery person put his comfortingly warm hands on my shoulders.

I was grateful for the heat of him. The simple touch after the long moments of distance between us held an erotic charge that shot through me. I realized the weight and energy of the hands on my skin were soothing and familiar, which allowed me to relax. He knelt beside me, hands wandering through my hair, and suddenly pulled me against him.

One hand brushed hair away from my ear to expose more of my skin to him. The other went around my neck with a careful pressure bordering on a caress, meant to remind me that I could breathe only because he allowed it. As he increased the pressure on my throat, stealing my next inhalation, I felt his mouth on my ear. His breath tickled across my neck as he waited to speak.

Though his lips were so close I felt them brush against my ear, his accented voice was barely audible over my thumping heart. "Good girl."

My eyes popped open as I heard the phrase that melted me and went straight to my cunt. Only then was I positive that the man was my lover, not a roommate or a lunatic off the street. And yet, knowing whose arms I was in made my heart beat faster with fear. My muscles softened into his touch, breathing him in, the masculine smell of his skin and the hint of his fabric softener. A smell edged by the scent of his own excitement melding with mine.

"You're beautiful like this." His hands released my hair and throat to travel slowly down my arms, darting to my nipples, squeezing them sharply. His fingers twisted and pulled the tender flesh, the pain highlighted by his tenderness a moment earlier. My hands lingered in the air, wanting to defend myself, but the closer my fingers got to his, the harder he pinched.

His lips were against my ear again. "You don't move unless I tell you to." Distracted as I was by pain, it took a moment for his words to register. The delay caused him to squeeze more roughly, tugging my nipples away from my body, stretching them painfully to punctuate his statement.

Against the urging of my body, I placed my hands in my lap and leaned into him. As his fingers continued their work, I grunted and moaned while trying to remain still, a task that felt impossible while unbound and in pain. He laughed at my struggle, twisting my nipples again for further reaction. When he suddenly released me, my nipples were raw and I bit my lip to keep from fighting back verbally. He grabbed my long hair, wrapped it around one hand, and pulled my head backward, almost knocking me off balance.

"Good girl," he said again in my ear, which he drew back to meet his lips. This time there was an edge of sarcasm to his tone. "There's just one problem." My heart skipped, and I ran through his instructions from over the phone, wondering what I could have forgotten. "I said, clean off the table. That means everything, silly girl."

I stared at the candle flickering in front of us as if it had personally wronged me. "I'm sorry . . . I thought . . . " I barely managed the words before he used the hand in my hair to force my face to the table, inches from the offending object.

"Shh, don't argue." He pressed my face into the cold wood with one hand while bringing the candle closer with the other. I saw my future flash before me as each flicker of the flame seemed to mock me, reminding me how much trouble I was in.

"Hands on the table," he said. He reached for something in his bag and, finding it, grabbed my hair again while repeating himself with a firm edge to his voice, emphasized by his harsh German tone, that I didn't dare disregard. "Hands. On. The. Table."

I reluctantly placed them on either side of my head and waited. His torso was pressed against my behind, so I could feel how excited he was already. He grabbed a nipple between each thumb and forefinger, twisting until I cried out, barely able to stop myself from reaching for him. Even through his jeans, I could feel his cock stiffen at my reaction. While I was distracted by pain, he grabbed my hands to guide them into the small of my back, where he used the weight of his body to pin them between us and force me farther onto the table.

My abused chest, pressed against the cold wood, ached under the weight of our bodies.

I could feel the steady rhythm of his breathing as he leaned against me, which made it difficult for me to breathe. I stopped fighting, giving in to exhaustion, though I desperately wanted to sit up and take the pressure off my breasts. He used this momentary acquiescence to place a large, rubber ball gag in my mouth, cinch the leather strap tight, and buckle it shut. My will to resist was deflated, as I became pliable and obedient as soon as he put anything between my lips. His cock, rope, a gag; I'd gladly opened wide and accepted them all.

He pulled my head off of the table to rest my body against him, continuing to trap my arms between us. I could barely see him in my peripheral vision, but I felt the warmth of his breath on my face. He remained still as I longed for him to do something or touch me anywhere. My body was thrumming with desire.

Soon he turned my head to face him and ran his tongue around the edge of my lips where they stretched around the ball in my mouth. It both tickled and sent a chill of humiliation through me. He was illustrating that I no longer had control. I closed my eyes and whimpered. I was desperate to return the kiss, moaning against the gag, wishing I could tangle tongues with him. When he tired of the game, the German rested me against the table again. "Stay," he said, and I did.

When he returned to my side with his bag of tricks, he'd pulled out tangles of rope. Stretching my arms out in front of me, he bound each wrist to one of the sturdy wooden legs of the table. The synthetic rope bit into my skin, pressing my arms into the firm edges of the table leg, just tight enough to discourage me from struggling. Next he ran rope above each knee, forcing them wide apart as he also tied my thighs to the table legs. This put me off center and exposed me thoroughly; I blushed.

He stood and walked in a circle around the table, making me wait. I could feel him appraising me, enjoying the view as I drooled and struggled against the ropes. When he was in my sight, he tormented me further by undoing his pants enough to expose his cock, stroking it several times before returning it to his jeans. He was so hard I could see the outline of him pressing against the fabric. I wanted so badly to touch him, but I could only groan around the gag. He smiled and finished his lap around the room, coming to a stop behind me.

He knelt down to slowly run a hand up my leg, feeling the slick trail that started halfway up my thighs and led to the puddle between them. "Someone is enjoying herself."

What he didn't know was that my pussy had been wet since I'd heard his voice on the phone. This was the sort of scene I'd been longing for since voicing my desires to Married Guy all those years before. The waiting, anticipation, and fear even before my lover arrived had me excited. Once the German actually had his hands on me, I was a lost cause; there was no hiding how much I wanted him to have his way with my body.

His hand traveled higher to finger me roughly, just long enough to make me crazy with lust. He stopped the moment I rocked against his hand, trying to force his digits to hit my sweet spot. The sigh that escaped his lips made it seem as if he was as disappointed as I was that he couldn't continue. "If you could have just followed directions . . ."

Rather than complete the sentence, he grabbed the candle. Holding it above me, he tipped the candle in small increments, maximizing the anticipation, drawing out the moment until the wax fell. The aroma of the hot candle teased as I waited, watching him in my periphery; I still didn't understand the appeal of this game. The first hot drips hit my lower back and behind, causing me to jump, but only out of shock at the heat of the wax in the cold room. Next I heard him riffling through his bag again. I didn't know what to expect, only that it wouldn't be gentle.

The first stroke was always the worst. It landed flush in the middle of my ass, a sharp, stinging *thwap* that let me know he'd hit me with a cane. I struggled against the rope, fully aware this would only result in rope burn but unwilling to admit defeat by remaining still. His wrist arced back for the next swing, and I yelped at the pain. He swung again, this time hitting harder.

I was learning this was both my favorite and the most painful device for him to wield. It delivered the sharp and focused kind of pain that I craved. He was talented at dancing around that border between pleasurable and too intense by alternating between hard and soft strokes. At times he hit me in quick succession until I felt unable to take more, only to switch to soft taps with the tip of the cane, beating me until my ass throbbed and I was dizzy with endorphins.

At the start, all the strokes landed on my ass, where they were severe but pleasant. Eventually he moved on to interspersing these with strikes to my thighs on more sensitive flesh. With my legs forced apart by rope, I couldn't protect myself. He seemed to enjoy these strokes and the noises they elicited most of all. Soon much of the attention he provided with the cane was focused there, on the tender flesh of my inner thighs.

I could no longer calm myself by quietly moaning through the gag and grasping at the table legs to which I was bound. Each stroke of the cane burned through my flesh, and I cried out, attempting to angle away from him. This thrilled him, creating an excuse to beat me harder, punishment for my mumbled dissent. All the while, he mocked me, claiming he'd stop if I would only cease moving. "Oh, I'm not even hitting that hard, just hold still." But we both knew he wouldn't be satisfied until he had his fill.

This went on until he dropped the cane, breathing heavily. As I collected myself, coming down from the beating, I heard his pants drop to the floor, and again I was on edge.

"Poor, silly girl, it must hurt." He tickled his fingers over my sore flesh, soothing the areas that had received the worst of it. "Shh, poor thing," he whispered, comforting me with his words and hands as if he weren't the same person who had doled out the cruelty moments before.

His hands wandered gently over my clammy body, a pleasant contrast to the pain, which softened to a tolerable throb. I was so focused on the discomfort that I didn't notice him slip a hand between my legs until he had two fingers inside me, enjoying how much wetter I was after the pain.

I should have known better than to allow myself to enjoy his touch. Just as I relaxed, he slipped his fingers out and slapped my clit with his palm hard enough to make me jump.

"Sorry, I missed a spot."

He slapped my wet lips several more times for his amusement, hitting the one part of me between the thighs that was not yet in agony. Just when I could almost anticipate the next blow, he slipped his cock inside me, penetrating so deeply that I sighed at the suddenness. He fucked with the same thorough roughness with which he had beaten me. Regardless of how hard he thrust, he couldn't make this unpleasant—I moaned, bucking against him, begging for more.

Pausing, he unbuckled the gag and removed it from my aching jaw. Then, without warning or slowing his pace, he pulled out, and I groaned in disappointment. He made his way in front of me, lifted my head from the table, and pressed his cock against my lips. It tasted like a combination of the two of us; I couldn't get enough, sucking so hard I was nearly choking.

He helped, grabbing my hair in both hands to force himself down my throat, grinning at the gagging noises that preceded me reflexively pulling away to breathe. I choked and drooled as he fucked my mouth, my eyes watering, which made a further mess of my face. When I hadn't had a breath for so long that I was near panicking, he looked at me seriously, holding my head firmly, with his cock deep in my throat, and came.

I swallowed the hot, sticky mess as best I could with him still in my mouth. He pet my head, using his other hand to untie me, managing to keep himself between my lips throughout most of the process, allowing me to lick and savor him. The German untangled me gently and with purpose, unknotting each rope before placing it back in his bag. When he was finished, I lay on the table in a heap and he moved everything down the hall to my bedroom. On his final trip, he blew out the candle, scooped me up in his arms, and carried me to bed.

As he closed the door to join me under the sheets for the next round of debauchery, the front door opened. We listened, wide-eyed, as my drunken roommate talked to himself while stumbling to his room. Once his door closed, we laughed at the perfect timing, knowing if he had come home only a minute earlier, he would have gotten quite the show.

CHAPTER 4
THE TANGLED MESS

Life wouldn't be complete without making the mistake of moving somewhere for a relationship at least once. Especially a relationship that couldn't be more obviously destined to fail. I got this particular undertaking out of the way early on, just after everything in my life in Milwaukee came crashing down.

The drunken sex with a new man every week had quickly led to me using the Internet to meet men to dabble in D/s (Dominance and submission) in unhealthy and dangerous ways, meeting them and jumping right into their handcuffs without a second thought, much less negotiation. At the time, the instant gratification of consensual pain and the thrill of being powerless was worth the favors these near strangers expected in return. I was lucky to have simply met men who were simply sexually manipulative; no one crossed any firm boundaries or was physically dangerous.

The German was the only man I met in this self-destructive period who treated me like an equal. He was my first regular and satisfying experience in giving up control and the only person I was playing these games with in a sane or safe manner. He never asked me to clean his apartment or do his laundry the way the so-called Dominants I'd known previous to him had.

He and I got ourselves into some epically twisted adventures. We scared my roommates with our spanking games and my muffled cries. We had long, lingering dinners out in restaurants while he had various vibrators locked inside me. Once he kidnapped me, leaving me wrapped in duct tape and a blindfold in his front seat during the two-hour-long drive to his house, a city away. And there was no way to describe the intense pleasure of being yelled at in incomprehensible German while bound and being beaten in a strange, cold basement.

What we couldn't manage in the years we had known one another was to live in the same city at the same time. The distance combined with my inability to communicate what I wanted from him meant that we were never more than occasional play partners. Instead of doing the hard work of seeing whether he shared my feelings and wanted a real relationship, I acted like a coward and left town. I so desperately wanted the real thing—sex, love, and kink—that at the first glimmer of it, I jumped.

At the time, I thought I saw something in the newest fellow to capture my attention that no one else was offering. Besides, there was nothing to keep me in Milwaukee; I had a shitty job, a noisy apartment, and none of my relationships were satisfying—I was everyone's casual thing on the side. Moving to Iowa didn't seem like a terrible idea, compared to what I was leaving behind.

I had no idea how unhealthy my habitually meeting strange men for sex and BDSM without negotiation was, or how lucky I was to weather these escapades without any real harm. I did know that these kinky experiences provided me with some level of satisfaction that was missing from the rest of my life. They quieted my head, allowing me to lose myself in the desires of the other person. I was free to simply follow their commands.

Subconsciously, I wanted someone to provide this guidance in all areas of my life. Instead, the universe was insisting I make tough choices in order to lift myself out of the post-college slump I inhabited. My lack of ambition led me to confuse the satisfaction I felt in being submissive with needing someone to make all my life decisions because I didn't feel qualified or able.

It never occurred to me then that this was a sign I should stop sleeping around, do some soul-searching, and find a therapist. Instead, I moved to Iowa, only a month into a long-distance relationship with Guitar Guy. It wasn't until I was there, terribly alone and far from everyone I knew, that I realized the depth of my mistake.

Like everyone I was fucking at the time, I had met him on an online BDSM site. His profile assured me he was an experienced Dom interested in many of the same things I was (including rope) and looking for a long-term kinky romance. It seemed like I'd hit the jackpot. So when he offered to visit one weekend, I didn't hesitate to agree.

The date was all right once I recovered from the surprise of Guitar Guy being much heavier than his profile stated. His photos had hidden his bulk but accentuated his flowing blond hair. His white lie about his appearance—the first of many half truths—didn't faze me; that level of honesty was what I thought I deserved, so calling off the weekend never crossed my mind.

That night he pulled leather cuffs from his gargantuan biker's jacket—which I would later learn he wore in all seasons—and strapped my wrists to the bedposts. My thoughts were at direct odds with one another as I lay naked and stretched across the mattress.

My rational mind questioned these restraints. He had voiced fascination with rope and a curiosity about elaborate bondage, so I was curious why he'd pinned me down with the quickest, most utilitarian option. But the other part of my mind, the part that always seemed to win out, was thrilled to be bound in any form.

He went on to add a blindfold, leaving me to wait in the darkness while I listened to the sound of him removing his clothes: the jangle of cumbersome pants full of loose change, the grunting effort it took him to remove his shirt and socks. Then the rustling of him searching through his seemingly bottomless jacket, an endeavor that culminated with the snap of elastic.

When he finally came within arm's reach, it was to rub his crotch on my hand. "Feel that?"

I nodded, unsure what I was touching, the pride in his voice making me worried. Exploring with my fingers, I was eventually able to understand that this was his package, covered in cheap pleather. He *mmm*ed as I felt around further to determine that this was an ill-fitting thong of some sort.

"You like that dick?"

Nodding again out of politeness, I continued to fondle him, searching for the impressive member he'd promised. A big cock was by no means a requirement for me, but he had talked about his genitals at such great length that I was waiting to be awed. Instead, I found a smaller-than-average penis topped by a large-gauge Prince Albert piercing. I was beginning to wonder if he had been honest about anything.

That first evening together, the restraints only stayed on until Guitar Guy wanted his cock sucked. He then forgot about the kinky activities we had discussed and transitioned into standard (and subpar) sex. His idea of being dominant was to lie like a beached whale in the center of the bed demanding that I do all the work. Lazily bossing me around didn't seem very Domly, but I was all too eager to please.

Our second rendezvous was nearly identical: me bound but otherwise unmolested until he bored of the scenario and commanded, "Blow me, let's get something going." Yet I held desperately to the promises he'd made online, sticking with him and waiting for the kinky dream to begin. I was so desperate for a new life that I agreed to move in with him.

What he forgot to mention when suggesting that I shack up with him—after our second date—was that he didn't technically have a home. Instead, he was illegally squatting in the back room of what had been his recording workshop—a studio in name only, since the music he made now was with a thoroughly unremarkable Christian rock group. Only the guys he played with found this gig glamorous: working in various capacities at the motor home plants that made up the entire economy of this particular small town and playing the church every Sunday.

Guitar Guy's eagerness to have me move in with him a month into our long-distance liaison should have been a red flag that this was not going to be a healthy relationship. Putting all my belongings in a van, only to be made aware that I was moving into a back room of his unsuccessful business, where there was no shower or kitchen, also should have been a sign to go back to Wisconsin and straighten out my life. Instead I stayed, codependently lulled into this situation with Guitar Guy out of fear of being alone and by the dangling carrot of a life of kinky sex.

He tricked me into coming to Iowa, but I fooled myself into staying. The kinky fantasy life of whips, cages, ropes, and endless pleasure we'd written about together during the online stage of our relationship blinded me to our reality. So while the scenery changed, my indecisive fumbling continued in Iowa.

After our first strained month sharing a space, Guitar Guy ended any ruse of BDSM interest, alleging it had never been that appealing to him. He claimed ignorance of any promise of kink. Soon even the vanilla sex stopped, leaving me bereft and frustrated, sneaking out of bed to masturbate in his cold studio while he slept, resigned to the mess I'd gotten into until I could afford to leave.

Furious at myself for moving to an even shittier city and accepting an even shittier job, I took my anger out on Guitar Guy through industrial-strength silent treatments that occasionally went on for months. When he acted as if my refusal to respond to his berating was a reward rather than a punishment, I escalated to carrying on deeply sexual flirtations with men online.

The German and I picked up where we'd left off when I'd rushed out of Milwaukee without saying a proper good-bye. He had made a similar mistake, moving in with a nearly asexual alcoholic whom he couldn't seem to break it off with. We tried to fulfill one another's fantasies with kinky emails and exchanging photos of ourselves in compromising positions.

It felt a lot like cheating, but since Guitar Guy had made it clear he was uninterested in a physical relationship, I felt justified finding satisfaction elsewhere. I wouldn't learn about polyamory for another year, so I continued guiltily courting the German from afar instead of having a difficult conversation about my needs with Guitar Guy—as if he would have listened.

Meanwhile, Guitar Guy seemed perfectly happy with the state of things. Cooking everything in a microwave and showering in the spare bathroom at his parents' house didn't strike him as childish; it was part of the grungy aesthetic he wanted to inhabit. For me, it stopped being a rousing adventure in slumming it—writing by day and wiring expensive recreational vehicles by night—when a storm drove a tree through what remained of the roof of our makeshift bedroom. I found moving into his mother's spare bedroom more appealing than living with him another day after that.

Guitar Guy was unconcerned, both with the gaping hole in the studio and the one in our relationship. He had lured me away from everything I knew and loved; where was I going to go? So he was shocked when, after a year with him, I found an apartment in Madison and left.

For several sane months, I had a new life and apartment in Wisconsin—one with indoor plumbing and a roof. I was close enough to the German to partake again in our kinky games and rough sex, things I had thoroughly missed. Feeling strong and smug, enjoying occasional forays into beatings and bondage and working in a wine store, was as close to living my dream as I'd yet gotten.

Life was good—until I took pity on Guitar Guy, who had never stopped calling me with his sob stories and eventually moved to Wisconsin to be close to me. This seemed vaguely romantic, so I allowed him to move in. Obviously, the year in Iowa had mangled my last sane brain cell to the point where staying in an endless cycle of verbal abuse seemed reasonable.

Like a typical victim of an abusive boyfriend, each time I got the ovaries to leave, I would take him back a week later, trusting that this time would be different. And like any talented abusive boyfriend, he played the sweet, attentive significant other when he caught a hint of me getting ready to leave. This was a role he inhabited just long enough that I would think he had changed.

Now, during the good periods, he would pretend an interest in bondage. During one of these smooth patches I was able to convince him to attend the monthly fetish night at a Goth club. It turned out to largely consist of people dressed up in leather and lace standing around in a dark bar listening to industrial music. There was a bit of dungeon furniture strewn around so that some bondage and light flogging could go on in the darker corners.

Everyone stayed fully clothed the entire evening, sipping watered-down drinks and nodding approvingly at the few people brave enough to play. People rarely made eye contact or talked to anyone they hadn't walked through the door with.

Then I noticed a man in a ridiculous lace-up silver lamé shirt doing amazing things with beautifully colored rope. The women he tied up seemed transported to another universe when he put his knots on their skin. I stood on the upper level of the club, breathless, in awe of the connection between the rope and their reactions. Guitar Guy was in the bathroom pouting after I'd refused to take his argumentative bait, leaving me a few minutes alone to enjoy the show.

When the Rope Guru was finished untying the last in his long line of victims, he wrapped her in his arms. The contrast between such tenderness and the rough way he had treated her earlier was hypnotic. I was so enthralled, I was initially oblivious to the fact that he was gazing back at me over her shoulder, smiling.

I blushed a deep red when I noticed his attention, and dashed out of the dungeon just in time to encounter Guitar Guy in the bar, who was ranting about what a traitorous whore I was for making eye contact with another man. It was late, and there was a lot of arguing to do before he would allow me to sleep, so we left.

That night I snuck out of bed to play with myself while imagining being the girl the Rope Guru had put in rope. This fantasy and the plethora of rope porn I found on the Internet got me through a lot of long nights of jerking myself off and hoping to find the courage to create a better life.

Eventually I bought my first piece of rope, 200 feet of stiff purple nylon from the farm-supply store, which I used to practice on myself, sharing the results virtually with the German. Soon I figured out just enough to do the basics on my own body—always when Guitar Guy was away, never revealing what I was doing. Soon the monthly fetish night was all I could think about.

At the next event I convinced Guitar Guy to talk to the Rope Guru with me. Once he was assured that no one else would be touching any of my important bits, Guitar Guy was even okay with learning how to do a simple tie. The whole time Rope Guru was demonstrating a simple chest harness, Guitar Guy kept a jealous eye on him, daring him to do anything he could construe as untoward. Arguing with me about flirting was small time compared to the bickering he could start if a man actually ever laid a finger on me in his presence.

Though Guitar Guy was only partaking in this moment for argumentative fodder, he couldn't put a damper on my excitement. I stood there in Rope Guru's chest ropes, floating off into another world, not wanting the moment to end, so nervous and shy that I didn't say a word. The men talked about the gorgeous red rope on my body while I dreamily listened. The rope was made of something called hemp. It was soft and firm at the same time.

The nice man did eventually want his ropes back, and in exchange, he hugged me good-bye while slipping me his card. Now I knew how to get in contact with this magical person who was doing things with rope I didn't know were possible in real life! I counted down the seconds until the next fetish night, hoping I would be brave enough to talk to him then.

When that night came, the Rope Guru was raffling off a kit of sky-blue hemp rope. To get in my good graces after our latest epic argument, Guitar Guy entered many times and won. We then had our very own rope to take home—where it sat in a locked case in his closet. All the BDSM toys were under lock and key so I couldn't use them without him. Still, the motivation never appeared for him to learn to tie, so this beautiful rope sat unused, which was so heartbreaking I almost couldn't cope.

One night he was taking his time getting ready to go out, so to pass the time I took off my dress and dragged the conveniently unlocked case full of unused floggers and blue rope into the middle of the bedroom. He didn't even notice what was happening until I was most of the way through hog-tying myself.

He gave me a passing glance on his way to grab a towel. I asked him, "Can you tie up my hands before you go in there?"

"Fine!" He rolled his eyes as I handed him the rope with the pre-tied cuffs in the middle and cinched them behind me so I couldn't get loose. "There," he said, deeply annoyed.

Backing out of the bedroom, he tripped over the Hitachi that had rolled out of the box while I was untangling the rope. He slipped it between me and the bed, trapping it between my thighs so that I couldn't wiggle away from it. "Is that what you wanted?"

While I was distracted by this sudden turn of events, he grabbed the rope I'd braided into my hair, yanking my head back until my chest was lifted off the bed, and tied that to my ankles. I was curved at such a sharp angle that the pressure on my diaphragm made it difficult to breathe, let alone speak to tell him that this position was too much. When he put an oversized ball gag in my mouth and tightened it behind me, I was getting scared; he was upset and not a trustworthy Top at the best of times. All of my fears were realized when he added a blindfold.

I could barely hear the bathroom door slam and the shower turn on over the buzz of the Hitachi coursing through the mattress. He'd left me alone, likely not realizing how dangerous it was to leave someone bound and unattended. Knowing him, he would shower and primp for an hour or more, and I was unsure how long I could hold this position. I worried about choking on the gag or a rope shifting in a dangerous manner while no one was there to save me.

I was so mad at him, and the vibrations were so intense, that my body worked against me by causing an endless loop of climaxes. The orgasms were so powerful I was having a difficult time breathing around the gag.

It would serve him right if I died here in a puddle of my own girl mess! was my last thought before things started to feel blurry around the edges. Then I felt a hand on my back, holding me still so the ball gag could be removed. I gasped for a much-needed breath, realizing he had been there the whole time, watching. The noise of the shower had been a fake out. That asshole!

That was the last time he agreed to do anything rope related. By now I knew there was a lot more to life and love than I'd found in my flawed relationship with Guitar Guy, if I could just get away from him.

After an especially hurtful argument I showed up to the wine shop barely disguising my tears. After I related the story of my seemingly inescapable relationship, a coworker confessed to being in a similar situation. She was preparing to leave her husband; the only delay was being able to afford a place on her own. So the two of us secretly found a bachelorette pad, left our abusive relationships, and moved on.

As I packed to leave, Guitar Guy was uncharacteristically kind. I thought that perhaps we'd both grown up, that everything would be okay between us. This hope disappeared the moment I asked him to help me move my couch.

"Fuck you, asking me for help after everything you've done . . ." I didn't bother asking what he imagined those things might be, or feeding his rage by responding. Instead I dragged the monstrous piece of furniture down a flight of stairs, across the apartment complex lawn, through the parking lot, and into the truck I'd borrowed from my father.

Guitar Guy possessed many dollies that would have made moving easy, all of which were missing when I came to retrieve the last of my things. I quickly realized those dollies were hidden for the same reason he was at the apartment when he was scheduled to work: so he could torment me one final time. And he did, in full view of the watchful neighbors, who looked out their windows as if this were the greatest live-from-the-front-yard episode of *Jerry Springer* ever.

Guitar Guy continued screaming at me as I held out my hand to return the keys; when he refused to take them, I dropped them on the concrete at his feet. Realizing this was his last chance to be cruel, he paused as I walked away, calculating the best insult to use as his parting shot.

Closing the truck door, I heard, "You're a whore and your brother cheats at Risk."

I laughed hysterically, tears filling my eyes, as I pulled away.

CHAPTER 5
THE WET SPOT

As my life with Guitar Guy was coming to an end, I cashed in my wine-shop tips and planned a trip to Seattle to visit the Nurse. He was an actively kinky Internet acquaintance who seemed to be doing all the things with his life I wanted to do with mine. Hoping to lure me out of my doomed relationship, he promised to show me the fun I was missing. I thought it would be good to get some distance while I decided whether or not to sign the lease with my work friend and leave Guitar Guy.

When Guitar Guy's van literally burst into flames on the way to the airport, I quickly got perspective. Even while pushing the smoldering vehicle to a service center in a shady neighborhood, he found a way to turn the situation into an argument—followed by a jealous rage and publicly humiliating me when a kind stranger drove us to the airport. Relieved to get there on time, I thought things were looking up. But that didn't last long.

Guitar Guy took me aside as I was checking my bags to say, "Today seems like an obvious sign that we shouldn't be together. Good-bye."

He removed his hands from my shoulders and walked away. Apparently it had taken a flaming vehicle to drive home for him what I'd known all along but was too cowardly to say. This was the conversation I'd been trying to have for what seemed like forever, but even when the other person is an abusive waste of space, breaking up hurts. Especially when they time the split to conveniently coincide with a much-needed vacation that would no longer be the hoped-for relaxing getaway.

I cried myself through the flight across the country and a lot of the sightseeing that ensued. I was the worst possible houseguest, moping around and obsessing about what waited for me at home. It didn't improve matters that it was obvious from the moment I walked into their house that the Nurse and his girlfriend were themselves in the midst of a breakup. He hadn't so much as hinted at this in our conversations.

The tension in the air was as thick and unpalatable as tar, and my being there only made the situation worse. I was giving them an audience and acting as the face of all his girlfriend's jealous fears. Everything he had been telling me from afar had been a lie; this wasn't the blissfully easy, open, and kink-filled relationship he had dreamily described.

I tried to make the best of things by becoming as invisible and self-sufficient as possible. I made the girlfriend dinner to prove I wasn't there to wreck her relationship, even while taking the word of the Nurse that it was okay that he and I fuck whenever she wasn't around. At the time it never occurred to me to ask about her feelings on the subject, so I let his word speak for her. Poly was a brand-new concept in my world. Not understanding that boundaries were an important part of open relationships, I assumed he was free to sleep with anyone.

When I wasn't leaving rooms to avoid their arguments or secretly fucking the Nurse, I spent as much time as I could entertaining myself in order to give them time alone. But tiptoeing around their breakup was shining a brighter light on the heartbreak I was feeling. Mostly, I cried everywhere I went, ducking down alleys or into bathrooms so as to not be obvious, barely able to enjoy any of the beauty of Seattle.

The only thing that briefly got me out of my funk was the promise of seeing The Wet Spot, the local sex-and-kink-positive club. It was so infamous that I had heard about it in the Midwest, and experiencing it was more than half the reason I had jumped on the Nurse's offer to visit.

From the second the Nurse and I walked in, I knew The Wet Spot was going to be different from the fetish scene I was accustomed to. This wasn't a glorified Goth night with floggers and nipple clamps in a dark and dirty bar like the one where I'd met the Rope Guru. This was a converted warehouse decked out in hard points and comfy couches, a huge space dedicated to nudity and hedonism. And that was only what I could see from the entrance.

When we finally got through the heavy-duty security at the door and into the main room, it was a naked free-for-all. Throughout the space were hordes of people in various states of undress dancing to a loop of remixed Nine Inch Nails songs. Boas, lamé, and striped knee socks seemed to be popular with this crowd. People here were wearing colors and smiling while gyrating under the strobe lights, which was unheard-of in Madison. I felt overdressed and out of place in my purple corset, fishnets, and boots. Nudity wasn't an option at the fetish nights where I came from, which were held in public bars, so overcompensating with sexy clothes was the only way I knew how to dress at an event like this. The Nurse kept assuring me I looked fine.

People were making out or chatting on the furniture strewn everywhere. It was all lovely, voyeuristic eye candy, but after all I'd heard about the city's rope scene, I was expecting to see more people doing rope. Momentarily disappointed, I settled for a tour of the private rooms at the back of the club where all the action was that night.

I wasn't comfortable in the sex room, a collection of twin beds covered in white sheets with fabric hanging between them to create an illusion of privacy. At the time, watching—and especially hearing—other people fuck was distinctly not my thing. I pulled my friend out of that room quickly and on to the next.

There a group of women were beating a skinny boy tied to the rafters of a canopy bed. They were the only ones in this room, and they made so much noise that my friend and I were invisible to them. If I was going to do something sexy in public for the first time, this seemed like the place for it. This room was private enough to feel like a comfortable place for taking my initial baby-deer-standing-for-the-first-time steps into exhibitionism. And it was obvious that a scene was the price the Nurse felt I owed him for bringing me here. He hadn't stopped hinting at this since we'd gotten into the car that evening.

As I was busy overthinking what was about to happen, the Nurse cleaned off and claimed a heavy wooden table padded with leather and hard points at its edges for securing limbs. It was at the center of the room, so everyone could see him with the pretty new girl. He stopped unpacking his toy bag and looked at me with noticeable impatience.

"Well? Are you going to get undressed?" He turned back to his bag.

My top and corset were easy to remove; I had plenty of practice being topless at events (though always with electrical tape over my nipples), so this seemed like the next logical step. But looping my thumbs into my skirt gave me pause. This was as far as I was comfortable disrobing. Playing in public was new to me, and I wanted to start relatively slowly, which disappointed my friend; he pushed at this boundary, getting increasingly frustrated.

"Just your skirt? You can keep the panties. At least take off your stockings. How about just the underwear?" His bedside manner left a lot to be desired.

I refused to give in. Boobs were all he was getting from me here. He sighed again and went back to untangling his new wine-colored hemp. The grassy smell of the rope calmed me so that I could almost forget how pushy he was being, along with the frightening noises coming from the other side of the room. This was the start of a lifetime of Pavlovian stirrings in my cunt at the faintest whiff of natural-fiber rope.

Still, the evening continued to get more uncomfortable. My desperate desire to get tied up was in direct opposition with how uncomfortable I was at the time with doing anything slightly sexual anywhere even slightly public. The two emotions were at such odds that I couldn't enjoy myself as he bound my arms behind me in a simple chest harness. I was so worried about whether the Nurse was having a good time or which boundary he was going to push next that the rope was a blur of awkwardness as I stood there, stony with tension.

The Nurse was so inexperienced that he couldn't even understand how to unwrap his new hemp; this wasn't filling me with confidence.

Today, I would know better and insist on going home. Younger, inexperienced me was half-naked and had agreed to come to this party. I thought this meant that following through with a scene was a requirement or that I owed him play, even though I didn't feel assured he knew enough about topping to be trustworthy.

This was before I had learned how to play safe, when I mistakenly thought people who neglected negotiation and prodded at boundaries were Domly, when in actuality they were dangerous assholes. I didn't know enough to distinguish pushiness from dominance. It took me a long time to figure out that the talking and anticipation while discussing what each person wanted out of the scene was the part of the power exchange that made the whole thing hot.

Meanwhile, the Nurse was operating under the beginner Dom illusion that asking the bottom what she wanted or liked equaled weakness. This was how he ended up doing little that I enjoyed and caused me to feel even more uncomfortable. He carried on as if my getting any gratification out of the evening wasn't on his list of priorities; I was merely an object to decorate with his rope and had no say in what occurred.

He probably thought that if there was rope on me, I should be grateful for the attention, and if I was a good bottom, I would do anything he wanted. This had already been made clear during our earlier play at his place. I'd let him fuck me without a condom, thinking that as a Top he got to choose what to do with my body, so I didn't think to say no to him while bound and gagged. After all, I'd agreed to sex, largely because I was unaware it was okay to negotiate it out of our play. I'd never been told I could voice my preferences and didn't have the self-esteem at the time to advocate for myself.

I didn't know stopping him was an option, wrongly thinking that sex and kink were inexorably linked and that he got to choose when and how the penetration occurred. I considered it part of the game, so I wasn't traumatized, simply made aware that this was part of his repertoire, something I wanted to prevent from happening again.

So, with the afternoon's activities fresh in my mind, I made it a point to fight for keeping my clothes on at The Wet Spot. I would feel too exposed being naked there, especially with a partner who was quickly losing my trust. Even while tied up, with a gag and blindfold on, I fought him all night, crossing my legs so that he couldn't pull down my skirt or panties. He didn't realize or care how much it meant to me to not be fucked or fingered in front of strangers. The person I am now would have untied myself and given him a stern lecture on "no means no." But then, days after breaking up with an abusive long-term partner, it didn't occur to me that it was in my power to just ask to go home.

Eventually he tired of me refusing and moved on to using a paddle to strike my ass. Spanking, I understood: it was the first thing he had done since getting out the rope that I enjoyed. As the paddle made contact, things were briefly right with the world. The sexy high of riding the increasing amounts of pain momentarily removed my doubts.

The pleasure only lasted until a blood-curdling scream emanated from the far corner of the room. I assumed it came from the man tied to the oversized bed in the corner. The chorus of maniacal female laughter that followed each bellow of pain confirmed this. Stiffening every muscle in my body and trying to stand up from the table, I longed to be untied immediately. I hadn't gotten my mind around screaming being a sign of pleasure, so there was no way for me to relax and carry on.

The Nurse eventually stopped spanking me long enough to hold me from behind and whisper, "I want to keep spanking you. It's okay." When I shook my head and stayed rigid, he continued, "I need to keep going. Unless you want to fuck instead." At this I leaned away from his body, shaking my head more aggressively. This was my first act of defiance to a Top and it felt strange, as if I'd done something wrong.

He exhaled deeply as he took off the rope and gag. The disappointed look on his face almost made me apologize. Being a submissive people-pleaser, it pained me to think he wasn't happy. I almost gave in, but then the tiny bound man screamed again, making me shiver with discomfort. I put on my clothes and asked to leave as soon as possible. The Nurse fumed while putting away his toys, and there was an awkward conversation on the way back to his place about how I was a tease.

"I'm so disappointed," he whined, sounding a lot like Guitar Guy. Tired of his manipulative bullshit, I stopped listening; it was all too familiar. This was exactly what I had left behind on the other side of the country. I didn't need any more of it.

The rest of the trip was a flurry of breakup drama as his relationship fell apart. Going back home to iron out my own breakup actually seemed appealing right then. My vacation from reality had gotten far too real; I couldn't wait to get back home and start a new chapter.

CHAPTER 6
THE PROFESSIONAL

"Hey, stranger," I whispered into the ear of the tousled-haired older gentleman sitting at the bar, scribbling away in his notebook.

"Nice corset." His raised eyebrow and flirtatious smile told me I'd been right to dress up.

When the Rope Guru had invited me to be his date, it was such a flattering proposal that I couldn't imagine turning him down. He had already worked his way through most of the other women in our erotic writers group, so it surprised no one when he turned his attention toward me, the newest addition. Rumor had it that he was trouble, which at the time made him impossibly intriguing. He was popular and well known in the kink and poly communities, while I was relatively new to it all: Madison, kink, dating after a breakup, everything. On top of that, a fetish bar on Halloween was out of my comfort zone. So it was nerves, and not my lack of practice in wearing heels, that made me stumbly and awkward.

Looking around the bar, I noticed I wasn't the only one who didn't appear comfortable in the dark, dungeon-y space with blaring music. With the number of half-dressed sorority girls and beer-bellied, pleather-chap-wearing fellows around, I realized Halloween was the kink world's version of amateur's night.

"So, what are you writing?" I removed my jacket, making sure to brush my thigh against his as I sat down, hoping to get his nose out of his notebook.

"Just some ideas for next week." He continued scribbling.

"Must be something good, if that's all you're going to divulge."

"Something like that." He was being quiet, which meant he was up to something. "Want to get a drink and look around?"

I glanced at the wooden cross in the corner and the dangerous-looking woman standing beside it, who was holding a whip in one hand and a leash connected to a mostly nude man in the other. "Yes. Please."

He waved down the bartender. I drummed my fingers nervously on the bar, willing the confidence-imbuing liquid to appear quickly. The Rope Guru gently bumped my shoulder with his to get my attention and gave me a wink that managed to be simultaneously alluring and fatherly. My heart raced, and my pale skin gave my blush away even in the dim light; the sight made him laugh sinisterly.

Feeling bolder after the whiskey, I agreed to a tour of the club. Standing, he pulled a bag out from under his seat. When he slipped his writing notebook inside, I saw the endless coils of multicolored rope it contained. I tilted my head, looking at him askance.

"Oh, that?" he asked. I nodded, encouraging an explanation. "I didn't want to be presumptuous, but you never know. I wouldn't want to be caught without it."

"Oh no. Of course not. Heaven forbid."

Sarcastic as I was, I could also feel myself blushing again as I wondered what he had in mind tonight. We'd been flirting at fetish events for a year now, but it wasn't until he invited me to join his erotic writing group that I began getting to know him through the strange intimacy of reading and editing each other's stories. Reading his well-written erotica (which focused on bondage and power) only heighted the crush I had on him. But he made no secret of his three partners, so I was sure the desire was distinctly one sided; even if he noticed me, I doubted he had time in his life for another lover.

As if reading my hesitation, he gently propelled me in the direction of the other room. As we passed into the back of the club, I realized this was the play room. This space was empty and dark, which made it feel much more intimate than the bar. It also had floor-to-ceiling mirrors on two walls, which I briefly imagined watching myself reflected in while being bound. In reality, I nervously stood in the best-lit corner of the room, taking it in. The Rope Guru gestured for me to come closer.

I was relieved when he pulled out two chairs rather than guiding me to one of the more taboo pieces of furniture, like the spanking bench at the other side of the room. He sat provocatively close. As we talked about writing and fellow acquaintances, I loosened up, letting my guard down. I was genuinely having a good time.

Then he asked, "Would you like to do some rope?"

I opened my mouth to search for an answer, eventually coming up with, "Sure, I'd love to. I haven't had much chance to do rope since that time with you at fetish night."

"That was months ago! Now, that's just a shame."

"Well, I don't have anyone to tie me these days. Actually, I rarely have." Suddenly my hands urgently required my attention as I nervously played with my fingers in order to avoid eye contact.

"So let's change that."

"Okay." My heart raced in anticipation.

He reached out to softly touch my wrist, causing me to look up shyly at him, licking my lips. "Well then, would you let me do the honor of tying you?"

I smiled and giggled, amazed that even at twenty-something, the right question from the right man could still make me feel like a giddy teenager. As I grasped for a response, my gaze returned to my hands, which were now being caressed by his.

"We won't do anything intense, just bind your arms. Maybe go from there if you like it. You can stop me at any time if it's too much." He ended our touch, returning his hands to his side: this simple break in physical contact, a deliberate act to break me from my reverie, captured my attention. I wanted his touch again. After many months of friendly flirting, there was something electric about that touch.

He and his mysterious rope had starred in my fantasies many times, so I was intrigued enough by him to be bound in public and see whether he lived up to the picture in my head. I'd come a long way in the months since Seattle and breaking up with Guitar Guy, getting bolder and longing for new experiences. And it felt ridiculous to turn down a chance to get tied up by someone famous for rope, especially since he was so obvious about his concern for my comfort.

Nervously, I smiled at him. "Yeah, I'd like that very much." His adorably cocky grin let me know he hadn't expected, even for a second, I would turn him down.

"Good. I'd like you in my rope." He took my hand in one of his and picked up the suddenly portentous bag with his other, guiding me forward. This time he led me to the corner of the room where both walls were mirrored, with a wooden ledge at chest height, just deep enough to set down drinks.

I stood, immobile with anticipation as he knelt, searching for a certain length of bubblegum-pink rope before standing up again. With deft hands he unlooped the line with one flick of his wrist and let the length of it unfold to the floor. He slowly ran his hand across it, ultimately finding the middle, watching me watch him while my pulse raced. Gripping my shoulders, he quickly turned me away from him. I looked down to see the loop of rope passing above my breasts and upper arms. He cinched it behind me, using this as a handle to pull me back against his chest.

"This is hemp rope. And this is my favorite piece of rope because it was made special for me by a friend. It's what I want to see against your skin tonight." All of this was said in the crook of my ear, just loud enough to be heard over the music. The warmth and wetness of his mouth against my skin made me melt against him.

I closed my eyes to focus on his voice as he continued. "Do you like the way it feels?" He tilted my head to the side and ran the rope along my neck, causing my breath to catch. Nodding, I allowed myself to be pressed more firmly against him. It seemed a safe bet that he was referring to the texture of the stiff, slightly scratchy rope, but I was also enjoying the feel of the none-too-subtle bulge of his crotch against my ass.

Releasing my face from his hand, he passed the rope over my chest again just above my breasts and then secured it behind me to pin my arms at my sides. "I like hemp because it gets good and tight but still feels nice." He punctuated this statement with a tug on the rope, tightening it before passing it in front of me again, so that the next loop was under my breasts. He cinched this in the back as well.

We made eye contact in the mirror, which was inches from my face. Gone was the sensitive writer I had met at the bar. His eyes had changed him into something darker, more dangerous. Before I could wonder about his transformation, he gripped my hair where it was bound up in a bun and gently pushed my face to the mirror. I was pressed against my own reflection, and my breath fogged up the glass as I exhaled.

"Enjoying yourself?" That deep, sultry voice was in my ear again, making me boneless with lust. I nodded, allowing him to toss me about like a rag doll. "Good girl," he snarled, simultaneously releasing my hair and guiding my wrists together at the small of my back, where he did what felt like magic to bind my hands. He had made me helpless with one short piece of ridiculously pink rope, and I loved it. This was what it felt like to be bound by someone with skill in bondage, someone interested in my comfort and safety. Trust, I could see, opened up a whole new world of hotness.

He pulled me away from the mirrored wall to lean me against his chest, and I sighed at the feel of our bodies against one another—fully clothed, yet doing something so erotic in a public place. As time went on, people danced around us to the loud techno music, occasionally stopping to watch. The vibrations of their movements and the heat of their bodies in this close space added to the allure of trusting the Rope Guru to keep me safe.

Purely by accident, while stretching my fingers to keep numbness away, I learned that in this position, if I wiggled my hands, my fingers brushed his cock. It was so tempting that I couldn't concentrate on anything but him pressed against me.

"You dirty little cock slut." I must have smiled and given myself away. He pushed me up against the railing along the wall again as he reached down into his bag. "I've read your stories; I know what you're thinking."

The stories I'd been submitting to the writing group explored some of my darkest masochistic fantasies in graphic detail. It was all under the guise of fiction, but I realized just then that he knew more about my secret desires than any lover or play partner before him. I wasn't talented at communicating my needs aloud, but my written words had been crystal clear about what I longed for.

I gave him a look in the mirror that I hoped said, *Yeah? So what?*

"Since you write such dirty things, I also know you like this." At that moment he slapped my ass with a small wooden paddle. More than anything, it was the shock at his audacity, calling me names and spanking me in public, that caused a sting. He hadn't hit me hard, but I closed my eyes and tried to catch my breath as he hit me once again. "You like that?"

The stubborn part of me wanted to fight, refusing to admit that I enjoyed something so taboo. Of course I'd been beat before, but there was something about being asked to be up front about this desire that was erotic and embarrassing at the same time. Luckily, the part of me that noticed how wet I was while playing this game won out. I nodded, consenting to more.

"Good." He nuzzled up against the nape of my neck as he spanked me several more times, none of them any harder than the first but all charged with more erotic thrill than the few other bedroom spankings I'd received. By the time he concluded, I was certain my panting was audible over the music.

He dropped the paddle, carefully undid my hair-clip to use my long curls as a handle, and pulled me against him, and then away, just to prove he could. It was a sort of perverse dance. Arching my head backward at a dangerous angle, he exposed my neck, running his free hand to the top clasp of the shirt I wore under my corset. He undid the top button while releasing a sound of mock shock, pantomiming surprise at his own actions.

We locked eyes in the mirror, and I watched as he undid the next few clasps, until my shirt was open to where the rope and corset met at my breasts. He grabbed both sides of the fabric and opened the shirt, exposing my cleavage. The amount of skin showing was nothing racy, and yet the grace and stealth at which he enacted these small gestures made it feel naughty.

"Should I continue?" he asked, fingers on the next button. I shook my head and he stopped. "Thank you for letting me know."

Boundary created and respected, he spun me around to face him, pulling me in. We were now so close I was sure we would kiss; I assumed that would be a part of our play, though we'd never discussed it. As I moved toward him to offer my lips, he moved away at the last moment. My whimper of disappointment seemed to be exactly what he was looking for. He pushed me back against the wall, pinning his knee between my legs. The heat of his leg radiated into my cunt, making me dizzy with the thought of moving against him. It took every ounce of control I had to not buck my hips.

Perched on his knee, I watched as he undid his dark tie and pulled it out from the collar of his shirt. He unknotted it, smoothing it before shoving a length of the tie into my mouth and knotting it off behind my head. It was tight enough that I was losing control of myself and beginning to drool. He smiled while turning me back around so I could look at my predicament.

"What was it you wrote? 'The only thing better than a man in a tie is watching a man take one off.' Where does this fall on the scale?" I smiled around the fabric at his smart-ass comment.

He pinned me to the wall with his knee between my legs again, this time from behind, as he bent to pick up another piece of rope. This he looped around my waist multiple times to make a sort of belt. Soon he was looming over me, pressing me to the mirror as he handled the lines very near my cunt. "Now this, this is called a crotch rope. The fun thing about it is tying a knot at just the right spot." There was a devious twist to his voice as he finished fiddling with the rope and pulled it tight between my legs, fastening it in the back.

It was an odd, slightly uncomfortable sensation, until he began tugging on the rope. He must have gotten the knot in the right spot, because that simple movement sent chills through me. I couldn't hide my pleasure as I fell against the mirror and writhed as he pulled the rope in different directions and different rhythms. The necktie gag muffled my moans as he continued.

Just as I was on the verge of coming due to the sheer novelty of the experience, he turned me toward him once more, grinning at my obvious frustration. "Poor girl." While brushing the messy hair out of my face, he brought his mouth close to mine and removed the tie from my mouth without backing away. Any movement of my face toward him, however, was met with a perfectly opposite movement on his part. I was beginning to wonder whether I should be offended—or if perhaps kissing was off-limits to girls he tied up in bars.

I was starting to feel mocked, and as I turned my face away from him, I thought this would probably be a good time to ask to be untied. I could feel my arousal turning to anger. Not fully understanding yet that rope didn't always equal sex, I wondered what cruel game he was playing by tying me up but refusing the basic familiarity of lips on lips.

Before I could open my mouth to speak, he placed his finger on my lower lip, allowing me to taste the salt and hemp on his skin. He nudged my face toward him, forcing me to make eye contact. With his finger still in my mouth, he lightly kissed his way from the corner of my lips to my ear. "You do know I've wanted to get you in my ropes since the first time I laid eyes on you, right?"

I remembered that night well: the accidental eye contact across the bar as he finished untying someone, me caught in the act of watching. The dance of months of building up the courage to speak to him, then being invited to his erotica group when he found out I was a writer. Everything falling into place as I became single and deeply interested in rope but unable to voice my desire for him.

My blank expression surely told him that the thought had never crossed my mind. But this was quite the way to find out otherwise.

He kissed my forehead tenderly and untied my hands; the remainder of the chest ropes stayed on for the moment. I faced him, locked in a hug I couldn't return as he continued untying. Once I was free, he stepped away to coil the rope up while I watched.

"Let's dance," he said after returning the pink rope to the bag.

"What? No, I don't dance." While I was bound, there was a protective bubble around us that kept me from focusing on anyone else in the room. Now, looking around, I realized how full the club had become. Underdressed and obviously drunk college-age bodies were filling every inch of the space, crowding us into the corner of a room that an hour ago had been empty. I blushed at the realization that these dozens of people had been privy to our scene.

"I bet you do, you just don't know it."

My face and body stayed rigid, refusing to move toward the gyrating mass of bodies.

"Come on!" He insisted.

As much as I disliked dancing, I had little choice; he pulled the rope still cinched between my legs hard enough that the knot rubbed enticingly against my clit, shocking me into compliance. My knees went rubbery, and I followed him to the dance floor in order to use him as support. He took advantage of this by bucking his knee between my legs, against my pussy, in time to the music. With his tie draped around my neck, he had another convenient handle.

At this point I could either ruin the moment by holding my ground and refusing to dance or I could play along by grinding against his leg and "dancing" with him. Considering the pleasant rhythm in which his knee was moving, I chose the latter.

I surrendered, grabbing the lapels of his jacket while moving in time to the music, and was transported back to that lovely headspace where the people around us disappeared. We locked eyes, him smiling at my obvious pleasure, now timing the thrust of his leg and the pull of the ropes against my crotch to keep me on edge. I was panting and near crazy with the desire to orgasm, but he wouldn't let me off that easy. Anytime I would close my eyes and become distracted—or neglected to move with him to the syncopation of the music—he would go still until I regained my place in our choreography.

This wasn't exactly dancing, but it was close.

Though I knew there were throngs of people around us while his nearly endless tease went on, I was no longer aware of them. Even the music faded to a dull beat that I wasn't so much hearing as feeling as it vibrated off the walls, floor, and his knee. My heart was thundering at the same pace. Everything else faded away as I focused on him and the hope that he would eventually let me come.

When he used the tie to pull me closer, I was so lost in a happy mixture of brain chemicals that I wasn't aware of what was happening. Again I found myself painfully close to his mouth, this time not bothering to tilt my head and hope it became a kiss. Instead I held the up-close eye contact, feeling his lips move only molecules from mine as he playfully whispered, "And I thought you said you couldn't dance?"

The smile barely had time to form on my lips before he thrust the meat of his thigh into my pussy at the same time that he pulled the crotch rope to line up with my clit. He meant business now, moving his leg in time to the thrust of my hips against him as he held his position, finally allowing me to come. I grasped onto the front of his jacket as my head lolled against him. We were still moving to the music, but only we knew I was coming.

As the waves of climax washed through me, I moaned with abandon into his neck, daring the music to go quiet. When the bucking of my hips lessened, he dropped his knee, releasing the pressure on the rope by reaching around me, holding the small of my back as I regained composure. With my face still resting on his shoulder, we undulated to the electronic beat in a more traditional form of dance.

The Rope Guru finished the untying slowly, removing the rope from my body with as much intent as he had shown in putting it on. He then took my hand, parting a path through the crowd to the bar, where he proceeded to revive me with water. After our performance on the dance floor, we were quiet, all flushed cheeks and coy smiles. Just when the silence was becoming awkward and I was regaining enough of my self-control to think I should leave, he took a firm grip on my upper arm to suggest I stand. Once I was in front of him, he sat, patting his lap, a suggestion to sit on him here in the bar in front of everyone.

I paused. He was the sort of person who had a charisma so magnetic it was impossible to resist; when he turned the spotlight of his attention on someone, she felt like the most important thing in the world, blessed with the gift of his sexual prowess and rope skills. I knew there was a line a mile long to be in my knee-high leather boots, and that I was special to him, the only thing on his mind. But only for the evening.

Was it worth it? A night of bliss before potentially going back to being the platonic editor of his stories? I thought back to the mind-bending orgasm on the dance floor. If that was what he could do while we were both fully clothed . . .

Before I could change my mind, I straddled his lap and slipped my sweaty body close to him. He licked his lips and tried not to grin. Already I could feel the excitement building, the slight bulge in his pants stiffening between my spread thighs, an arousal I could feel myself reciprocating. I leaned in close, our arms instinctively clambering around one another, the same adolescent pawing that every first time with a new person inevitably leads to. Few things are more exciting than the first exploration of every inch of a new body.

Drawing my mouth close to his, I was positive now that he was playing a game in which kissing was off-limits, and I could play that game equally well. Before he could turn his face away, I put my hand to his chin, running my fingers along the stubble on his cheek and into his damp curls. I licked my lips deliberately, knowing our faces were close enough that my tongue would brush his lips momentarily. He sighed and moved his head back to look at me.

I pulled my hair clip out from his chest pocket and leaned back to put on a show of repinning my hair, fully aware that by leaning backward I was also grinding our hips together provocatively.

With my hair out of the way, I leaned in to kiss his neck tenderly and was rewarded with another sigh. I continued this until he returned the favor, his goatee tickling my neck. "So," I said, "no kissing, huh? Is that the game we're playing now, Mister? Wonder where you got that idea? Perhaps from a story in group a few weeks back?"

He pulled away, as if offended that I was drawing attention to his scheme. That's when I was positive he was acting out a scene from a story I had read aloud once to our group but nearly forgotten about since. He was pilfering my fantasy of sadistic-but-sexy kissing deprivation and using it against me. I was impressed at his cockiness.

"They do say that imitation is the sincerest form of flattery," he called out over the music.

"Cliché, but I'll take it."

For the next blur of hours, we played the push-and-pull game of not kissing. We did everything but actually lock lips, nibbling, licking, sucking on neck, ears, and throat. I unbuttoned his shirt and licked at his chest. He bit at my already exposed cleavage and boldly managed to snake his way under my shirt to roll my hard nipples with his fingers. I bucked my crotch against his lap, torturing him, grinding myself against the bulge in his jeans, and then against his hand, him *tsk*ing at the knowledge of how wet he had managed to make me.

I had no idea how long this went on, tormenting one another in every way possible while fully clothed and surrounded by drunk people. Eventually, neither of us could stay locked in that position any longer, but both of us were too stubborn to be the first to suggest we end the game. It became a mutual understanding that we would leave the bar when he stood and deposited me on my shaky feet.

The bar was still packed, making the room feel tropical, though it was frosty outside with an early hint of winter. We were both dripping sweat when we stumbled out of the bar, drunk on one other. The chill of the wind instantly cooled our skin, taking us from overheated to chilled through in seconds.

It started to snow, the first of the year, and we looked up to laugh—it was such a cheesy romance-movie cliché, but it was really happening. We weren't going back into the bar but didn't want to go home. Both of us were trying to hold on to this delightful, light-headed moment as long as possible, but the cold wasn't going to allow us to linger much longer.

"Let me walk you to your car." Once there, he pushed me up

against the driver's side, dropped his bag, and kissed me. Our tongues tangled together in a frenzy, the long, lingering lack of kissing finally at an end, which made for a very intense kiss. In this inevitable, inexorable moment, we wrapped our arms around each other, trapping body heat and the warmth of the kiss between us.

The icy pricks of snowflakes hitting my exposed skin contrasted with the warm and wet heat of his mouth against mine. Neither of us acted with rhyme or reason any longer. There were only our bodies reacting to each other's passion, our heads tilting perfectly to kiss more deeply, our limbs intertwining without any conscious thought. We were so lost in one another's embrace that we lost track of time, the cold, and the fact that we were quite literally standing in the middle of the street.

CHAPTER 7

THE SPIRITUAL ENLIGHTENMENT

"A priest and an erotica writer walk into a party . . . " was often how we were introduced to new people. It was a great gag that few people fully believed. We both looked so normal it rarely crossed anyone's mind that it could be anything other than a joke. Once they were clued in to the reality, though, they would really get interested in our relationship.

"How does that work?" strangers would inevitably ask. It didn't seem possible that a man of God could reconcile his religion with my interest in bondage and writing about it. Nor could they understand how I found any excitement in his conservative, buttoned-up nature, given my wild and adventurous ways.

We laughingly inhabited this paradox for six years, making a joke of the cliché that opposites attract. It was amusing to have so little in common on the surface and yet get along so well. The notion that no one else could understand how we worked so well together seemed to make our bond stronger.

There was one thing we could always agree on, the thing that brought us together: words. They were the reason we'd met, when I'd found myself at a reading one evening, scoping the crowd for a man in a clerical collar. That was one of those times when I had to stop and look at my life, realizing how odd things had gotten.

As the Rope Guru and I had become an item, it had also become obvious that he didn't have nearly enough free time to have the sort of relationship I desired. We managed the occasional rope tryst, but his having multiple other partners—and a predilection for flirting with every kinky young woman who looked in his direction—left me wanting more special attention. So when the Rope Guru met the Priest, he insisted I meet this person as well, seeing as, aside from bondage, we had so many similar interests. The Priest was looking for romance and someone to do bookish and foodie things with. And these were my favorite activities outside of rope, the sort of everyday things the Rope Guru wasn't available for. So the Rope Guru coached me through setting up an excuse to run into the Priest, both of us excited about the possibility of me finding another partner. This was the beginning of me doing poly ethically. It was complicated and exciting.

In his black suit with the hint of a white collar, the Priest stood out amongst the tweed-and-wool-coat University of Madison intellectuals. There was no way he was going to spot me in this throng of college kids, so I had to work up the courage to walk across the crowded room. This was before my modeling and storytelling days; shyness and social anxiety still ruled my interactions. Approaching him was well outside the realm of things I would ordinarily do. Yet it felt necessary, as though if I didn't cross the room, the choose-your-own-adventure series that was my life would take an unpleasant turn on the next page.

For something that felt so inevitable, the Priest and I shared some very ungainly small talk as I introduced myself as the woman the Rope Guru had probably suggested that he meet. The Priest seemed happy to finally connect but forgot to stand up to shake my hand. I kept forgetting what I was saying. We both forgot that we should probably sit together in order to get better acquainted. So I went back to my seat at the back of the room and we separately listened to the author on stage. Afterward I hurried out of the auditorium so we wouldn't awkwardly run into one another on the way out. I walked home thinking that was that.

"You're so dumb. That meant he likes you! You should have waited around and gone out for drinks after." This was my roommate's response when I replayed the interaction. I shrugged, believing nothing would come of it.

To my surprise, he got my information from our matchmaker, the Rope Guru, and emailed later that week to suggest we get together that weekend at the Goth-meets-fetish-wear dance night at the industrial music club where the Priest regularly danced and I often networked with kinksters. My life wasn't weird enough, so I figured, why not?

I was then faced with the problem of figuring out what to wear to leather-and-lace night when going on a first date with a priest. An open-minded, Gnostic priest, but a priest nonetheless. (His was a religion concerned with spiritual *gnosis* rather than restrictive rules like celibacy.) I tried on everything in my closet before settling on tight dress pants with a red waist cincher and boots.

I searched the bar for a bald man in a tuxedo with tails and a top hat, but as I looked around, I didn't see anyone dressed the way he had described himself. The anxiety that accompanied being at an unfamiliar social event alone grew as I wondered if I'd been stood up. It wasn't until I sat down with a drink and looked in the direction of the flashing lights on the dance floor that I recognized his silhouette and smiled.

He was dancing in a way that was both embarrassing and endearing. Later I would find out he called this maneuver—which he did on a regular basis—"embracing the bat." It involved cupping hands to his chest as if holding something delicate, tossing his hands in the air to release it, then doing the same motion repeatedly while stomping in place. This perfectly showcased how little he cared about the opinions of the cool kids all around him, who were barely swaying to the music.

Amused, I watched this for a while, until he started dancing with an acquaintance of mine. This was the perfect opportunity to approach him with minimal awkwardness, so I jumped up and pushed my way through the dancers. Trying to play it cool, I greeted the woman I vaguely knew and pretended to just happen to notice the Priest.

His lips moved, but I couldn't hear a thing he said over the thumping bass. Smiling, I pantomimed heading toward the bar. It took a bit of convincing in this impossible sign language to drag him away from the dance floor; I resolutely refused to sway my body despite the efforts of multiple people to lure me into their arms.

I needed to stop going to events where dancing was a requirement.

Once we were sitting, my worry that we would have nothing to talk about turned out to be for nothing. We easily fell into conversation about books (we both dug Chuck Palahniuk), writing (he wrote sci fi, in contrast to my smut), and how glad we were that the Rope Guru had helped us meet. This transitioned into the typical brief version of life stories (we were both from small-town Wisconsin, but he had moved to New Orleans for a woman while I was busy in Iowa), all the while tiptoeing around sex (I knew he had a wife and they were poly, but I didn't know if I was allowed to sleep with him). We sat side by side, not touching, screaming over the music until leaving... to get pie.

"There's always room for pie," he said while walking to my car.

This was one of his many catchphrases, cute at first in their unironic cheesiness and often repeated throughout our relationship. The air of casual-yet-secure nonchalance about him was comforting. He knew who he was and what he wanted, and he would settle for nothing less. I had never had so much fun or been so at ease with anyone. We laughed, a lot. Talking didn't come easy to me then, but here I was, chatting away without a care or worry.

After that, every date together was an adventure. We ate at nearly every restaurant in Madison, made excuses to get dressed up and go out, and went to an endless number of book readings and wine tastings. We had a lot in common for seeming so different, and we were both so glad to have someone to relate to that we became addicted to each other.

I had to force him into a friendly hug good-bye that first night, which was my first clue that things were going to progress slowly. But once we finally got naked, a month into dating, we never looked back. For the following months, we were so busy exploring one another that there was little time to sleep. He taught me to be self-assured, happy, healthy, and communicative. I taught him to let his freak out, gave him an excuse to be naughty, and tried to make being poly as painless as possible after his wife left him for a monogamous relationship elsewhere, thus allowing the Priest and me to became a full-time item. Finally I was feeling like a whole person again.

There was just one problem: the lack of rope. I was recently out of a long relationship with Guitar Guy, in which I'd had almost no kinky fun, and I was not going to live without being tied up and beaten on a regular basis again. For as perfect as the Priest was, BDSM appeared to be the only secret society he had no interest in. I felt selfish being so insistent about it being a requirement in my life, as it had become the only thing that caused issues in our relationship.

It nearly broke us up for good when he ran out of a New Year's Eve party where my friends playfully spanked one another while one laughingly played the victim by saying, "Oh no, please don't."

The Priest deemed this lighthearted beating inappropriate and disgusting; he couldn't understand why anyone would do such things. I reminded him in an unkind tone how we'd met, that he should know full well I was a part of those activities myself.

"Is that how you feel about what I do when I'm not with you?"

He didn't respond, but I got the feeling the answer was *yes*, so I went back to the party, ringing in the new year with people who didn't find my hobbies unappealing.

I thought we were finished until the next day, when he stubbornly sat on my front steps, refusing to leave until I agreed to sit and talk our guts out about the situation. If kink was that important to me, he promised we would find a way to make this relationship work: it and I were worth it to him.

That night, as we played big spoon/little spoon just before we fell asleep, he reached to the side of the bed where our pile of clothes was and wrapped my scarf around our ankles. We slept curled together, tied limb to limb, all night. This was the extent of his bondage knowledge and interest, but he became insistent that I find what I needed elsewhere.

This was when it was especially pleasant to have the Rope Guru as my other partner. I would have kinky adventures with him and come home to whisper the filth of what I had done with another man into the Priest's ear. It worked for us. I got my needs met, and he got to live vicariously through me and my delight with bondage without having to learn any knots or confront his discomfort about consensually inflicted pain. And he would date women who could feed his love for theology, which was delightful for me, as it was the one area of his life I had little interest in.

We easily fell into a healthy and communicative polyamorous relationship, largely by accident. Since we both had other partners when we met, it was obvious we wanted an open relationship, but we never sat down and created rules or expectations for dating other people. Instead, we talked endlessly about our other lovers and dealt with the pangs of jealousy or resentment as they popped up, trusting one another to make good choices and respect each other by being smart about sexual health when sleeping with other partners. We were very fortunate to be a couple for so long with almost no issues. When people would ask us how we did it, I would confess that I had no idea. The Priest and I worked together nearly effortlessly; I'd found the love of my life.

Along the way, the Priest even seemed to pick up a bit of rope knowledge and comfort with bondage through osmosis as I talked about my rope adventures. I would occasionally find myself tied to a chair or bound to a post at a party and have the odd thought, *This feels dirty, I'm doing kinky shit with my own boyfriend.* Then I would smile at the knowledge that by letting time pass and not forcing the issue, I had allowed him to come around to enjoying a few of the spanky bondage games I loved.

For the most part, however, kink only interested him when he had a partner in crime, when he could gang up on me with one of my other lovers—of which there were many in our time together. Yet there was never any true jealousy; instead, we felt camaraderie with the other people each of us dated.

After each of our brief kinky interludes I would hope the Priest's taste for the ropey would endure. To my increasing frustration, however, as quickly as his urge would appear, the Priest returned to being my sweet, vanilla boyfriend. He was always more interested in leading church services while I went off to get tied up by strangers than in tying me up himself. That was never going to change. And as I allowed myself to come to terms with that fact, my heart broke. The time we spent alone doing vastly different things was a great way to grow as individuals and always have the space to follow our passions—until it wasn't. Eventually the excitement associated with being very different people wore off and the not wanting to be at the same place on the same night wore on us.

After six years and a move across the country together, we were almost always apart. Most of our interactions occurred in text messages while we pursued our vastly different interests separately. If scheduling went well, we spent one evening together each week. I jokingly began referring to my pillow as my boyfriend, since that's what I curled up with nightly.

With the Priest, I had a long-term partner whom I adored—we shared bills, a house, and a dog—but I felt strangely single. I went to events alone, with no regular partner to share my passion for rope, kink, or dirty sex. He felt the same. I was never going to want to go to church, make cookies for the potluck, or talk philosophy with his congregation. Eventually, the together-but-alone got old.

I couldn't have become the person I am today without him. And I would never have had the courage to follow my writing or rope dreams without him pushing me in that direction. But those same passions were part of what drove us apart. The wild, creative, passionately slutty person I had become didn't fit into his hopes of a white picket fence and babies. So after those glorious and adventure-filled years, we went our separate ways with no hard feelings, to live our own separate dreams: his, a life packed with religion and a big family, and mine, full of kinky sex and adventure.

CHAPTER 8
THE GAME CHANGER

Frustrated with the lack of rope community in Madison, I'd started a group in my living room by gathering people together who were open to sharing their knowledge. Though I was moving to the other side of the country in a couple months, this was something I'd wanted for a while. Others were longing for a rope community, so I used my obsessive organizational skills to create one; it would be a small part of me I could leave behind, a legacy I could hope to visit from time to time. Besides, if I could decide to relocate to Portland, Oregon, in order to start a new life in a place where I knew no one, running a rope meeting should be simple in comparison.

Mr. Photo was the second person to arrive. Having seen his photos online, I was instantly stunned into silence and disbelief that he was in my home, leaving the other attendee to do all the talking.

Mr. Photo's images were black-and-white pieces of art. Using perfect soft lighting and gorgeous rope work, the models in his photos looked otherworldly in their grace and curvy perfection against stark backgrounds. No two pictures were the same, though they all shared a similar color palette and austere tone. In one, the subject was contorted in the air with only a few lines of rope suspending her from an unseen point in the sky, bliss on her face contrasting with the stress her muscles were exhibiting. In the next, the woman was standing, tied elaborately, but her eye contact with the viewer spoke to her being in charge despite her predicament.

In his khaki shorts, work-dirtied gym shoes, and polo shirt, Mr. Photo seemed too ordinary to be the person who created such dreamy images. His thin frame and lined skin made him seem too unintimidating to be the person who controlled the bodies of so many young women. Only his frequent smirk hinted at his dark side.

I was tongue-tied while trying not to be a fangirl, and I didn't know what to talk to him about. This man was doing exactly what I'd been looking for all these years: safe and artful rope bondage. He was my fantasies made real. And his portfolio site even stated, "Always on the lookout for willing subjects of all shapes and experience levels." Yet I couldn't find the courage to ask if he would be interested in collaborating. Instead, I sat across from him silently while he shared ties. I nearly cried out in joy when other people showed up, adding bodies to the room and voices to the conversation.

I continued looking at Mr. Photo's images online, too shy to write to him. So when a message from him appeared in my in-box, I was almost too nervous to open it, only to realize it was simply a polite note thanking me for hosting and offering to help the next time around. But what started as a discussion of rope and possibilities for the new group became more flirtatious. Finally, he asked the question I was too scared to put into words: "Shall we work together?"

Until Mr. Photo, I'd only been bound by people I was sharing some sort of ongoing physical intimacy with, and I had only been naked with those I slept with. I was having a hard time wrapping my head around sharing those activities in the context of creating art. But ever interested in an adventure, before I could talk myself out of it, I wrote, "Yes! Where and when? Tell me more."

Driving to meet him that first time, I was anxiously aflutter. Especially when the end point of his directions took me into an industrial parking lot with a sandwich-board sign pointing in from the highway that read *Fine Family and Senior Portraits*. It didn't seem possible that in such a tiny, rural town, the same person could be both a family and fetish photographer. I had to be in the wrong place.

As I gathered my courage, the sound of my idling engine seemed to catch the attention of someone inside the brick building. I watched as a finger opened the shade and an eye peeked out the window, a shadow traveled the length of the rooms inside, and the front door opened. Out came Mr. Photo. He brought in the sign with one strong, deceptively skinny arm and smoked a cigarette with the other.

I gathered my bags slowly, delaying the moment as long as possible before entering his building. He held the door, waiting patiently, likely accustomed to first-time models and their uneasy butterflies.

Given the caliber of his photos, I was expecting a fancy studio full of complicated equipment, things I didn't understand but would learn how to interact with quickly in order for the shoot to go well. Instead, walking through his front door, I saw a busy but well-ordered workshop.

"This is my day job, fixing crap for the locals. It pays for my photography habit." With childlike pride he showed off the project he'd been finishing before as I arrived. This was so endearing I forgot to be nervous.

He pointed to the wall of pinup-style photos he'd done of ladies and vintage tools—samples of his photography that were acceptable to the townies who came in to talk about whether he could fix their tractor or store a piece of equipment for them. These were a higher class of the typical pinup calendar babe, managing to be subtly subversive. The women were powerful, able to operate the tools they were holding. They were dirty, dressed for the job, and amused at being observed.

I smiled and nodded as he told the story of each one. It was easy to see he enjoyed his job and had an affection for the women he worked with. The way he spoke of them was sweet, never creepy. He had a tale to tell about each model, as well as most every item in his shop. Mr. Photo had a lot of stories.

After a full tour of his space, he ushered me into his studio. The space was both impossibly dark and painfully bright. My eyes were drawn to the raised platform to the right of the door, where several complicated-looking lighting systems were pointed. From the bare-beamed ceiling hung a system of chains and carabiners that ended with a large silver ring he utilized to suspend models. I knew this, because it featured prominently in many of his photos.

Behind the platform was a simple gray backdrop. This was momentarily baffling, given the fact that various images of his depicted women in brick rooms, near gorgeous wallpapers, and other elaborate scenes. It occurred to me then that these were only Photoshop fantasies he later added. Seeing how relatively ordinary this room was, when the images made it seem so grand, helped to ease my nerves. If he could make this space seem magical with his camera, I had no doubt he could make plain and simple me look fabulous as well.

The other two-thirds of the room was lit and decorated like a cozy waiting room with a large leather couch and interesting wooden chairs. Compared to the shooting area, this section of his studio was extremely dark. I stumbled into it, carrying my bags.

Mr. Photo showed me the changing room and wardrobe closet where he kept his props. I opened my bag to show him the various items I'd brought, including a vintage-inspired garter belt that looked like something out of a Betty Page picture and some sassy heels.

"Okay, I like it. My thought is to put you in some rope. That will be the real deal; everything else will mostly be fantasy with a little reality mixed in. We'll do pretty much whatever you want. First I'm . . ."

I smiled at his excitement, until we seemed to have the same thought: we were getting ahead of ourselves. Since I had never done this sort of thing before, and wasn't sure how comfortable I would be with the level of nudity he was accustomed to, I asked if we could start with some simple head shots. If that went well, we could move on to the more risqué photos. So we switched gears, placing Mr. Photo's rope ideas on hold.

Now it was time for me to climb atop the stage and into the light. As I was blinded by the brightness, Mr. Photo became a voice in the darkness. "Relax. Shift your head to the right. Straighten your arm. The other one . . ."

It didn't going well. I was too stiff, which made my smiles look forced. Mr. Photo joked to lighten the mood while coaching me on how to stand, where to place my limbs in relation to my body, and at what angle to position myself in relationship to the lights. Soon I was keeping so many instructions in mind while posing that I forgot to feel ill at ease. I was playing to the camera and finally letting loose when he said, "Okay, I think we have what we need."

We looked into the tiny viewfinder at the back of his camera. As the photos progressed, they got better, culminating in the final images, which I couldn't believe were of me. My smile was genuine (in response to one of his quips), my hair was perfect, and I looked sexy and confident. I knew it was largely a matter of lighting and perspective, but there was a fair amount of me there as well, and I was impressed.

"Wow," was all I could manage.

"You done good. What do you think?"

"I like them!"

He laughed. "I mean, what do you think about . . . " He nodded toward the pile of rope at the corner of the stage. I wilted, the creative high melting in an instant, leaving nothing but nerves. Heart racing and visibly sweating now, I could feel my face flush.

"Tell you what, I'm gonna go out for a smoke. You put on whatever you're comfortable shooting in next, and we'll go from there when I'm done with my bad habit." He smiled boyishly while tapping out a cigarette and walking out the door with a thump. Suddenly I was alone to make a big decision about whether I wanted naked pictures of me to exist in the world forever.

Before I could change my mind, I lifted the dress over my head. I didn't bother using the dressing room to put on the lingerie we'd decided on earlier, including vintage back-seamed stockings that I pulled on carefully, seducing myself with the feel of the soft nylon on my skin. As I sat to force myself into high heels, the door opened, bringing in the grassy smell of summer air and a faint whiff of tobacco. Though Mr. Photo loomed silently, in my armor of confidence I was no longer nervous. I smiled at him over my shoulder, asking, "Are my seams straight?"

I stood, turning so he could look at my stockings and barely covered behind, knowing full well I was being a tease. He kept his distance, a question he wasn't asking twisting his lips; I guessed at the answer. "You can touch me. It's okay. Just don't be creepy about it. Or at least not until we talk about creepy, anyway."

Breathing a sigh of relief and laughing, Mr. Photo knelt to hold my thigh and jiggle the stocking until the seams were straight. "Smart-ass," he said under his breath.

"Thanks for noticing." I grabbed my ass and contorted my expression. He continued primping me, being less careful now that we were joking. Once we'd crossed the border of touching, our interaction became more relaxed. We bantered sarcastically to combat the tension between us. I wasn't sure if it was just creative energy attracting us, nor did I know whether I wanted to act on it, but I felt safe poking at the edges of this flirtation in the name of photos.

When it was time to get down to business, Mr. Photo pointed at the stage, playing at being stern. "Get up there!"

Again I stood on the X at the center of the lights, which were now turned down low as Mr. Photo retrieved the pile of bundled rope. He juggled a piece between his hands, seeming to weigh a thought. Following his gaze, I noticed he was looking at my bra curiously.

"Do you want that to go away?"

"Underwire?"

"Yes."

"Then yes. I mean, if you're—" I unclasped my bra with a flourish and tossed it away, finding that if I feigned boldness, real confidence quickly followed.

"Better?"

"Yes, ma'am." He spun me around by the shoulders, and I heard the rope bundle snap open—even in the heat of the stage it gave me a chill. Wrapping his arms around me, Mr. Photo ran the first line under my breasts. Cinching in the back, he pulled the rope so tight it took my breath away, putting me off balance during the rest of the tie. He continued working quickly, moving me this way and that, pulling everything snug and corset-like, which distracted me from any other thoughts. But a twinge of nervousness briefly reappeared when, finishing the decorative chest wrappings, Mr. Photo turned me to face him. I could feel the intensity of his gaze on my breasts as he adjusted the design by tugging the ropes.

I wasn't accustomed to being this casual about nudity. In my experience bare skin was necessarily a preamble to sex, but that wasn't the case here—this was purely professional. A near stranger was touching me but only to create art. This was when I realized my life was taking another strange turn. Not only was I comfortable sharing this moment with Mr. Photo, I was enjoying it.

Along with the excitement of exhibitionism, the rope was working its magic on my senses, leaving me flushed and quietly aroused. But I was careful to be satisfied finding pleasure in the experience of riding the sensations without any urge to escalate our interaction to a sexual plane. Because of the exchange of power and energy, being tied was nearly always sensual for me, but I'd realized that it wasn't about sex unless both people chose to make it so. I found that bondage was often more akin to meditation: a centering experience that made it enjoyable to inhabit my skin.

During the beginning of my journey into BDSM, rope had everything to do with sex, as back then it was hard for me to imagine being bound without it leading down that road. But since becoming a part of the sex-positive and kink communities, I understood the appeal of being tied just for the sake of feeling rope on my skin and interacting with another person in an intimate way. So my senses were awakened by being tied by Mr. Photo, but I had no intension of doing anything more than flirting with him.

Mr. Photo grinned, lowering himself to one creaky knee to pop open another skein of rope and continue the pattern down my belly with knotted diamonds. At my crotch, he stopped to look up again with another silent question.

I spread my legs in response, nodding and smiling. He didn't hesitate to reach between my thighs. The lines tucking into my labia made me keenly aware of my body as he pulled the rope tight. Behind me, I could feel him mirroring the diamond pattern, then tightening them all. The lines were boa-constrictor tight and getting snugger each time I took a breath.

Stepping away, Mr. Photo started on the support lines that ran from the ropes around my chest to the dangling silver ring. Tugging on this pulley system like a leash, he was able to bring me closer to him by forcing me into motion. I tottered in his direction, trying to keep my balance in tall shoes on the slippery floor.

Shocked at his forceful manhandling, I furrowed my brow; after all, we were here for photos, not play. The loaded eye contact we maintained as he tied off these lines felt a lot like both of us were toying with the idea of making this into more but resisting. I dropped my head and leaned into the pressure he put on the harness. He lifted the lines that led to the ring until I was standing on tiptoes.

"Stay here one second. Don't go anywhere," he said quietly near my ear.

"Haha," I managed, but I wasn't laughing—instead, I did everything I could to stifle a moan. He had every iota of my attention and was totally in control. The last thing I wanted was him to leave my side, but he was merely retrieving the camera.

"Can I take your hands away?" He held yet more nylon rope, shaken loose and ready. I nodded, offering my hands, which he bound together then tugged behind my head before tying them to the ring above. This nicely exposed my chest, making me more vulnerable. I could feel myself getting wet, willing my body to not go so far as to puddle my underthings in a way that would show in the photos.

There again was that eye contact, him taking in his prey and me trying to guess his next move. As was our agreement, he didn't touch me except where it was required to place rope on my body or get my attention. That didn't stop very inch of my skin from wanting his hands near. I closed my eyes, waiting, trying to remain professional.

He backed away, and the camera clicked, but I wasn't present enough to be aware of what he was shooting, too rope-high to pose. I felt his hands on my shoulders again, moving me to a new angle. *Click, click.* He would pace to a different spot, adjust the lights. *Click, click.* I looked at him, at the camera, my eyes glazed, blissed out on the dopamine and endorphins that being bound released.

The next time I felt his touch, it was at my knees, a gentle pressure and a tap that I recognized as him wanting me to spread them. As I did, the sexual nature of this gesture snapped me to attention, forcing me back to reality as he turned my ass to the camera. He lay on the floor to shoot, accentuating the curve of my behind. I arched my back to make it pop even more, and he grunted softly. *Click, click, click.*

He raised one of my legs, tying it to the ring so that I was careening in circles, pivoting on the toe of my single grounded shoe on his glossy floor. *Click, click, click.* He tried to catch my giggling surprise as I attempted to find traction.

"Well, how about we just take care of this one too?"

I wrinkled my nose at his lack of assistance.

"Yeah, sure, why not. I'm not feeling quite helpless enough yet."

He chuckled and bound my remaining unrestrained limb. Kneeling, he looked up at me, peering between the elbows framing my vision.

"Ready to fly?" This hadn't occurred to me. Of course, if he lifted that leg, I would be suspended. It made sense, but I hadn't thought we'd get this far.

"I never have before."

He looked taken aback. "Well, I'll go easy on you . . . for now."

He cradled my thigh in the crook of one arm, used the other to tie my ankle to the ring, and then lifted my leg to shoulder level. When he stepped back, there was only rope holding me above the floor. I refused to panic, but I'd never felt more vulnerable. And yet, imagining how beautiful I must be with these lines wrapping me securely, I felt powerful as well.

Click, click, click. He was everywhere at once, working quickly to get images before my muscles tired. It wasn't easy to dangle there as the rope dug into my skin, getting impossibly tighter, but I endured the discomfort. It was simple to masochistically twist the pain into pleasure, so that once the endorphins were coursing, I could barely tell the difference. It worked like a runner's high does in keeping the runner unaware of how sore her body is until the run is finished.

It was only when my muscles started to burn that I had to squeak out, "I'm done."

Mr. Photo sprang into action, lowering my legs so I could breathe easily and loosening the lines holding my torso so I could touch the floor. He stood at a polite distance, looking concerned, with his arms outstretched in a pantomime of an embrace. I nodded, granting him permission for more touch. The hug was fatherly and not at all sexual—it was aftercare, his body simply reminding mine of its place on earth and urging my limbs back to reality. It worked; I felt able to go on.

"Do you need your hands?"

"Nah." I smirked, daring him to return to his camera.

The shutter popped as I writhed in the ropes, playing at arousal until I realized I wasn't playing; the pressure of the rope between my legs was extremely pleasant. When I stopped, the camera did as well.

Mr. Photo came into the light, and we locked eyes. He stayed silent while walking around behind me, circling like a predator on his way to undo the diamonds around my torso. I let out a sigh at the sudden relief when the rope loosened and popped free from between my legs, releasing with it the obvious smell of my excitement. Blushing, I hoped he wouldn't notice.

"Having fun?"

"Uh yeah, just a little."

"You look a little . . . disheveled. Mind if I help with that?" He looped a finger under the band of my panties but didn't go any further. "The only thing that would make these rope marks better is if these weren't in the way."

What the hell, I thought. "Go for it."

He shimmied them over my hips and stopped when my pubic hair was exposed, which felt more scandalous than if he had taken them off fully. It was hot and demeaning at the same time, like so many things about being a rope bottom. *Click, click.*

I grinned at the camera as he captured a final shot then put down his camera to finish untying me. Once free from the rope, a beautiful network of marks was exposed on my skin where it had pressed. We both traced them at different parts of my belly, laughing to catch our actions being mirrored in the other.

"If you're up for it, there's one more thing I want to try." He disappeared into the dark, leaving me wobbling, thrilled, and alone in the lights. When Mr. Photo reappeared with an evil smile and a leather cube that looked like a mini ottoman, I knew he was up to trouble. "I have an image of your ass bent over this thing in some low-key light. It will make that butt even more epic, if that's possible."

I laughed at the delight on his face. "And what would I be wearing during this adventure?"

"Ideally? Nothing." He held up a leather flogger that had been hidden behind his back. "Except maybe this to pinken you up." With an expectant expression, he waited, looking me up and down.

Somehow he could get away with being lecherous without it seeming creepy. Any other near stranger holding a camera would've gotten slapped for suggesting we play spanky games for photos after having just met. Mr. Photo, however, was endearing in his dirty-old-man nature. It was part of his persona, the veneer that made him a memorable local character. He knew everyone, and everyone knew him. That was the way of small towns. So Mr. Photo was a rarity in that many people were also aware of his bondage hobby but he was so jokey and harmless that it didn't bother anyone. That was just Mr. Photo, one of his quirks alongside bad puns and wearing white socks with sandals.

The innocuous nature that he exuded—not a mean or pushy cell in his body—was also why I trusted him to go further. After all, it wasn't the activities he was suggesting that were causing my hesitancy—bondage and floggings were a regular part of my life by this point. Instead, I was tentative about crossing a line with a photographer, knowing our interaction was supposed to be professional. I'd also toned down on casual sex since meeting the Priest. Having a satisfying sexual and emotional relationship made random encounters so much less appealing. But I'd had a crush on Mr. Photo since discovering his photography, so I felt comfortable exploring further with him and seeing what came of it.

"Let's do it." I kicked off my shoes and began the project of taking off my stockings.

"Do it? I was suggesting flogging not . . . going all the way." He winked, and I squished up my face in response to his sarcasm; it was rare to meet someone who made more terrible jokes than I did.

Mr. Photo set up the impromptu spanking bench while I undressed. Hitting a switch, he changed the bright lights we'd used for head shots and rope to a chiaroscuro of extreme shadows, the stage barely lit.

"Assume the position."

I bent over the square with my ass in the air, surprised at how quickly I had become comfortable with the camera; it didn't faze me any longer to be aware that every aspect of my body was being captured. *Click* went the camera shutter behind me.

After taking dozens of shots, Mr. Photo seemed to remember that the rest of me was there too. "More rope?" he asked, already fondling a length between his fingers.

I perked up so noticeably that I didn't need to say a word. Mr. Photo belly laughed. "Of course you do. Why did I even bother to ask? You crack me up, gal."

He put simple rope cuffs on each wrist and tied them down to the sides of the cube. My waist was next, bound tight around the cube so I couldn't sit up. "Ready?" The flails of the flogger tickled my ass.

I steadied myself, preparing for the bite of the flogger. The smack and hot impact of the leather across my behind were almost instantaneous. I inhaled sharply, trying to process the sensation as it was repeated. Arching my back to the pain that danced along pleasure, I was glad for the rope holding me. While bound I could endure this at length—if I could get past the initial fight-or-flight mechanism and sink into the moment.

Mr. Photo replaced the flogger with his palm, soothing my goose-bumped flesh, a kind contrast to the wickedness. I melted into the solid leather device holding me in place, moaning, still unsure whether we were playing or shooting, or where the line was between lover and photographer.

He returned to smacking me with the flogger until I lost track of reality. When he stopped, I had no sense of where I was or how much time had passed, just that I was desperate for touch but being denied that closeness. Mr. Photo tossed aside the instrument of pain and replaced it with the camera, snapping several photos before refastening the lens cap and setting it aside.

I lay there, ass in the air, and I couldn't imagine what came next as Mr. Photo disappeared into the darkness.

When the shooting lights on stage went out, I jumped. There was only the sound of my breathing for what seemed like forever, until Mr. Photo reappeared, holding a powerful Hitachi vibrator. He circled, not getting close, just looking. I wanted to cry out in frustration, unable to wait any longer for contact.

Finally, kneeling in front of me, Mr. Photo held up the vibrator. "May I?"

"Please," I whispered, embarrassed at my need, my body desperate for release. It had been so long since I'd engaged in kinky play that this mild scene was driving me wild. It was unexpected and thrilling.

The loud hum of the vibrator caused me to startle again. Mr. Photo edged in closer, tucking it between my thighs. He explored until coming to rest on a sweet spot that made me buck against the vibrations. Holding the device steady, Mr. Photo gave no reprieve as I wiggled in bliss. Moaning, I no longer held back.

With his free hand, he pressed against the small of my back so I had no choice but to ride the vibrations. I was panting, nearly in another dimension of joy, so it took me a minute to understand him over the humming motor. "It's so red."

His palm sweetly grazing my throbbing ass created so much sensation it became maddening. I was struggling so frantically against the border of release that when he used his open hand to spank me, I was caught off guard. Forgetting to keep up my defenses, I came, undulating against the vibrator. Mr. Photo alternately pet and hit my behind until I couldn't come anymore.

When I started giggling manically from overstimulation, he clicked off the vibrator, untied me, and came close enough to touch. I wrapped my arms around him, falling into his chest; this hug wasn't platonic. The touching after being denied so long made it seem like the only option was for our hands to be all over each other. I didn't bother to stop and think if this was professional.

Reading my one anxious thought, he joked, but with a grain of seriousness, "Don't worry—I don't do this with all the girls."

• • •

Our acquaintance started in the name of photos—me as his model and muse—but quickly became more. He wasn't like the men I'd known before him, who largely played with rope as if it were a sexy party trick. Mr. Photo transferred a part of himself into his rope, and then into the person he placed it on. It was a passionate, shared experience that left me changed. Soon I was driving to visit his studio multiple times a week, where we would play out a variation on the same ritual with rope.

The slick surface of the nylon rope would kiss his skin at a frequency akin to the sound of a person brushing her long hair as I knelt in front of him, watching. Rope run through deft hands makes a meditative sound that I know now as the song of bindings about to be put to use. It was a noise I never thought much of until those evenings spent dreamily observing Mr. Photo seduce his lengths of nylon, longing for him to put his hands and ropes on me.

The calm before the struggle put my synapses on edge. I saw the same lust for it reflected in his ice-blue eyes. He combined the artistry involved in wrapping lines around a body with the perfect dash of sensuality and sadism that made the experience addictive. It was all I could think about that summer of our brief acquaintance.

After caressing the rope, he would begin the task of coiling his lines around me, and at last I would feel the warmth of his rough hands against my skin. That first brush of fingers adjusting a line, his arms looped around me in an embrace I couldn't reciprocate, was like lightning through my veins. Suddenly my full focus was on this man and his silvery rope; this was the perfect place to find peace from a restless mind. No matter how many times we interacted, that first touch was electric.

The dance would continue until I was bound to his liking. Our gaze meeting across the distance, me packaged nicely upon the floor and him standing above me, taking in his prize. His puckish blue eyes were impossible to hold for more than a moment without a full-body blush taking over. Like his well-lined hands, they had a story to tell, one that I got in bits and pieces each evening when the rope came off and we curled against one another. But when bound, the only promise in his stare was of flight, freedom, and the furious intensity between us.

Some describe being suspended in rope as like flying, but the truth was, it was like nothing else, which was a large part of what made the moment so appealing. I've spent a significant amount of time trying to recapture those moments of bliss when Mr. Photo would haul my body off the floor and into the air. There was something in that room and in his touch that couldn't be reproduced—the grace and beauty of a body defying the laws of physics thanks to a few simple pieces of rope and the talent in his fingers.

His hands would flicker across my dangling body; they were soft, tender, and giving at times, then they turned into hard, malevolent tools of pain. Sometimes they would own the very air I breathed, curled around my neck, putting my blood and breath on hold for his amusement. Those brief seconds would feel like hours, our pulse one, his touch so close to my jugular it was hard to tell whose heartbeat I was hearing.

After that, when I drew a well-earned breath, he would twirl me through the air, a dazzle of sensations flooding my rope-drunk brain. There was something genuine and zygogenic created out of the energy between the two of us and this specific confluence of lust, limbs, and loops of rope. This lack of gravity was better than anything else I'd ever experienced.

After an evening of breathless experiences in his ropes, I would leave his studio to drive the thirty minutes home in the darkest dark on curvy, small-town Wisconsin roads, full to bursting with new experiences and stories, wobbly with pleasure and the high of artistic creation. The center of my brain remembered how to get me home, while the rest of me reveled.

Before drifting off to sleep, I would check my in-box to find photos showing me what we had created. These images, which he had tweaked while I was traveling home, welcomed me like a long-distance goodnight kiss. When I looked at these pictures, I was barely able to recognize the person in them. Captured there was the me he saw and found with his lens, the one he was forcing me to notice.

He took me into the world of his rope and camera to show me my beauty and transformed me into who I always was on the inside but had never given myself permission to outwardly express. I was now free to be this bold, bright, shiny thing that could say and do anything and be part of any story I put my mind to. He inspired me to start writing again (after a long hiatus) by gifting me with experiences that insisted on being recorded.

Our interaction began with me as his muse, but in the end, he became mine.

CHAPTER 9
THE SHOW ME THE ROPES

It was the first time I'd invited someone over for a rope date, and I didn't know what to expect. The Doctor's muscles, shaved head, and stern features made him as physically intimidating as the stories I'd heard of his inventive cruel streak. He had a way of talking to the women he wanted to play with, subtly getting them to reveal themselves and learning what made them tick so he could poke at their deepest fears and desires. I was curious to find out where we could go together, what dark place he would dream up to explore. This all made me feel like a giggling schoolgirl on the sweltering afternoon he stopped by with his bag of tricks.

Since meeting Mr. Photo I had developed enough confidence to ask people to tie me up, and I was finding that I was willing to try nearly anything once. And having seen the Doctor across the room during a rope meeting, I knew I wanted him to be cruel to me.

My partner, the Priest, was 2,000 miles away in Portland, hunting for a house and job while I stayed behind one last month to fulfill our lease. I was pent up and sexually frustrated in a way that only getting beaten into a masochistic frenzy would satisfy. The Doctor seemed like the perfect man to fill that need.

I welcomed him to my largely empty living room. After the requisite small talk, he said, "Get undressed."

He leaned back to take in the show while I removed my dress. The moment I was naked he was behind me, tugging my arms straight back, where he started a strappado, which is perhaps the most uncomfortable way to bind arms (and likely why he chose the tie). It was a strain on the body, with elbows locked straight and the rope cinching in the entire length of both arms where they were bound parallel and tightly together. My neck, shoulders, and chest started to burn instantly.

Even through the continual blowing of the central air, we were both already covered in a sheen of sweat. It was that oppressively hot. I could feel the perspiration dripping down my body. Wet spots quickly spread at the small of his back and underarms as he worked. And yet he refused to remove any clothing throughout the ordeal, perhaps to further accentuate the power dynamic between us.

I didn't feel nearly as awkward around him as I'd expected to. Largely, I supposed, because he had solved the eternal dilemma of what I should do with my hands. Whole sections of my brain ordinarily portioned out to being anxious about what to do with my body had been relieved of their duties. As long as his rope was on me, he could tell my appendages what was required of them. This feeling of instant calm, even around an unfamiliar person I trusted, was one of the reasons I loved rope so much. The only thing I had to worry about now was how sadistic he would be.

He had a way of tying the ropes tight around the tender bits of the upper arms with well-placed knots that made the position surprisingly comfortable. It occurred to me then how much his knowledge of anatomy must have come in handy. Ordinarily, I would lose circulation in my hands once my arms were bound behind me this way, but he had placed his lines perfectly, so that I didn't feel a pinch of discomfort. The Doctor knew just where to place ropes so his victim could stay in them for a long time.

As he walked to my front, the grin he gave me through the glow of sweat on his face let me know he also knew how to provide pain with equally little effort. It was only because we didn't know one another well that he was being kind. We had negotiated for some casual nonsexual play, with just enough sadism to keep it interesting. This was our first time interacting outside of rope group, so he wouldn't be doling out anything heavy unless I explicitly asked for more. But the promise that he could change his mind and mess with my mind or body at anytime was palpable between us. He didn't have to touch me for me to be intimidated by him.

The intensity with which he held my gaze caused me to look away;

he made me nervous in the best possible way. Using this moment of distraction to his advantage, he grabbed the ropes around my body to lower me facedown onto the wooden table near the couch. This moment of flight made me gasp, surprised that he could lift my weight. Not being petite, I was very seldom tossed about by anyone, so this display made his strength suddenly real and intimidating.

Once I was chest down at the table's center, the Doctor bound my ankles together and then secured them to the arm bindings, fastening me into a hog-tie that arched my body in a difficult position. My chest was bent off the table to strain closer to my feet, which were angled toward my bound arms. He then added more rope in the form of a gag which had the tripled usefulness of holding my head in an uncomfortable position, keeping me quiet, and if he was lucky, I would make his day by drooling, which was his favorite sign of helplessness.

When he started going through the pile of packing supplies sitting in the corner, I had a moment of concern, especially now that I was gagged and unable to ask questions. Noticing my grunts of struggle as I shifted, trying to follow his movements, he quipped, "Don't worry. I'm not planning anything too crazy. Not today, anyway."

He returned to fingering through a box, making a show of lifting a wrench or hammer as if questioning their usefulness, keeping me on edge with concern. I soon realized that it was likely the collection of pens and markers that he was truly interested in. Having them out in the open was making enacting his plot far too simple. He grinned sadistically while uncapping a Sharpie, which he brandished like a weapon.

He kneeled close, threatening me with the open marker, its distinct chemical smell teasing my nose. I soon discovered how little I could move as he brought the tip near my face. All of my strength was focused on using my core muscles to hold my shoulders back in order to breathe, so I couldn't get away, but I could watch in my peripheral vision as he sidled to the other end of the table. When I couldn't see him anymore, I felt the cold Sharpie make contact with my thigh.

"I thought we'd combine two of our favorite things. You know, aside from rope, of course."

The one thing I enjoyed nearly as much as rope was writing. Occasionally I'd been blessed with partners who would take pen to my skin and treat it like paper. Something about being written on was maddeningly hot: the objectification, combining words and sex, the taboo of marking someone's skin. There were enough pictures of me used as a canvas that anyone who had looked at my modeling profile would be aware of this fixation.

The Doctor had done his research and managed to get in my head. "Tell me when you figure out what I'm writing."

I darted him a look. As if I could tell him anything with scratchy straw-flavored rope in my mouth, burning at the corners of my lips.

Sinking into the predicament, I enjoyed the soft strokes of the pen on flesh. It was a soothing tickle, one of my favorite sensations. I tried to follow the movements of his hand to guess what he was writing but quickly got lost in the moment. The Doctor finished with a self-satisfied expression, and I waited for him to end the mystery by telling me which words would be on my skin for the next days.

"Usually I stick to simple stuff like 'bitch' or 'whore' for this sort of thing, but I figured something poetic would be more fitting here." He brought his face kiss-close to mine, making me wait as he blew down my chest, his breath hot on my sweaty skin.

Finally he rasped in my ear, "I went with my favorite Elvis song." He dragged his nails down my ribs to watch me wiggle while he moved closer to his artwork again.

"*We're caught in a trap, I can't walk out* . . . Let me know when you've figured it out."

"Haha," I tried to quip back at him, but it came out as a muffled *mrph, mrph.*

He read the remaining words off my thigh, the beginning lines of "Suspicious Minds." I smiled around the rope, amused that he had found a way to combine our interests, his in Elvis, mine in all things body-writing related.

The Doctor lowered himself toward the floor to look me in the eye while explaining his theory that the song is much darker and kinkier than most people think. "Well, of course he can't leave, because she has him tied up. And the tears are real because she keeps flogging his balls." I would have laughed at his rant except there again was that pleasantly scary look in his eyes, rendering me silent.

"The only problem is, I ran out of canvas because I'm a fucking physician, so I'm legally required to have shitty-ass handwriting. I'll have to be more meticulous next time. Also, you're not drooling enough." At that he gave me an open-handed slap across the ass where the beginnings of his lyrics were written. The surprise of the sensation made me jump. He laughed and proceeded to whack me several more times for further amusement.

"Hey, check this out." He displayed his palm, which looked like he'd been handling charcoal. It entertained him endlessly that with each smack of his hand, the Sharpie wore off slightly, transferring from my ass to his hand. He periodically continued to show me proof of how much of the marker he'd removed and therefore how much work he was doing.

Fixated now, he continued to spank that one side of my ass exclusively until the first words he had written were largely erased. When I got too tired to hold my neck at that angle any longer, I started shaking my head with a pained expression until he caught on. "Head getting heavy?" I nodded as best I could. "Too bad!" He returned to hitting my ass as I grumbled at him. "Oh . . . just kidding."

He leaned over me, his crotch purposefully close to my face while he untied the ropes in my mouth from the ones on my feet. With a great sigh of relief from me, the pressure was released from my neck. I leaned my head into his leg until he lowered me to the table, carefully untangling the gag from my mouth. "You didn't even drool? I'm so fucking disappointed."

"Yeah, well, I was busy doing other things."

"Like what?"

"Um, lying here."

He tickled the bottom of my feet to punctuate his amusement at my sarcasm. This silenced me for the moment.

Curious, I squirmed around to admire the partly smudged words that curved around my thigh. It looked like a kid had gotten ahold of the art supplies when no one was watching, but the writing hadn't been about artistry—rather, it had been about the shared experience of playing with words. I laughed. "You weren't kidding about your calligraphy skills, Doc."

This earned me a sharp tug on the arm ropes as he loosened them, bringing me against his chest so he could pinch a nipple until I giggled. This annoyed him further. "Masochist."

"Thanks for noticing." He pinched again, and I turned my head to smile at him. "Yeah, pain isn't really a punishment for me."

"So I see."

When my arms were fully free, I stretched and massaged the muscles back to life, shaking out the stiffness until circulation returned to each finger. I've never been able to stay in that tie before without them going instantly numb, so I was impressed with whatever technique the Doctor had used to make it so sustainable. As I rested my muscles, I questioned him about what he'd done differently, and he happily explained his methods while cooling down from the effort of slinging rope in a 100-degree room.

I was impressed by his knowledge and willingness to share it. While he explained the most important knot in the tie, I grabbed a piece of his rope to wrap it around my legs as he talked, following his directions to see if I could in fact re-create this tie later.

"You got it!" he exclaimed, yanking at the ropes to test my knot.

It was a heady experience to have learned something so quickly and easily, and it made me want to try more. This marked the beginning of me hoping to understand what the Top was doing. I was starting to get curious about how doing the tying worked, after spending so much time with rope geeks. Maybe I'd get good enough and brave enough to bind someone other than myself eventually. So I spent the afternoon filing away for later the information the Doctor was sharing.

"Anyway, enough of being nerds. You up for another thing?"

I smiled widely.

"I'll take that as a yes?"

I feigned distress. "Uh yeah, I just hate getting tied up so much. Oh no, please don't practice on me anymore."

"Okay smart-ass, come here so I can figure out this hip thing."

It was something that the rope group had been learning the weekend before. The Doctor wanted to go over it again to save the steps in his muscle memory. I was more than happy to stand still long enough for him to figure it out.

This tie was especially pleasing in the way it lifted and framed the booty. When he had finished, several lines of rope hugged my upper thigh just under my butt then looped around my hips to create a handle. It was called the gunslinger because it looked like a ropey holster when one was tied on each side. I watched while he experimented, asking questions and eager to try it on myself later, the intensity of my curiosity amusing him.

Having engineered this tie to his liking, the Doctor waggled his eyebrows as he picked up another piece of rope. "I don't think I'm done with you yet."

"Okay," I said softly, a little unsure of the sinister energy radiating off of him.

He grasped my wrists in his strong palm to effortlessly bind them together and pull them behind my head. The Doctor loomed over me, so close we were breathing the same air as he made me wait before further amplifying the vulnerability of my position by forcing a rope around my bound arms and into my mouth. This he anchored in place so I wouldn't be able to push it out from between my teeth. Once again I was unable to speak or escape.

Using the rope on my hips as handles and a handful of my curls to drag me, I was lifted onto a small, firm, cube-shaped ottoman. We were both breathing heavily as he slapped at my thighs to suggest I spread my legs. I grunted at his cruelty and its suddenness but acquiesced so the Doctor could tie an ankle into the waist rope on each side. This placed my legs in an extreme frogged position, my heel touching my thigh on each side. With my legs bent thusly I balanced against the edge of the cube, unable to shift except to hold my balance. My chest and cunt were on display, and he was looking at me like I was dinner.

He wasted no time yanking a flogger out of his bag to brandish it theatrically in the empty space of my living room. Periodically he threatened with the crack of the leather as it wrapped around itself in the air, moving closer to me with each stroke. The dark expression on his face made his desire to provide pain obvious; I didn't mind that I would be the focus of his cruelty.

Still, the first blow was a shock as it landed directly between my open legs, the thump of the leather exhilarating and painful. With the corner of the ottoman between my thighs and the rope holding me tight, I couldn't close them to protect myself. I could only moan into the rope between my teeth that was making me drool as I endured the flogging. The moisture from my own mouth trickled down my chin while I remained as still as possible, not wanting to risk rope burn on my face.

The Doctor grinned manically each time his blows made purchase, enjoying my surprise as much as my drool-gurgled whimpers. The flails of the flogger bit into my bare thighs painfully. I was sweating, equally from the effort of holding myself centered and from arousal. The smell of our humid bodies was mixing with the aroma of soft leather; it was heady and delicious. I closed my eyes to enjoy the heavy flogger striking me several more times.

Just as I got invested in the rhythm of the pain, wondering if it was possible to get off from being hit, he stopped suddenly to untie me. Bringing his large, sweaty body close enough that I could feel the heat coming off of him, he worked from behind me while pressed alluringly against my back. He pulled his ropes off slowly like a tickle or a tease. The stiff lines of hemp running over my skin gave me chills even in the heat of the room. He breathed near my ear while untying everything but the rope gag—which trapped my hands at the nape of my neck, leaving me unable to touch him or relax—while watching him re-coil his ropes.

Our play ended so suddenly that a million anxious thoughts ran through my head. When I was fully unbound and his rope was packed, the Doctor hugged me and left with the smiling assurance that he had enjoyed himself. Though I longed to have him stay longer, I remained silent and let him get away. Like any good Top, he had likely stopped when he did to leave me wanting more and to prevent us from crossing a boundary during our first interaction. It just happened that I was leaving the Midwest permanently soon, so we would never have an opportunity to finish what we'd started.

Regardless, I was happy to have managed to play with the Doctor once. Planning to move across the country had been strangely motivating; knowing I wouldn't get another chance, I began befriending interesting people and jumping on experiences I ordinarily would have been too shy to participate in. It was a little disappointing to finally meet these fellow rope lovers now, when I would only have the opportunity to know them for a short while. But it was a powerful experience to have finally found community. I would find it again in Portland as soon as I got there, refusing to ever go back to being kink deprived again.

CHAPTER 10
THE LONG GOOD-BYE

I'd been tempted to cancel my date with the Gamer all that day. It was flattering that he'd asked me out for drinks and rope before I left town, but since I generally wasn't attracted to younger men, it was hard for me to ignore our seven year age difference (which made him barely old enough to drink). Plus, the next day was my last at the call center I was working at, so getting to bed relatively early seemed prudent. I only followed through because I was sure we wouldn't have enough in common to make it through one drink.

We met at my favorite French bistro, the only place in Madison I would miss. Sharing drinks at the bar and flirting, the Gamer effortlessly held up his end of the conversation, making his youth and ego more charming than laughable, even as he tried to explain his passion for competitively fighting with foam swords. Our legs touched periodically under the bar, and despite myself I felt that spark of warmth, the thrill of a new body. He was tempting.

That he didn't shift away during this accidental contact let me know he was receptive, that I could have him if I chose. Blame the wine or his smile, but I stopped moving away. Our thighs rested together comfortably as we carried on talking as if this wasn't happening, almost as if daring the other to mention the sudden intimacy. Neither of us did.

Drinks became a walk around the lake. The cavalier way he draped his arm over my shoulder while we strolled was oddly appealing; he felt alluring tucked in next to me, our bodies moving in rhythm. Somewhere along the way I let my guard down, allowing his cocky attitude and sense of humor to win me over. By the time we were sitting, watching the sun drifting lower over the water, I was returning his touch, cuddling in closer.

Several times our faces turned to one another, millimeters separating us, neither moving in to make the kiss official. This would last until one of us would turn away smiling. After a beat of silence we would continue the conversation as if nothing had happened. The sexual tension between us was so great I was surprised we weren't risking arrest by making out, hands all over each other right there in public.

During the next spell of staring at one another he broke the silence with, "Should we go back to your place? I want to make good on my promise to tie you up before you abandon me for the West Coast."

His forwardness made him even more appealing. "Absolutely, yes."

We walked back to our cars so he could follow me home through the maze of cookie-cutter suburbia I lived in. Finally, standing outside my place, I nodded toward the living room. "Come on up. I hope you don't mind dogs. Mine is up there and she'll be all over you."

"Ah man, a doggie? I love 'em. Bring her on."

The second the front door opened, my giant, four-legged best friend was doing figure eights between our legs, trying to say hello to us both at once. True to his word, the Gamer seemed to be enjoying the attention almost as much as she was. I stood back and laughed at them being cute. Playing with my furry gal was an absolutely necessary part of the courtship ritual for anyone who made it into my home. If my dog liked someone, they were much more likely to be allowed in my bed. So it was nice to see him passing this unspoken test. I sat nearby to remind him why he was there.

"Hi," he said, looking at me seductively.

As he brought his face close, I felt certain the moment we'd been denying ourselves would occur. Then, just as our lips would have met, the dog forced her head between us, showing her displeasure at not being the center of attention. We laughed at our adorable chaperone as I stood, taking his hand to pull him up as well. I gave the dog one last ear rub before leading the Gamer down the hall to my bedroom and closing the door on her protests. I pulled out the bag containing my small collection of rope, a recent gift from the Priest, and spread the various lengths of red hemp on my bed. "Well, here it is, if that offer of getting tied up still stands."

He smiled, grabbing one of the longer pieces. "Come here."

I pulled off my sweater and walked to him, eager to find out what he had in mind. He spun me around to pull my arms together in back, binding my wrists. Working the ropes up my straightened arms in a ladder-like pattern, he created an arm binder, a lot like the one the Doctor had placed on me the week before. To use up the leftover rope, the Gamer ran the remaining bit around my chest, making the tie feel more restrictive.

I continued our snarky banter as he worked. "You know, for someone who claims they don't know shit about rope, you're doing pretty well."

"That's because you're seeing the one thing I know how to do. Don't bother being impressed yet." But I was. He'd only been experimenting with rope for a short while—long enough to find our practice group, but not long enough to have his own rope. So his tying effectively without fumbling was notable.

"I'm gonna keep on being a little impressed, regardless."

"Suit yourself."

In case he was feeling too shy to ask, I mentioned, "You know, I'd be happy to get undressed." My tight skirt was perfect for a dinner date but overkill for bondage situations. I was feeling stifled by all the fabric.

"Girl, I've seen it all on the Internet. I'll get around to that when I'm ready," was his response as he continued to tie. This was a first: a guy who wanted me to keep my clothes on. My first instinct was to feel insulted, but before I could overthink his words, the Gamer tossed me onto the bed, knocking the breath out of me.

I lay there facedown, stunned and watching him in my peripheral vision. The Gamer sat close, looking at me as I wondered what to expect from him. When he reached for me, I wasn't anticipating that he would have tickling in mind. So when he poked at my ribs, I was surprised into laughing with a snort.

"Not so mouthy anymore, are you?" he playfully mocked now that I couldn't fight back.

We joked while he poked and tickled, making me squirm and laugh uncontrollably. It was fun rolling around in rope, but I wasn't sure where this was leading, if anywhere. This felt a little too much like childhood wrestling with my little brother to be sexy.

That all changed when he pulled me on top of him.

He slid back in the bed effortlessly with me on his lap. Leaning back against the headboard, he situated my body against his chest facing away from him. Silent, neither of us moved; I was focused on resisting the urge to move my fingers as they lay on his crotch. I was breathing fast from the giggling and the excitement of our bodies touching.

The Gamer's fingers tentatively traveled along my arms, skipping across my neck and clavicles. I closed my eyes and melted into him, waiting as he became bolder. We hadn't had an explicit conversation about our expectations, so each time the intimacy progressed, he paused to give me a chance to stop him if need be.

He released the handle of rope around my chest so his fingers could have access to my breasts and explored them, running circles around my nipples. He then moved on to the expanse of my legs not covered by my skirt. I squirmed for a different reason now. He stopped suddenly to put a hand on my chin, guiding my face toward his.

There was a beat as we breathed each other in, and I wondered if he planned to follow through with bringing his lips closer to mine. I smiled nervously, and this is when he placed a hand at the back of my head to pull me in. There again was the heat that started in the bar, the sweet newness of an unexplored lover's mouth making itself available. The rush of the first kiss, the first touch, of not being sure of anything.

We continued to tangle tongues as he put his hands all over me, everywhere except between my legs. I tried lifting my hips to bring myself closer to his hand, only to have him move away at the last second with a chuckle. The teasing followed by yet another level of the same had me moaning into his mouth. He cradled my head in his palm, drawing me close so I couldn't break the kiss.

Just as his deprivation was about to become irksome, the Gamer pushed my skirt up and flickered his fingers toward my crotch. Meticulously he worked a hand down the front of my panties to slide a finger between my wet lips. I breathed heavily into his mouth, causing him to moan in return, wordlessly voicing his pleasure at how well his teasing had worked.

His finger hovered above my clit, allowing me to grind against it. I could hear how sloppy wet I was as I moved against him harder, desperately wanting him to shift his fingers. Somehow I subsisted on his kisses, in such a frenzy that I kept forgetting to inhale. When he did decide to graze his finger over my clit, lightly at first and then more purposefully, I finally broke the connection between our mouths. Gasping in a full breath, I bit down on my lip, coming within seconds of him moving his digits against me.

The anticipation had made me liquid in his hands. He used this against me, continuing to finger me quickly, refusing to give reprieve. I came again while working myself against his hand. Kissing him between breaths, I humped the fingers he'd maneuvered inside me, enjoying the wet thrusts of his hand manipulating me within the confines of my panties.

It seemed likely he would have kept at this all night if it wasn't for my hands going numb. Nothing ruined the mood like begging in a desperate, unsexy way to be untied because of tingling limbs. Except in this case it gave him an excuse to drag my exhausted body off the bed to untie and immediately retie me while I was still ragdoll-limp with pleasure.

This time the Gamer tied me face up, my arms spread eagle to the headboard, my ankles bound together at the foot of the bed. I was puzzled at his decision to keep me clothed under the enforced chastity of my closed legs, but it soon occurred to me that the tease was what really appealed to him.

Standing at a distance so I could watch, he took off his shirt, revealing his trim body before climbing under me again. The restraints were loose enough that I could lift myself in order to make room for him under my body, where he wrapped his arms around me. Feeling him close, I was already aching to spread my legs, but he wasn't finished with his pleasant torment. And I didn't have the inclination to complain as he alternately kept me just on the edge of orgasm or in the middle of an endless cascade of them by sliding his fingers expertly between my bound thighs.

Though I longed to touch or kiss him, the Gamer kept me in such a whirlwind of pleasure that I couldn't find two brain cells to rub together in order to ask for such things. The heat of his naked chest bled into my body through my shirt, making me long to feel his skin on mine.

In the fog that was the aftermath of so many orgasms and so much teasing, I didn't immediately realize he had crawled out from under me, but I did pull myself together enough to notice, with a mixture of sadness and relief, that I was being untied. It was always a melancholy moment when the rope was all removed and I was loose, not knowing the next time I would have a chance to be tied yet happy to be able to move my sore muscles.

To celebrate my freedom, I helped the Gamer get undressed, enjoying unwrapping him like a present. He didn't argue as I unclasped his pants and let them hit the floor then reached to remove my clothes, kissing him the entire time, only pulling away to drag the shirt over my head.

Our bodies were already sweaty in the end-of-summer humidity, but I was so desperate to have him pressed against me that neither of us was bothered by the heat. I ran my hands along the length of his thin body, feeling the bones under his tight skin, taking my time now that I could touch him. His cock jumped to attention when I reached it. I stroked it as gently as he had rubbed me, and it continued to grow impressively with his excitement.

Once I was free of the rope, we didn't dance around the main course any longer. The Gamer pushed me away from his big cock and back onto the bed. Knowing what came next, I tossed him a condom, playing with myself provocatively while watching him put it on. Even after the endless orgasms, I still wanted more. I couldn't get enough—of him, of his touch, or his tongue in my mouth, his cock in my hand. And I had to be crazy with lust to believe it possible that we would fit together.

I've enjoyed a variety of cocks and never been a size queen, but the Gamer was extraordinary. This was the first time I'd ever felt trepidation in regards to being penetrated, but I wanted to feel him inside me so badly that I was willing to find out if it was possible. He nudged the head of himself against my lips and gradually added pressure, inching his way in slowly, allowing me to become accustomed to the girth of him. I held on to his hips as encouragement, trying not to make any noises that he would misconstrue as a hint to stop and kissing him when I needed distraction. I ached with the difficulty of taking his cock but wanted all of him. He had pushed me over the edge of pleasure where nothing was enough.

The long and difficult work of relaxing so I could accommodate him was well worth the payoff. Once the Gamer was able to fully slip inside, I was lost to the intensity of it. My eyes rolled back in my head, and I moaned unrepentantly while I waited for him to really fuck me. Instead he was still, looking at me with concern.

"I don't want to hurt you. Tell me to stop if I do."

"What if I want to be hurt?" He looked taken aback. "Fuck me." It came out as a plea. I wanted him so badly that it was all I could think of.

This seemed to satisfy him, as he thrust in earnest. It did sting as I grew accustomed to him, but with each buck of his hips, I enjoyed the Gamer more. His size and boyishness made me feel so wicked that I came again, wrapping my legs around his waist, pleading for him not to stop as I babbled a crazy stream of syllables.

"No, ouch, more, yes, fuck, oh, ow, stop, please, don't stop."

So he didn't, ramming himself inside me until I was so enraptured that I couldn't move, able only to hold on to him while begging for more. Occasionally I would look up, amused at his grin, knowing he was obviously enjoying himself as well. It was about then that I realized the benefit of younger men was their endurance.

In time, the boundless pleasure became an altered state. I held onto his sweat-soaked body and let him fuck me, enjoying every minute but unable to contribute anything other than orgasms. The amount of dopamine in my system was making me high, and I passed over from moans into giggles; every nerve in my body was awake and on fire.

We eventually gave up on satisfying one another, falling into a pile at the center of the bed. Sometime later I woke up wondering where—and even briefly who—I was, lying on the sleeping chest of a man who had almost literally screwed my brains out.

So as not to repeat the cycle all over again, we vowed to keep our hands off one another long enough to find his clothes. I had to somehow work in the morning, and his primary poly relationship didn't allow for sleepovers. If reality hadn't intervened, we likely would have fucked until the sun came up, napping between bouts of bliss.

After one long, distracting kiss I got him into his car and watched it disappear. I was thrilled, full of pleasure, exhausted, and slightly disappointed I would never see him again. In a perfect world we would have the opportunity to repeat this evening again and again. Now he would become a long-distance flirtation.

I locked the door and barely made it to my couch before passing out with one hand petting the dog. And to think, I almost stood him up.

CHAPTER 11
THE KITTEN, THE SWITCH & THE VACUUM BED

Though I had no idea what to expect and didn't know anyone else who would be there, I couldn't imagine turning down my first invitation to a play party, which wasn't an offer that came along every day. I talked myself into attending by reasoning that, at worst, I could add "seeing a pro-Domme's dungeon" to my list of crazy experiences.

The Mistress and her husband put on gatherings that were the stuff of local kink legend, so, having only met them once, I was shocked and flattered to be invited. This had been happening a lot as the date of my departure neared. Suddenly people wanted to hang out and invite me to events. I'd been on more dates and met more new people in the last month than I had in all my years in Madison combined. Knowing I would never get another chance to make good on their offers was a great motivation to agree to many of these opportunities.

So I put my anxiety aside and now, deep in the suburbs, I stood listening to the beat of party music on the other side of the Mistress's door before timidly letting myself in. The room was crowded with people in dark, Goth-y clothing and unusual hair and makeup. They turned to look at me oddly as I entered, making me instantly feel like an outsider. Moving through the crowd, which barely acknowledged my presence, I made my way to the kitchen to get a glass of water that would occupy my hands. Recognizing many of these people as the same impeccably dressed crowd that filled the local fetish night events but never participated in the actual kink scene, I knew better than to be offended by their lack of friendliness. My people were downstairs in the basement.

Holding my red Dixie cup full of fizzy water as my wingman, I tottered unevenly down the stairs. The lower I got, the darker and warmer it became, until I found myself in a low-ceilinged, crowded wonderland of perversion where a cute girl was getting flogged on the Saint Andrew's cross at the center of the room. All heads turned briefly to see who had joined the party, then turned away to continue watching the scene unfold in front of them.

Not recognizing anyone, I worked my way into the back of the crowd to lean against a concrete wall. Once the flogging was over and people were mingling, the man of the house saw me gawkily standing around and approached me with a huge smile. He was pleasantly androgynous with bleached hair and eyeliner. Tight leather pants hugged his butt and crotch in a way that made it difficult to keep my eyes above waist level.

I was surprised he remembered me, even more surprised when he said, "Did you come just to watch, or are you going to play?"

"Well, I would be up to play, but I don't really know anyone here."

"You know me."

I blushed and looked away. It felt like a practical joke that after so many years of not experiencing this world, I was now being welcomed into it with so little effort. "I guess you're right." He looked at me and waited. "Oh wait," I said. "Are you offering?"

"Yes, I'd love to flog you."

I wasn't keen on being the center of attention, but it could be fun and perhaps melt away some of my anxiety by giving my mind something else to fixate on. "Okay!" I smiled and shrugged.

"May I?" he asked, gesturing with his outstretched palm toward the hand I had wrapped around myself.

"Of course."

He took my hand and led me to the cross, still warm from the other girl's body. Gently pressing me against it, he whispered, "Grab the rings, the ones above your head."

With a shiver of delight at being given instructions, I did as told. As I faced away from the crowd, the other people all but disappeared. I focused on this man, his already sweaty body, topless, tattooed, and lovely. I was feeling exhilarated at stepping out of my comfort zone to try something with a new person in a new place.

"Tell me what you like. What do you want to do?" He asked close to my ear, not quite stepping close enough for our bodies to touch.

"What?" I'd never been asked questions like this before. Usually Tops did whatever they were into and I trusted them to be reasonable while hoping they wouldn't go too far. I let the men do as they pleased, using each experience to learn whether or not I liked what they did. I didn't know yet about properly setting up a scene or asking to get my own satisfaction from the interaction.

"I know you like rope, obviously, but what else?"

"Um, pain, I guess. And trying new things," I said, hoping it was enough. Even admitting to that much out loud felt strange.

"Okay." He took one wrist in his hand, pressed himself against me, and reached for a leather cuff, which he tightened on my arm then connected to a point on the cross. My heart sank, as it does whenever someone forgoes rope for something more utilitarian. Any other restraint and my mind wandered, making it difficult to remain in the moment.

I assumed it was no secret that rope was the most important part of play for me. After all, this fellow and I had met at a rope practice and we'd mentioned the word during our negotiation, so I thought he would magically know what I desired. Now I know better, that being a Top doesn't make a person clairvoyant; his comment was an opening for me to mention if rope was a requirement.

Instead of expressing my lack of interest in buckled restraints, I made a quip while he bound my other wrist. "Aww, no rope?"

"The way I figure, you probably get more of that than you know what to do with. And as you'll see, I'm far more into leather." He clipped the other cuff to the cross with a clack, and I decided to roll with it.

He grabbed a flogger off the pegboard near my head, and I closed my eyes as I leaned into the cross, anticipating the impact. Instead of hitting me, he moved close, breathing down my bare back. "Is there anywhere you don't want to be touched?"

The me of that moment was impatient for him to get on with things—she hadn't had anything unfortunate happen to her, didn't know how dangerous it was to play haphazardly. The me of now realizes what a gentleman he was, how sexy it was to ask for consent and set boundaries.

"Let's say, not between the legs," I managed after a long pause.

"Okay. Is this all right?" He moved his hands to my waist while leaning in close.

I nodded, enjoying the heat of him near, his attention glowing down on me. In a roomful of other willing people he already knew, this man had chosen me. As he ran his hands up and down my corset, I felt the boning pressing into me, and the contrast of hard metal and soft flesh gave me chills.

Putting a hand on the muscled center of my back, he pushed me into the cross. "How hard can I hit?"

"Hard? You won't break me, that's for sure."

"Understood."

The whoosh of leather filled the air as he got a feel for the flogger's balance, leaving me to wait and anticipate. The first impact struck my back with an impressive snap. I sighed as he repeated this gentle massage on my shoulders, thoroughly warming me up, as this was our first time playing. Next he focused on my ass. Alternating between several hard thwacks with the bulk of the flails then a couple light brushes of the leather tails to create juxtaposition between soft and hard, he left me wondering when each sensation would hit.

Just as the feel of leather making contact with my back and ass were becoming intense enough to get my attention and incite a moan, he stopped. I thought he was ramping up for a heavier beating, but instead he put down the flogger and immediately unclasped my wrists.

Holding me tight from behind, he kept asking if I was okay, seeming to have miscalculated my level of experience entirely. This happened frequently. People often mistook my quietness and sweet-seeming face as innocence and an inability to take a beating.

He wasn't the first nor the last person to think they were being too rough on me while I was wondering when the fun was going to start. I didn't know yet that I could ask for more.

After I convinced him I was fine, he leaned his gorgeous body against me, caressing where the flogger had left temporary marks before helping me to step down from the cross. We embraced before he sent me on my way.

"See you around. Thanks for coming! And make sure to say hi to the lady of the house."

"Will do! Thanks for the ouchies." He instantly turned to start a negotiation with someone else.

Not yet ready to head home, I wandered into another room, looking for trouble. He'd gotten my kinky libido going without satisfying it; hopefully, there was someone around who could help.

In a quiet room were two women I recognized from other events. This seemed like a good place to refuel and get away from the action, so I sat on the opposite side of the room, eavesdropping as one of them organized her toy bag. It appeared she was eager for someone to tie up, as she obsessively rewrapped the same length of hemp, full of nervous energy. Her friend wasn't taking the hint; she was more interested in talking about music than rope. So apparently I'd come to the right room.

The woman with the rope and I hadn't interacted previously, but the worst that could happen was she'd turn me down and I'd never see her again. So I got up the courage to say hello, casually complimenting her ropes before diving in. "Were you looking to tie someone up?"

There was a tense moment as she looked between me and the line in her hand, but eventually her furrowed brow turned into a smile. "Yeah, actually." She put out her hand. "Cat."

I stood to shake with her. "Hi. Emily."

"Cool, so where should we do this?" We looked around for a comfy place to play, ultimately staking out a spot on a leather-covered bench, where she spread out her rope. We continued sharing nerdy details about our favorite rope venders and knots while she tied.

It wasn't until Cat had me in a tight chest harness with my arms trapped behind my back and secured to the bench that I stopped to realize this was the first time I'd been tied up by a lady. Things happen at the strangest times: I'd been longing to know what it was like to be topped by a woman but hadn't found the opportunity to pursue it. Now it was happening almost on accident.

"I like to start it in the front, do all the cinches, then wiggle it to the back to finish it off," I said, casually bantering with Cat about our about favorite methods of self-tying a certain harness while she added another rope to the harness on my body. On the inside I was all aflutter.

"Never thought of that. I'm bendy enough to do all the tying behind me." She finished the rope she was working with and picked up another from her bag. This one she looped around her own body. She spun to display all sides of a well-executed chest harness she had tied on herself, all without being able to see behind her.

I was impressed. "Nice!" Cat definitely knew what she was doing.

It was different being tied by someone who, like me, had learned rope by practicing on herself. She knew where the lines felt best, where to make them tight to dole out the most pain or pleasure. And it was obvious that she loved bondage, from either end. I'd watched her suspend herself at an event, and she had the same gleeful smile then as she did now, tightening the ropes looped around my arms.

Her energy was a big change from the rope slinging of most men, who knew the method and technique of tying but very rarely agreed to actively experience what the ties felt like on their own bodies. It was the first time I noticed the difference, how it affects the tie and flow of the scene. There was no ego, nothing for her to prove—she wasn't trying to impress or control me. Instead, we were equals enjoying the feel and the movement of her lines together.

We were still casually conversing when she started putting clothespins on my exposed skin, which got my full attention, causing me to forget what I was saying. About that time we locked eyes and mutually shrugged; we'd reached the end of what two strangers that were sexually uninterested in each other could do with rope, and that was okay.

As she untied and I helped her coil her lines, we heard mumblings through the wall. The group in the main room was getting excited about something being set up that they kept calling a vacuum bed. Once Cat's ropes were stowed away, we headed in the direction of the rest of the party, where there was a lot of giggling and the purr of a Shop-Vac—not a sound I would expect at a play party.

A woman was about to be sealed inside this latex bed. I wasn't sure what this piece of equipment did, but I looked forward to finding out. The room got quiet as she held the breathing tube—a shortened snorkel that added the air of a kinky DIY project to the scene—in her teeth. Then the loud hum of the vacuum sucking all the air out of the bed filled the room and we watched the shiny black sheath of latex shrink tight around her curves.

This was essentially a human-sized zip-up bag made of shiny black rubber. Along the edges, a border of PVC piping held the sack in a rectangular shape as the air was forced out through the vacuum hose connected to it. This created a seal that pulled the latex tight, reducing the person inside to a faceless, three-dimensional outline with only the breathing tube connecting them to the outside world.

Once the woman was trapped inside, the people in the room passed around a bottle of silicone lube, making their hands slippery, then took turns swarming to the bed at the center of the room to rub her body through the rubber. The lubrication made the latex glisten as she arched into the anonymous hands, hinting that being inside was somehow pleasurable.

Eventually she asked to be released, emerging bleary eyed from her slippery cocoon and looking a little shell-shocked as she curled up on the carpet in a corner. I desperately wanted to volunteer to partake in the experience that had had such a drastic effect on this woman, especially since this was another opportunity I might never have again. But I was having difficulty overcoming my vague claustrophobia. Anything that covered my face had historically caused me to panic, so I stayed silent, allowing my shyness to get the better of me.

The Mistress's eyes rested on me for a moment as she asked,

"Anyone else?" She raised an eyebrow flirtatiously.

"Okay, I'll go," I called from the corner, her face having convinced me.

"Well, come here." I knelt to listen to her instructions. "Take off anything sharp that could tear the rubber and crawl in."

As I removed everything but my skirt and stockings, the Mistress lifted the top sheet of latex, making a gap for me to slide under it and into the bed. The latex was surprisingly slick and wet feeling as I slipped inside. This was so different from the rubber I was accustomed to, the squeaky, often uncomfortable, and industrial-smelling latex of condoms and gloves. This was buttery soft and luscious, silky and infinitely touchable.

Lying there, I was feeling uncertain about what I'd agreed to, and my confidence wasn't bolstered when she handed me the snorkel. "Hold this in your mouth, and I'll situate it while zipping you in. If you want out, wiggle your fingers." She pantomimed the exact motion.

I nodded, worried that the moment the latex cinched around my face I would be terrified. Despite realizing how hot and sweaty the bed was, even unzipped, I convinced myself to relax. Once I was situated, the Mistress grasped the outside of the breathing tube and zipped me into a dark and womblike world. I closed my eyes, hearing only the loud connecting of the teeth on the heavy-duty zipper echoing all around me.

Inside the bed was comfortably quiet and relaxing. I listened to the muffled sounds of the party outside and the whoosh of my breath through the snorkel. The vacuum clicked on, creating a comforting hum that stole the air from the bed, sucking the rubber tight against me; it was like being sealed into a giant uninflated balloon. The rubber pushed tighter until I couldn't move. Wiggling my body up and down against the floor was possible, but none of my body parts inside the latex could shift. I was trapped.

It was startling at first, but I forced myself to concentrate on breathing, noticing that every exhale brought the latex in tighter. This full-body hug was everything I enjoyed about being restrained. In here it was calm and quiet, and there was nothing for me to do or worry about; I was just my body and it was blissful.

The Mistress startled me out of my near meditative trance, yelling so I could hear, "May we touch you?"

I nodded and felt someone's hands on my belly. It was oddly sexy; the warmth of their skin transmitted through the latex, and the sensation of their movement ran through the entire sheet of tight rubber. Soon I felt another anonymous set of hands running up my legs, pushing the slick rubber to feel the curves of my flesh through it. More hands touched my chest and arms. Someone else gently fondled me between my legs. The tightness of the bed made every touch magnified, so to be denied all my senses but still experiencing sensory overload was an odd juxtaposition.

When the excitement of strange hands everywhere wore off, I wiggled my fingers to signal that I was done. The vacuum was turned off, jolting me back to reality. As soon as the bag was unzipped, the man of the house traded places with me and slipped into the bed, wanting to have a go at being fondled by a room full of people.

Woozy with endorphins, I sat back and observed, until someone handed me the bottle of lube. Now that I knew what it was like, I was excited to try touching him, so I made my hands slippery and reached for his abs. He felt firm and wonderful. The Mistress even played with his cock, which was amusing to observe as it tried to become erect against the weight of the suctioned-in latex.

Once he was released, I thanked the couple for their hospitality, got dressed, and headed home. The next day the Priest would be flying into Madison. He had succeeded in locating himself a job and a duplex for us in Portland. We would finish packing our things in a storage container that would meet us on the West Coast, put the dog and our essentials into my car, and drive across the country to our new life. Between the high of being on the edge of a new beginning and the excitement of the party, I didn't sleep at all that night. I was too excited about the new era that was about to begin.

CHAPTER 12
THE CHAIR

Perpetually clad in aviator sunglasses and a shit-eating grin, Mr. Vain was the first person I met in this strange new world of Portland. I was drawn to his gregarious size and demeanor, and I enjoyed standing on tiptoe to hug him. Just sitting near him made me feel engulfed in safety. So, having made no other acquaintances and curious about what would develop, I spent a lot of time with Mr. Vain.

We practiced rope several times a week, totally platonically, yet there was always a confusing energy between us. It felt as if we were about to become lovers, like he would kiss me at any moment while he had me bound. But each time we met, without provocation, as if reminding himself, he would offer the refrain, "I don't sleep with models." Thus referring to me with this title, he used to talk insultingly about the women he tied up.

He would flirt one day and ignore me the next, making it impossible to know what to think of him or what sort of relationship he was hoping for. I'd been very clear that I was okay with just being rope friends but found him attractive; if he wanted to explore a physical relationship, we could talk about it. He laughed this conversation off and childishly mocked me for hitting on him. It was only because he was the one person, other than the Priest, I knew in Portland that I even bothered to continue talking to him. This level of immaturity wasn't at all appealing.

So I'd stopped thinking of him as a flirtatious option by the time we sat in my living room—empty while my furniture slowly made its own journey across the country—passing a bottle of wine back and forth. Mr. Vain was quieter than normal that particular evening, distracted and pensive, with little of his usual showboating. Even his trademark smirk didn't appear until late in the evening when he reached for some bright-red nylon rope, and said, "Let's have you in that chair. I've got an idea I wanna get out."

I wasn't expecting much. This was how our days of practicing rope concepts usually started. It seemed like any other time with him: I'd sit still and give him pointers on making the tie more or less painful, and he would take me in and out of rope several times until he was satisfied. No play, no sex, no flirting, just rope while I listened to him talk about his favorite subject: himself.

He was binding an ankle to each front leg of the heavy antique chair before I'd even gotten fully seated. With the same exuberance, he ran a rope over my thighs, pinning them to the hardwood seat. He looped another line around my waist and then my chest to hold me to the intricately carved chair back. Finishing off the tie, he bound my hands together, pulling them behind my neck to connect the rope to the back of the chair, a very compromising position that didn't allow any wiggle room. My underarms and chest were vulnerable, my legs forced apart, leaving me feeling exposed even though I was fully clothed.

Normally he would walk a 360 around his tie, laugh at his genius, and immediately untie me, satisfied to have brought his idea into reality. This time he asked, "Hey, do you mind if I experiment with something? You know, proof of concept and all that."

His strange behavior already had me on edge. Nonetheless I said, "Sure."

There was silence before he asked, "Do you trust me?"

"Uh, yes?" It came out as a question and sounded obviously disingenuous. What I trusted was that he was more scared of me than I was of him, so I wasn't worried he was going to do anything untoward without my permission.

He continued standing over me, leering like the cat that was getting ready to eat a flock of canaries. "Do you like me?"

This seemed like an odd question to ask a person he'd bound in an inescapable position. I furrowed my brow, trying to puzzle out his plan. "I like you more than I did yesterday. The wine helped."

This was met with an unimpressed expression and an eye roll. "Good."

He lifted me and the chair off the floor suddenly. Midair, he redistributed this combined weight and lowered it so my shoulders rested on the carpet with the chair on top of me. My knees and elbows were holding the full weight of the heavy wooden monstrosity, the only furniture I owned at that moment. I was worried at first that the chair would break, but after wiggling and not getting an inch of give or hearing any creaking of the wood, I was more concerned about running out of breath. There was no way to get out of this mess. The arms of the chair meant I couldn't roll to the side, and having my hands behind my head didn't give me any leverage to maneuver. In fact, if I moved too much, I forced the air out of my lungs with the weight of the chair back. All I could do was twist my head to the side as far as possible between my elbows to look up at him.

He grinned cockily and lowered himself to lie next to me, eye to eye on the carpet. He moved near enough to put his mouth to my ear. "It's good that you like me, because after this, you won't." I felt his hot breath without being able to move away as his voluminous lips lingered near my face.

Still, I couldn't tell if he was coming on to me, because he was the king of mixed messages. We would go out on what felt like a date—fancy food, an excuse to dress up—then he'd kiss me on the cheek and go home. He'd invite me away for the weekend to do photos at some crazy location only to back out at the last minute and take another model. His mind games were baffling, but at that moment I wasn't in a situation to wonder about anything other than how long I could hold myself in that position. Already I could feel my arms getting weak. After they tired, the chair would be pressing into the back of my neck, making this situation a lot less enjoyable.

He lay there watching my predicament, doing nothing. Eventually, I had to use my last bit of air to eke out a tiny, "Please."

"Please? Please, what? Are *you* asking to be untied?"

I shook my head no as best I could while barely managing, "My arms, please." They felt like I'd been lifting weights all day, the lactic acid burning my muscles while my hands simultaneously went numb. It was excruciating, so much so that I had to overcome my pride and ask for help, something I rarely did in rope unless it was a true emergency and something I definitely didn't want to do with Mr. Vain. It felt like showing weakness to a bully.

He sighed while standing to lift me and the chair, putting it down awkwardly on its side so I could now breathe and rest my tired arms. I was sideways but still securely bound to the chair. While I recovered, he lay down beside me, smiling. "That was amazing."

We locked eyes, panting in the same rhythm. It was impossible to read him, and the uncertainty was both erotic and baffling. With anyone else this moment would be the prelude to something, but with him I had no idea of his intentions. Then again, most of my concentration was focused on making sure the circulation was returning to my arms.

While I was distracted, he methodically moved his face closer, so that when I noticed him again, it was obvious we were about to kiss. We made myopic eye contact the instant before our lips met. I closed my eyes to the sensation of his large, soft lips touching mine. Everything about him was double the scale of me, so his mouth engulfed mine in a very tender kiss.

I was desperate to get my hands free, this time because I wanted to touch him, to hold his face in my hands and keep him close now that this strange intimacy was finally taking place. It was torment to be unable to reach Mr. Vain as we locked lips and tongues, his hands all over me; they tickled my vulnerable underarms, fondling my chest, holding my hips in his huge hands. I was stuck, unable to loosen the rope no matter how hard I struggled. However, he was free to use his strength to lift the chair whenever he chose, keeping the kiss from breaking whenever he wanted to change position. When he tired of lying on the floor, he tipped the chair back onto all four legs and leaned down to kiss me.

When he finally backed away to watch me wiggle in his ropes and catch my breath, it felt like we had been making out nearly as long as we had been avoiding this sexual tension. My body was flushed with the heat of the moment as he leaned in for another endless kiss and caress. Lust combined with the flood of happy brain chemicals that came along with getting bound was making me dizzy and unable to think straight.

Without ending our lip-lock, he reached around my body to untie the rope binding my hands to the back of the chair, pulling them around his neck so I could embrace him momentarily. Just as I was enjoying the hint of freedom, Mr. Vain surprised me by briefly untying my hands only to then bind one wrist to each arm of the chair. I was torn between the desire to return his touch and enjoying the realization that this was the longest I'd ever spent bound. It was titillating to know he had the desire to toy with me while I was incapacitated for hours on end, so I yielded to his mouth, waiting to see what else he had in mind.

And yet I felt trepidation as well—since we were only practice partners, Mr. Vain and I had never talked about boundaries or safe sex. Thinking this was just another evening of practice, I hadn't thought to have this conversation before we got to this point. It was such bad form to negotiate in the middle of a scene when the sexual energy was already flowing, but that's where I found myself: left to hope Mr. Vain was mature enough to understand me saying no if he went too far.

The next rope he removed had been pinning down my thighs, which conveniently gave me more room to move as Mr. Vain ran his hands over my legs, purposefully avoiding anything higher than mid-thigh. I tried to angle my body closer to his fingers, but he removed his hands from my legs altogether. With his mouth was on mine, I was too distracted to notice his fingers on the button of my pants until he pulled away to ask, "May I?"

I lifted my hips to make it easy for him to slide them over my ass, signaling that I wouldn't mind if they were removed.

"That is the hottest thing a woman can possibly do." He groaned, carefully tugging the fabric down the arch of my hips. We kissed with new intensity as he slowly ran a hand up my legs, resting between them. I moaned desperately, moving myself against his fingers, hoping to convince him to touch with purpose. Eventually he did with tiny flickers of his huge index finger over my clit.

Snaking his hand further down the front of my panties, he noticed how wet I was and pulled away with a look that could have been horror or admiration. He leaned in for a kiss but tentatively now, so I whispered into his mouth, "I guess I still like you after all."

"Is that what this means?" He seemed genuinely curious. It occurred to me just then that his glacial pace, mind games, and cockiness were actually him overcompensating for sexual inexperience.

I tried to be helpful by raising myself into his hand and grinding against him. Finally Mr. Vain used his hands for something other than teasing, and he seemed to enjoy fingering and fondling me with his enormous digits. The eagerness and general hand movements were there, but his lack of deftness was troublesome. Each time I moved my hips in an attempt to angle him in the right direction, he moved away or started a different rhythm that threw me off, mistaking my squirming for a game.

Oblivious to what a mood killer it was, he periodically would ask, "You come yet?"

Having been bound to this chair for over two hours, even I was done being in rope. Assuming he wouldn't take it well if he heard the truth—that he wouldn't be able to get me off like that—I clamped down on the finger he had inside me while writhing and moaning, which seemed to convince him.

"Finally," he sighed while slipping his hand out of my panties to collapse next to me in a sweaty pile.

After removing the remaining rope and tossing it aside, he pulled me on top of him. We rolled around the empty room, losing more clothes and getting more daring with our hands until we were a naked, exhausted heap. The sun was starting to glow through the blinds when I made the first of many mistakes with him by taking him to the air mattress that was temporarily serving as my bed to sleep off the debauchery.

This broke all my personal rules of not getting too attached to casual partners, but especially to the childish Mr. Vain. I should have known better, having long ago learned the joy of rope just for rope's sake, but there was still a part of me that wanted to up the ante and bring sex into this equation. There were a million reasons I should have negotiated with him before getting to this point, but I was too loopy and high on chemicals to make good choices. And he definitely wasn't going to be the voice of reason.

Under my covers he was back to the nervous boy who didn't know what to do with himself. I thought we would finish what we started, but when I tried to put my mouth on him or hint that I would have sex with him, he retreated into making sarcastic comments. I gave up and rolled over to go to sleep.

The next morning I woke to a snoring giant and the obviousness of my error. This began several months of him pointedly not tying me up in what felt like punishment for something I couldn't fathom. Instead he called frequently to talk about his feelings and the relationship I didn't know we were having. In my mind we had fooled around once and we hadn't clicked, so we would go back to being platonic rope partners. But he wanted something he apparently couldn't ask for, an emotional intimacy, maybe, or for me to jump through some hoop before he could tie or touch me again.

There appeared to be no meeting in the middle. He was too emotionally immature for me to consider the relationship he hinted at wanting, and all I desired was rope, which was now distinctly lacking. So after one last confusing dance of our tongues and hands in a hotel room one weekend, we stopped talking.

I was done. We needed to be something or nothing, and this nebulous in-between thing that couldn't be defined wasn't making anyone happy. And yet it was like breaking up with a middle school drama queen.

By the time I broke it off with him, I had other friends in town, other rope partners, a community of support, and Mr. Vain made every attempt to turn them against me. He called me, angrily wanting to talk for hours, only to suddenly hang up on me. He gossiped to anyone who would listen, trying to get people to choose sides by making me into the crazy ex who was ruining his life. He would tie up my friends before casually talking shit about me while cuddling them in aftercare.

His gaslighting was so intense that I started to question what had actually happened, wondering if maybe he was a sweet, emotionally available rope Top and I really was ruining his reputation by mentioning my experiences with him to people who asked if he was a trustworthy person to play with. Luckily, the Priest was there through it all, my rock, my sounding board. He had seen Mr. Vain's interactions with rope bottoms and assured me that I was right to warn other women about his emotional volatility. If I kept my head up, Mr. Vain would eventually get bored and go away.

Through it all, I continued to go to munches, rope parties, and photo shoots despite the fact that Mr. Vain was often in the same room bad-mouthing about me. I put on a tough face and smiled my way through it, moving on to others more worthy of my energy, recalibrating my impression of people and being more careful in my interactions with the Portland kink community. Things were so much different here than in the overly polite Midwest to which I was accustomed.

Mr. Vain was a frustrating learning experience, and yet I still had the memory of that one evening with him, a hint of how it could have been, and a sexy reminder of why I'd gotten involved with him in the first place. The sight of a great chair can still make me warm inside.

CHAPTER 13

THE WATERFALL

During my first year in Portland I had a habit of saying yes to everything. So when a photographer asked if I wanted to dangle naked from a fallen log over a waterfall, I didn't pause before saying, "Hell, yeah."

The first step in this epic adventure was driving two hours to meet Mack Daddy, who was one of the riggers for the shoot, so we could carpool together. When I finally found him, the first of several long car rides I would have to endure that day began. I alternated between crossing my fingers that the truck wouldn't fall apart and hoping Mack Daddy wouldn't have a heart attack. Any pressure on the brakes caused the truck to shutter and jerk, the belts making terrible screeching noises. He made equally troublesome sounds, wheezing and coughing constantly. Between phlegmy performances he bragged in graphic detail about every event in his long and varied sex life. He repeated some of the stories several times like an elderly broken record, never pausing for me to contribute to the "conversation."

At first I thought this guy had to be a joke the photographer was playing on me. Mack Daddy couldn't be this lewd and be for real. (If he was one of the so-called legends of the local BDSM community, I wasn't sure it was a group I wanted to be involved with.) But when we pulled into the state park where everyone else was waiting, he hopped out of the truck and ran to the center of the group, continuing to tell the explicit story he was in the middle of reciting to me, without stopping to take a breath. The people gathered there smiled and gave him the look one would give a pet licking itself in front of company. So apparently this was his normal behavior.

Meanwhile, wondering how I drew the short straw in the carpooling lottery, I was trapped in the truck because the door handle didn't work. Eventually I got the attention of someone outside, who looked at me quizzically as I called out the small gap in the window, "Um, I seem to be involved in some sort of nonconsensual truck bondage. Could you see if the handle works from the outside?"

Once I was released from the vehicle, I was able to meet everyone, my regular awkwardness amplified by my ungainly entrance. With introductions made, model releases signed, and shooting plans finalized, there was still another hour-long drive up the mountain. That meant another hour of sex stories as told by a literal dirty old man while I reassured myself this would all be worth the trouble once we got there.

And it was. Words like *lush, vibrant, fertile,* and *shockingly green* ran through my head. The area the photographer had scoped out was beautiful and intoxicating, leaving me stunned that this forested wonderland was part of my new life. This wasn't the sparse-pines-and-shrubs type of wooded area I was accustomed to from the Midwest, this was nature gone crazy. There were so many trees, ferns, and flowers, and on everything, everywhere, was moss. It grew on the road and up the sides of the rocks and covered the trunks of most of the trees. Some moss hung down from those trees like tinsel.

Our pack of creative types hiked into the woods with our equipment. All of it had to fit through the narrow paths and under giant fallen logs, so that even a brief journey seemed to take much longer. We made nervous small talk while stumbling into the valley where the beautiful blue water of the falls sparkled at the farthest end. We went quiet with awe, listening to the rumble and hiss of the water.

The area was so remote that, aside from one of us talking occasionally, there was no sound other than the white noise of the water rushing down the rocks. It smelled alive and sensual here, which made me feel like anything could happen. Seeing how high the waterfall was also made the moment and what we were planning to do feel real.

The four models gathered in a flat open area with a log to sit on. We all looked at the fallen log dangling above the waterfall with the same expression of apprehension. While contemplating the wisdom of this plan, we huddled silently together for warmth, waiting for the men to be finished setting up. The longer we waited, the more time we had to think about all the things that could go wrong, feeling less confident as the creative high wore off and we were faced with the reality of the situation.

Hearing our murmurs of worry, one of the other riggers, the Satyr, offered to climb the log we would use as a hard point and personally check its safety. We were reverently silent as he donned a climbing harness, top roped himself to a sturdy tree, and walked out onto the log. No one breathed as he took the first step on the old fallen wood. We were a long way from civilization, and there was no phone reception; if someone got hurt, they would be in trouble.

The worst-case scenarios rushing through my head, I couldn't bear to look until the others gasped. My eyes popped open to see the Satyr smiling and having the time of his life, continuing gracefully to the log's center, where he bounced up and down like a rugged tightrope walker. It didn't move, which made the log as safe as it was going to get for our purposes.

The three rope experts began the laborious task of rigging a metal ring to the log. Soon they had finished with the log and were climbing across the rocks in front of the waterfall toward us, looking very serious. The photographer asked, "Emily, how would you feel about going up first?"

My heart was in my throat, as I was seeing renewed images of one of us falling to our deaths. I had hoped someone else would go first, but though I was consumed by second thoughts, I refused to let on that I was nervous. All cool and cavalier, I said, "Yeah, sure, let's do it."

The men stood together like boys waiting for a girl to pick them for the Sadie Hawkins dance. Mack Daddy clearly wanted me to choose him, assuming we were a team after driving in together. But there was no way I was going to trust him with my life.

The only thing I knew about the other rigger was that he made beautifully colored rope by hand and did suspension demos during fetish night. I understood he was talented from watching him perform, but I didn't know anything about him personally. His smile and long salt-and-pepper hair were endearing; I was definitely curious about him but unsure if this was the moment to experiment so drastically.

That left the Satyr, whom I had talked to for all of ten minutes in a rope class, but I was comforted by his energy and trusted him to be attentive if something went wrong. Besides, I felt certain a rope teacher of his caliber would know what he was doing.

"Satyr, will you do the honors, since we know each other so well?"

"I would love to. But we have to negotiate first." He looked at me very seriously. Caressing my arm, he looked at me earnestly and asked, "Once you're up there, can I fuck you? Can I? Can I?" He chuckled and waggled his eyebrow at me.

To deflect how flustered his joke had made me, I sarcastically said, "Classy."

We hugged while laughing; thank goodness he was joking. I had to recalibrate my expectations after spending most of the day with Mack Daddy, for whom that would *not* have been a question asked in jest.

The Satyr unpacked his khaki knapsack full of rope, and I got undressed. I tried not to freeze, and he attempted to not get mud on his rope during the long task of tying me up. Mostly I laughed at his smart-ass comments to stay warm while hiding under a large fleece blanket that he tucked out of the way when he needed access to a body part. Happily, the rope did have a strange way of making me feel slightly warmer, even though it covered very little surface area.

When he was finished, the Satyr ran his fingers along the lines of hemp where they looped around my chest and hips to make them perfect. It was then time for me to stand in the cold mist of a roaring waterfall, where the Satyr finished my rigging by connecting the rope around my body to the ring that would raise me off the ground. I was shivering; the spray from the falls was frigid, and after a minute of standing there, moisture was darkening the Satyr's gray jacket. I could only imagine how wet I was without even knowing it, having long ago become too cold to be able to process the wind and water on my skin. About then I understood the notion of suffering for art. Hypothermia crossed my mind as he increased the pace of his tying so that soon it was time for him to yank me up off the ground.

That first moment of weightlessness—when the earth wasn't part of my world any longer, and it was just the ropes holding me up in the air—was always odd. By then I'd been suspended dozens of times by Mr. Photo, but I still had a tendency to panic about the loss of control for a few seconds before realizing what a miracle being suspended was. Soon, swaying in the air like a pendulum between the Satyr and the water, I was entranced and feeling invincible.

"Ready?"

I nodded, and he began pulling, which lifted me up, the rush of the water growing in volume as I rose. My body rocked wildly back and forth, dangerously close and then far from the falls. Though it was bracingly cold on the ground, in the air it was the perfect temperature, which was likely a combination of adrenaline, endorphins, and no longer being in the spray of water.

It was amazing up there, hanging inches from a stunning waterfall, watching it tumble over the broken rocks and logs. Mist hit my face as I twirled around in the air feeling as if I really was flying. I felt so free that it was easy to forget there was rope involved until someone poked me with a branch in the thigh. Looking down, I saw the Satyr holding a long stick. While I was having an ethereal experience, the group on the ground was trying to get my attention. Their mouths and hands were moving, but I couldn't understand a thing.

I wanted to zone out and stare at the water, but the scrunched face of the photographer indicated that he had other plans. Focusing on posing now, I repositioned myself every thirty seconds to give him a different angle. It seemed like only a minute had passed when the Satyr lowered me. "How are your hands doing?"

In the excitement I'd been ignoring any pain or discomfort. All the while I had been pulling against the ropes with my wrists to arch my back or extend my legs to enhance the curvature of my frame. But once he brought my limbs to my attention, I noticed how uncomfortably tingly my fingers were from this straining.

As the riggers brought me down to quickly release my arms, the photographer complained, "Well, untie her for a second and send her back up. I want more angles."

The Satyr gave the man with a camera a look that silenced him. He wrapped me in a towel and pulled me to his chest to share body heat. The photographer sighed as the Satyr helped me back to the warmer area where the others were waiting. The other models high fived me as we excitedly babbled about how unbelievable this whole experience was. The Satyr and I did the reverse of our earlier dance, slower this time since his fingers were too cold to be as dexterous as before, the wetness of the rope making it difficult to remove. Over his shoulder I occasionally caught a glance of the next model flying upside down and loving it.

Coming down from my rope high, I watched as the other two models went up, enjoyed the show, and then helped to apply the cozy aftercare robe as soon as they were back on the ground. I held a blanket up against the wind for the model the third rigger, the Rope Maker, was untying. When he was finished, his partner was a happy puddle, but he was still invigorated from the last tie. He looked over the models, seemingly with the hope of getting one more idea out of his system before we left. It was getting dark fast, so if something was going to happen, it had to come together quickly.

I was warm again, and he seemed so adorably eager that I volunteered, touching the Rope Maker's arm to capture his attention. "I'd be up for doing another tie if you are."

Somehow his smile got even wider. Usually I was the only one so pumped from shooting that I refused to let the moment end, so it was a welcome change to have a partner in crime who was willing to make the most of this beautiful location. We tossed out ideas for poses that would be possible on the pile of logs at the base of the falls. The other two riggers were high above us, removing the suspension ring even as the darkness came on in a rush.

The Rope Maker wasted no time, putting rope on me immediately so that the photographer could capture whatever we created before it was completely dark. Using purple rope he had spun himself, the Rope Maker put a diamond-shaped *karada* harness down my body, using fancy double coin knots to embellish the spaces between the ropes. We didn't bother trying to keep me covered in order to preserve body heat; instead, he tied quickly with a precision and grace that was mind-boggling. The Rope Maker was finished before I had time to get cold.

"It's not real rope, but it will do."

I looked down at the gorgeous pattern he'd dreamed up on a whim. "Uh, what makes it unreal rope? Is it because I can still do this?" I reached out to pretend to tweak his nipple.

He laughed in a way that sounded thunderous in the waterfall's echo, and with the same swiftness, he bound my wrists together. "That's enough of that."

Against my squeals of faux protest, the Rope Maker threw me over his shoulder and carried me across the creek. He dropped me on the log I would pose on, and I looked at him, stunned to silence by the display of manpower. "Fair enough."

He laughed and removed the wrist cuff with a giddy grin so the photographer could go over long-exposure techniques. The instructions ended with, "You'll have to pick a pose and hold it for up to a minute." This wouldn't be easy under the slippery and cold conditions. Without any sun, it was positively chilly on that moist, mossy log, but I wasn't one to step down from a challenge.

I jumped up on that log and worked it. When the photographer said, "Hold it," I went to my happy place, which wasn't difficult considering I was naked and covered in rope. Forcing myself into a stillness that bordered on meditative, I held my breath, knowing that the slightest movement would ruin the exposure. When I started to feel swoony, wondering if I could hold on any longer, there would be an unnatural flash of light in the darkness. Totally blinded from the glare of the camera, I would hear from somewhere below, "Okay!"

Sucking in a breath, I would move to a new pose, beginning the ritual all over again. And as these things go, the very last photo we took was the keeper. I sat in the crook of several branches, legs dangling to mirror the branches behind them, my arms at my side as I glared into the camera as if this was my domain. The ambient light the photographer was able to bounce off the water and my skin bathed everything in an unearthly indigo that I later found it difficult to believe wasn't Photoshopped. He knew his way around behind that lens.

It was only when I felt the warmth of the Rope Maker's chest as he carried me back to my clothes that I realized how cold I was. Finished being tough and model-esque, I shivered uncontrollably. There was no light remaining at this point, just blurs of human shapes and occasional flashes of lights as everyone packed up. This added a level of creepiness to what was earlier an idyllic hideout.

Back at our pile of gear, I was the only one naked and covered in mud. So those undefined shapes stood impatiently watching, murmuring in the dark as the Satyr and the Rope Maker took turns untangling the rope from my body. Everyone was cold and hungry, eager to return to their vehicles, which added an edge of desperation as they rushed to pack my things before I'd located my pants.

The moment my clothes were on, someone handed me a light and we took off down the path. While I was still coming down from my rope daze, the entire crew hiked toward the cars. I was still loopy and full of endorphins, which made rushing to catch up difficult. At the truck, the Satyr tucked me back into the horrible truck to get warm.

The others were headed to a picnic area for dinner and wine in the photographer's camper to revel in the high of camaraderie and creativity. We were all feeling giddy after such a once-in-a-lifetime afternoon and the gorgeous photos that had been produced. Mack Daddy, however, refused to stop and join in the festivities. Instead, he sped past the campsite so fast I couldn't arrange a ride with someone else.

The upside was that he was so angry at me for not wanting to be bound by him that he didn't talk the rest of the evening.

His seething anger on the other side of the messy truck couldn't dampen my mood; I was thrilled. This was the shoot that got me hooked, letting me know that though momentarily jobless and friendless, I had moved to the right part of the country. Somewhere that a waterfall photo shoot—and so much else—was possible.

CHAPTER 14
THE ROGUE WITH THE ROPES

"I would like to ask you some questions now, laying down the parameters of our play, negotiating the boundaries, and feeling out your comfort levels."

When the Satyr began our evening by thoroughly mapping out the scene he wanted to enact, my body was already thrumming with anticipation though we weren't yet touching. I nodded as if this sort of conversation was something to which I was accustomed. In reality, after a lifetime of being shamed by lovers for asking them to tie me up, I didn't know how to be open about my kinky desires with a long-time partner, let alone with a casual acquaintance I was playing with for the first time. Until meeting the Satyr, I'd simply been playing with people who were into rope and sadism, allowing them to follow their bliss while hoping I would get something out of the scene as well but never explicitly telling them what I enjoyed. The Satyr's level of honesty intimidated me, but I followed his lead, knowing how important this conversation was and hoping my responses would come easier with practice.

"On a scale of one to ten, with ten being 'push my limits' and zero being 'just don't go there,' tell me how interested you are, keeping in mind that all of these elements are inherently present when one is being bound but knowing that I can try to avoid those that don't set your loins on fire." This is how he talked, like the sexiest college professor ever, who had obviously had this conversation a million times before and knew how to create a delicious and safe scene.

I did my best to communicate my wishes but was overwhelmed, finding it difficult to guess how attracted I was to him before we'd touched. But if I was too conservative in voicing my needs, the scene might fall flat because he didn't push me in any way. If I was too open, I might get more than I bargained for. So I tried to imagine a middle ground.

When we were finished negotiating, I was already a little exhausted and more intimidated than when I'd arrived. I wondered if there would be any room for surprise after talking about everything that would happen. His ability to communicate was erotic in itself, but I'd never experienced something so thorough. It was a lot to process just then, but the Satyr was a great influence, and soon his questions would become my preferred method of negotiating.

Finally the talking was finished and he stood, gesturing that I should do the same. I understood this was the end of our time as equals, because when he pulled away from an embrace and held me at arm's length, his entire demeanor had transformed; his eyes were somehow blacker, his mouth a tense line. It was such a drastic transition that a chill ran through me.

"Undress for me, now." The emphasis on the final word heated me through, melting me into compliance. I stacked my clothes neatly on the couch. He didn't speak or move a muscle, just stared unblinking at my nakedness. I felt so exposed that he could probably see through me to watch my heart thunder and the dirty thoughts race through my brain.

Breaking the silence, he said, "Kneel."

I obeyed while he loomed above, hoping he wasn't judging my chubby thighs and fluffy stomach. Then I realized he'd seen it all before and wouldn't have invited me here if he wasn't interested in my body just the way it was. So instead I focused on the thrill of the attention. There was an undeniable flush of excitement in being vulnerable to this man whose rope skills I'd been lusting over from afar while learning from him in rope group. I looked up into his eyes, daunting in their firmness, none of the humor remaining from minutes before. I looked away, submissively bowing my head.

Finally he moved, uncrossing his arms as he walked behind me, where I heard him rustle in his bag. There was a clank of metal and the brush of ropes against the canvas bag, the thump of it all hitting the floor. The only other sound was the whir of the forced air heat through the vents and the tickle of rain on the roof. It was then I realized that even after the half hour of negotiating I had no idea what to expect.

My blood raced frantically, making it hard to hear when, in a throaty voice, he asked, "Are you ready to begin?"

"Yes, please," I whispered back.

He uncoiled a line, and the hollow thump of the coiled rope hitting the hardwood floor startled me. The natural-fiber smell of the jute that was his preferred material wafted into the room. The barnyard odor was intoxicating as he took his time nestling in behind me, placing one knee on either side of my hips with his clothed chest against my back now, and the heat of him permeated my skin.

I closed my eyes. Gone was the snarky, bratty part of me. One stern look from this man and I was knocked into deference, knowing he meant business. His breath was on my shoulder as he allowed the moment to linger. Waiting for him to act made it feel a little like being trapped in a room with a beautiful, hungry animal.

To further emphasize the contrast in power between us, he remained fully clothed, and the rough denim covering his thighs chafed my skin as he pulled me into him by throwing the rope around my chest and tugging me in. Dizzy with the desire to be bound, I was compliant, melting against him, feeling his heat radiate into me. I didn't move while trying to anticipate the next step in this dance, knowing the basics of what would occur but not the details of how or when. So I felt the breath knocked out of me when he pushed me away into a bow that placed my forehead on the floor, exposing my ass to him.

"That's a lovely girl."

I sighed, thrumming at his words while nuzzling my face into the fleecy blanket. Inwardly I laughed at myself for being so drawn in by a compliment from the same person who had just cruelly exposed me.

He trapped my wrists in the curve of my back with one hand while pulling rope around them with his other; I was restrained before

I could process what had happened. It was so effortless as to seem magical. Skillfully and slowly, he created a traditional bondage harness called a *takate kote* or box tie that bound my biceps into the rope that looped around my chest above and below my breasts. There was no way to move my arms at all when he finished, the position restrictive yet strangely comforting.

It happened so naturally: the ropes zipping by without him stopping to adjust, me swaying under the force of his hands and the tugging of his lines. Each pull of the rope was carried out with such fluidity and grace it was as if the rope were a part of his fingers. There was no fumbling or second thoughts; his lines went on almost without exertion.

He pulled me to his chest, leaning me backward so he could admire what he'd created by running his hands over the rope and my skin. As he tugged on my nipples, he ran his nose along my neck like he was marking his territory. I yipped as he tightened his grip until I could no longer be stoic, and it was then that he pushed me forward to add yet another rope to the ones already holding me so securely. This bit was purely decorative, zigzags of rope across my chest in a pattern I would never be able to recreate.

I started out torn between giving myself over to the power of the connection he was creating and staying watchful enough to take in his movements, hoping to remember and learn from them for later—stuck between wanting to be taken by him and wanting to be him. But he was so deft with his lines that I was quickly in awe, having lost track of any attempt to understand what he'd done. It didn't feel like being bound so much as being painted with his rope—brush strokes of jute, flashes of bamboo. He was creating art. To think of anything but pure enjoyment—of how quickly he had incapacitated me, the efficiency and beauty of it all—would have ruined the moment.

Through it all, he never broke the contact between our bodies, even as he moved me around by the rope, using it has a handle to adjust my position. His breath, the heat of his mouth, in the crook of my neck each time he brought me close—it was a gorgeous dance.

His obvious abilities put me at ease to the point where I felt comfortable going to a quiet, meditative place inside myself. It was a state I only disappeared into with someone I trusted implicitly, which didn't happen often. It took a special person to make me feel this safe, having absolutely no fear a boundary would be crossed. I was still present but at a happy, altered distance, enjoying his every movement intensely, as he wove me further into his control.

The lines creaked and moaned like the sails of an ancient ship as he moved me around and used his fingers to deftly apply pressure to unexpected points along my body. These were nerve-centered places that could go from pleasure to shocks of pain in an instant, punctuating our moments together with deliberate discomfort to keep me in the present with him. The Satyr would press or manipulate a space—inner thigh, neck, shoulder, ear—until I sighed or cried out softly; the moment lasted another breathless beat and then it would be over. He would caress me, the soothing authoritative edge in his voice lulling me deeper into my head as he cooed, "That's a brave girl."

When he finished with a predicament, the Satyr would untie just enough of his lines to transition into a new position, reusing rope already warm from my body to contort me in a different way. There was nothing sexual about our dance in rope, but it was endlessly sensual: his mouth close to mine, the intense eye contact, his hands grasping flesh while mine flailed in vain to gain purchase, making contact, but only briefly. He occasionally leaned my body against his to where I could contort my hands to press against his belly, the warmth of him traveling into me as I felt his wiry and muscular frame or the brush of his long, silvering ponytail against my face.

It felt as if only seconds had passed when he began untying, piling the rope near my face where I was curled up on the floor so I could enjoy the closeness of it as he deprived my body of its touch. He left my hands for last, keeping me in his grasp, facedown and moaning, for as long as possible. As I bowed before him—his body over mine, holding me down as his rope soon no longer would—he finally untied that last knot, tugging it with a snap. My hands fell to my side, unfamiliar to me. I didn't know what to do with them after not having them in my power for so long. The Satyr helped me sit up and wrap my arms around him in a friendly embrace; the scene ended as it began as I came back to earth.

That first night led to a second. And then to many photo shoots.

I enjoyed his company as much as I enjoyed his rope, but there was something missing that kept us from taking things any further. As he tossed me about in his well-placed lines, any arousal I felt was centered on his rope and not on the man applying it. The Satyr was a sensual and obviously erotic man, but I couldn't imagine myself getting any more seriously involved with him. After my tryst with the Rope Guru all those years ago, I knew that I couldn't handle getting entangled with the premier rope Top of the city, competing with the entire city for his attention.

As much as it disappointed me to keep him at a distance, we naturally segued into being rope pals instead, finding ways to enjoy each other's company without becoming lovers. Rather than have a whirlwind affair that would end in hurt feelings and awkwardness, we had the opportunity to become muses for one another. He enjoyed rope and creativity as much as I did, so we began an artistic collaboration with his camera that had no limits. And he became my teacher as I tried to take in the wealth of knowledge he offered.

It's still a pleasure to see him tying his partner, the Librarian, and the beauty of connection between them. They are perfectly matched and living the ropey dream. I have moments of longing, wishing I could have that, or kicking myself for not pursuing the Satyr myself. Mostly when I see the Satyr and the Librarian kiss, the bliss in their eyes as they take in one another before or after rope, all I feel is endless joy for them.

Someday I'll find my Satyr.

CHAPTER 15
THE DAMSEL IN DISTRESS

I never quite knew what to expect when I went on a modeling gig. After seeing the photographer's portfolio and talking about our ideas, it should have been clear what he was looking for and whether we'd click. Sadly, that often wasn't the case. Photographers liked to play the same game as people writing dating profiles, omitting important details and fibbing to make themselves seem more appealing. So it was always up in the air as to whether the shoot would be worth putting on makeup for until I was actually face to face with the photographer. And yet I kept trying. My interest in modeling seemed to be equal parts creative expression and masochism. For every fabulous and productive shoot, there were twice as many experiences with photographers that made me temporarily swear off modeling.

Despite all the ridiculous or scary characters I'd posed for with little to no payoff, I was always more amused than angry at the situations I found myself in. Modeling was mostly a way to stay occupied while I was unemployed, and if I could occasionally make money while doing it, even better. And all the false starts would seem worth it when I met a photographer who went above and beyond my expectations. A few of the people I first met behind a camera are now my favorite people in Portland. So in the end, the pleasure of modeling always won out despite the close calls.

However, knowing the sort of odds I was up against in meeting someone new, there was a game I liked to play to keep myself sane. While driving to meet him I would try to imagine what the man with the camera would look like after only hearing his voice on the phone. Because, hypocritically, photographers almost never let anyone take photos of them, which meant they rarely had head shots of themselves. I didn't care what these guys looked like—I wasn't there to get laid—but it would have been nice to have some reference, a way to know if I'd wandered into the correct studio.

This game also gave me something other than nerves to focus on while driving to meet a stranger, which never stopped being unnerving. I was well aware how dangerous it was to drive to a private place to meet a man and take my clothes off. That was why I always let at least one person know where I was going and gave them the photographer's contact information just in case I ended up dead in a weirdo's basement. At least someone would know where look for me eventually.

The fellow I was going to meet on this particular evening had a strangely comforting and soft voice. I was imagining someone small and vaguely handsome. And I had a pretty good feeling about him; this didn't seem like an evening I would have to worry about the photographer.

So, after driving to an unfamiliar area in the outskirts of town in rain so heavy I couldn't see an inch in front of me, I was not expecting the door to be opened by a balding guy with a giant unkempt beard and a permanent frown. His appearance wasn't the only thing I wasn't expecting. Now that I was in his space—which he continued to refer to as his studio though it was obviously his bachelor pad apartment—he was a completely different person than he had been on the phone. Once he admitted me inside, he returned to the sofa to finish watching the action movie on his big screen while mumbling under his breath, "You're early."

Our appointment was for 7 o'clock, and it was 7:02. Usually photographers complained about models being late or not showing up at all, so this was an interesting complaint. I stood awkwardly in his entryway for longer than I should have before asking, "Should I change into something?"

With a sigh he stood up, resigning himself to pausing the movie, in order to give me the tour. His bathroom was huge, full of mirrors, perfect lighting, and a ridiculous amount of make-up and costumes. It wasn't until this moment I was convinced he was actually a photographer and not part of an elaborate prank.

After changing, I returned to the area he used for shooting to stand and watch him arrange lights. He seemed to be pretending I wasn't there. I asked him, "Where do you want to start?"

"Give me a minute."

He went on adjusting equipment as if I was inconveniencing him by being there. This is how things continued for the rest of the evening; he was largely silent, even when I asked him an easy, direct question. When I could get a response out of him, it was short and gruff. This was especially confusing because he had been a perfect gentleman on the phone earlier and had seemed excited about the shoot.

It was as if he hadn't gotten the memo that an attractive stranger had driven across town to get naked and prance around for him. He wasn't even paying me for my time, so I couldn't figure out what he was so mopey about, but it set an unpleasant mood for the evening. Then he put on a Death Cab for Cutie-heavy mix of emo music that did absolutely nothing to bolster the atmosphere in the room.

Attitude aside, this guy did really amazing things with light and shadows to create very neat film noir-ish images. The way he lit his models made them look transported back in time, like something out of *The Big Sleep*, all slick wardrobe, classy makeup, and pin curls. His giant, softly gleaming lights made skin glow and pop against his flat black background. Using this technique, he was in the process of working on a damsel-in-distress project. Many of the photos involved women bound in rope, so I was curious to see myself in his style of bondage. The whole helpless-woman-victim concept didn't do much for me—I've spent most of my life trying to get into rope, so I didn't understand struggling to get out of it—but I was willing to give it a try if he could make me look like a classic movie dame.

He grumped his way through some test shots only to get up and leave the room. Just as I was contemplating grabbing my clothes and going back out into the rain, he wordlessly dragged a giant plastic tub full of rope out of his spare bedroom. My inner rope slut drooled with excitement. I've known people who really like rope, but this was an epic amount, and when he dumped it on the floor, it looked like a nylon rope rainbow had exploded. With another person this would have cued the start of an amazing evening, but I reminded myself where I was at the moment.

However, the rope did give me some motivation to stay and endure his attitude a bit longer. I disappeared into the bathroom to put on some pinup lingerie, and when I returned, trying to make small talk, I asked, "Wow, so you really like rope, then?"

"No, not really. I don't get it at all, but weirdly enough, girls seem to like it."

"It's not that weird. I really like rope."

He ignored this and told a story of a time when he was interested in learning Boy Scout knots, so for practice he carried a length of cord with him everywhere. One day it fell out of his bag while he was shooting, making the model he was working with get wide eyed and excited. She asked him to tie her up for pictures, and he grudgingly assented. The next thing he knew, all the models at that group shoot were lining up to get tied up for photos. Finding it the easiest way to get women interested in doing photos with him, he decided to make rope his trademark though he didn't particularly enjoy it.

I almost bought his tale of abject disinterest, until he put rope on my wrists.

He was deft in his handling of the lines and seemed to purposely tighten them too tight. I could see the sadistic gleam in his eyes as he knotted the rope very restrictively when he could have done a simple fake-out tie for the camera. I stayed quiet, though it seemed obvious he was practiced in tying more than just knots, because he was talented enough to create some decorative and semi-complex work.

We shot this first tie with me sitting on a stool, hands bound in front of me, in a basic chest harness made of simple white nylon that looked surprisingly amazing against my skin and the dark background. This pose only lasted a couple minutes—as long as it took him to capture a couple photos—and he was eager to remove the rope as soon as possible.

Next he put me into a fancy arm binder that was totally hidden from the camera, and this was when I genuinely started to wonder about the guy, telling me he didn't understand rope but tying something complicated the camera would never see. Not only that, but he had again tied the ropes tighter than they needed to be, so that as soon as he knotted them off, I was already uncomfortable.

"So, here's the thing: I know you put a lot of work into that and it's beautiful, but my hands are going to go numb in about a minute. So just a heads up. Maybe we can loosen it a bit?"

"You'll be okay." It wasn't a statement meant to comfort—it indicated, rather, a lack of attentiveness. He was behind me, so he didn't see me roll my eyes. Beardy proceeded to make the tie more uncomfortable by using the wrist ropes to anchor a line between my legs. Pulling my arms lower and straining my shoulders, he created a crotch rope by yanking it tight and anchoring the ends of the ropes around my thighs. I like discomfort with my rope, but his lack of elegance left a lot to be desired.

I jumped at the amount of pressure that was now being placed on my cunt when he pulled the knot too tight. "Oh!" he called, my reaction causing him to jump halfway across the room and stumble over his pile of multicolored rope. Knots on the labia are supposed to be just tight enough to create pressure; this was ridiculous.

I had visions of him cracking his head open on the entertainment center while I was stuck, mostly naked, in a tie I couldn't wiggle out of. That would be hard to explain. Luckily, he and his verdant beard came out unscathed. "You're not one of those that gets turned on or something by this are you? Because I can stop."

I couldn't stop myself from laughing out loud. "As I've been explaining, yes, yes, I do enjoy the sexual aspect of rope. It's a big part of my life. But that will not be a problem in this situation. Somehow I will control myself."

"Good." He scrunched his features into an icky face, as if I had given him girl cooties by touching his rope with my vulva. "Note to self: sanitize this rope immediately after the shoot."

I glared at him.

"No offense."

"I fully support you washing rope in between models. It was the way you worded it."

Now he glared at me. I wondered why he was photographing women if he wasn't comfortable with their bodies.

Determined to make the rest of the shoot fun, I flirted with his camera until he was blushing constantly. Finally it seemed like photos were being captured that I would enjoy putting in my portfolio. That is, until Beardy revealed his obsession with gags. From there on out he put one on me for every set of photos we did that night. And if gagging women wasn't something that did it for him sexually, then I couldn't imagine what other purpose they served. In a photo shoot situation, a gag is a horrible idea. While wearing one, the model has no way to emote except with her eyes. With both my hands and mouth bound, my posing options were drastically limited.

When my arms inevitably fell painfully asleep after about ten photos, I tried to express this through the industrial-strength black gaffer's tape on my mouth. Which sounded like "*mph mmnds mr nmmb.*"

When he didn't respond to my repeated muffled distress calls, I still wasn't concerned, thinking this tape would behave like other tape. I knew from past experience that duct tape was easy enough to wiggle off one's face. However, the tape Beardy had used was not moving. In fact, it hurt to attempt a contortion of my mouth in the slightest. All I could manage was a muffled *mmphff* of pain as I wiggled my fingers, hoping for circulation to return.

He kept shooting.

Unwilling to sacrifice my fingers to this project, I stood and turned my back to him, knowing this would get his attention. Earlier when I had posed with my ass toward the camera, he had screamed as if he were terrified and told me never to turn my back on the camera. So I knew seeing my butt again would get his attention. He stuttered and stammered, asking me to get back to the kneeling pose he'd requested. He either couldn't understand my problem or was blatantly ignoring it.

I backed up toward him, wiggling my numb fingers and grunting through the gaffer's tape. It was like a silent movie routine gone wrong. As I got closer, continuing to snake my fingers around and refusing to back down, he finally got the hint to untie me. First he pulled off the tape in one quick rip, along with a couple layers of my skin.

"Ouch! My hands are totally asleep. The rope needs to come off now."

"Is that all? Why didn't you just tell me your hands were going numb? I was just starting to get something good. One more . . . come on."

He had to be joking. "Um." I stood there glaring at him as he looked at me completely without irony. When he finally realized that I couldn't be bullied, he roughly tugged the harness off, forgoing any finesse, knotting up the rope that had touched me and tossing it across the room so it didn't contaminate anything.

It was definitely time to go home now. "Are we done here, then?" I called after him.

"Yeah, I got what I needed."

I quickly got dressed so we could go through with the pleasantries of "thanks" and "it was fun" and "it was great meeting you." Or at least I did and he followed my lead. When the issue of when I might see some pictures from him came up, his answer was, "I really like to watch TV, so it will probably be two months before I get around to sending you anything."

This seemed about right, considering the fact that he plopped onto the couch and turned on the movie as soon as I opened the door to leave. He didn't even bother to see me out. This was a trade-for-finished-photos shoot and I was a beginning model, so I wasn't expecting photos tomorrow, but two months seemed a bit much.

Usually I came home amped up with creative energy. After this shoot, however, all I could say as the Priest and our dog met me at the door was, "Whiskey, *stat*, please."

And true to his words, Beardy sent me the photos two days before the end of the two-month deadline.

CHAPTER 16
THE HOUSEDRESS

It quickly became obvious that modeling only felt rewarding if I created a bond with the photographer. The act of taking photos, of getting drawn into the process of another artist's art was extremely personal, often nearly as intimate as sex. As much of a slut as I was, this wasn't an intimacy I wanted to share with random weirdos anymore just because they had a big sexy portfolio. At this point, photography had largely taken the place of the random sexual encounters that had ruled my early sex life, as I'd found that the mild erotic attention of a shoot fed the same need bed-hopping had.

So after a few too many experiences like that with the grumpy, bearded, gag fetishist, I began meeting men with cameras for drinks before going through with a shoot. It was sharing experiences that weren't quite scary but could have been with photographers like Beardy that made me rethink the way I had been going about modeling. Those moments illustrated that it was only my good fortune that nothing truly bad had happened. I'd gotten close, seen how creepy and uncomfortable that black hole of danger could be, and wanted to avoid it. Meeting photographers for the first time on their turf, without knowing anything about them, wasn't going to work for me any longer.

My new method came with its own pitfalls, however. Connecting with a photographer for the first time over drinks often felt a lot like going on a first date. So it was sometimes easy for one of us to catch a hint of chemistry and get confused, especially since at the end of this "date" there was no question that I'd soon be naked in front of him. The expectations were different—and the end result was lovely images rather than horizontal acrobatics—but both experiences started out the same.

We'd meet in a bar, have a few cocktails, do the mini version of our life stories, and then get down to the serious stuff: creativity, motivation, our individual muses. Once we got there, it became a matter of how soon we could get to his place and put the energy between us to use. That was when things went well. Just like in dating, for every successful meeting there was an equal number of drink dates with photographers that went nowhere (and during which I counted the seconds before I could politely escape).

Meeting Mr. Green at the dark neighborhood bar he had suggested felt a little more like a date than usual. He was attractive in a geeky sort of way, with a well-trimmed beard and sweet smile. He was endearingly reserved but easy to talk to, giving me the opportunity to be the chatty one for a change. After an hour we hadn't even bothered discussing photos. So there was a strange lull in the conversation that seemed to signal both of us realizing the real reason we were there.

Finally Mr. Green managed, "We should talk about photos, huh?"

After a momentary giggling awkwardness, we were babbling and talking over one another while piling up potential concepts, seeing where our interests lined up and which ideas would be possible. It was apparent we were clicking, both of us looking forward to putting his camera to use. If it had been a date, we likely would have ended up making out in his car to tide us over until the next time we could see each other. Instead, we scheduled a time to shoot and flirt over his camera.

Given how well Mr. Green and I got along, I had high hopes for the photos we would create together. I wasn't dreading our appointment or feeling uncomfortable showing up at his place with a bag full of vintage-style lingerie and a 1950s checkered housedress. This lack of nervousness was rare. Usually I spent an hour pacing my bedroom before a shoot saying, "Why am I doing this again?"

To which the Priest usually responded with, "Going to a photo shoot, where you'll be tied up and get pretty photos taken, also known as your favorite things? Gee, I don't know. Your life sucks."

I would roll my eyes and realize he was right. The introverted half of me was constantly trying to find an excuse to call off the shoot and stay home where it was safe. The extroverted part of me was thrilled to have a chance to cavort in pretty clothes and be the center of attention. I would spend that last hour before going to a shoot primping and attempting to meld those sides of my personality. And in the end the extrovert always won out.

When I got to Mr. Green's door, he ushered me in a bit frantically. "Sorry, I was setting up at the last minute, and I tend to get nervous working with a new model. Can I get you some water? What do you want to listen to? Let me give you the tour."

He showed me around his small but beautiful apartment, including his library full of rare erotica. It also doubled as an absinthe parlor, complete with an old-fashioned louching station that dripped cold water into the green liquor to make it drinkable. This room had me daydreaming of lounging with a dirty book in one hand and a tiny fluted glass of emerald liquid in the other. But this was not on the menu for our afternoon together.

Once we'd circled back into his open kitchen and living room area he stopped and looked at me expectantly, so I voiced my answers to his original rapid-fire questions. "I would love some water, and I will trust your taste in music as long as it's upbeat."

He led me to the kitchen where he showed off some samples of a few of his favorite shoots that hung on the walls, giving me a better idea of his aesthetic. Soon we'd exhausted our small talk and it was time to stop dancing around the reason I was there. He decided on a playlist of funky retro music that set the perfect tone for the lighthearted shoot he had in mind.

As he finished with the stereo and turned back to me, something changed in his expression and his features became firm and authoritative. "So, what did you bring?"

I showed Mr. Green the checkered housedress, and he deemed it perfect. He nearly danced his fingers together, Mr. Burns style, in his excitement about this dress, so I didn't bother with any of the other options. He jumped up to grab his camera and looked at me enthusiastically.

"Ready?"

"Yep."

When I returned from changing, he was at his computer contemplating old black-and-white drawings. "Come look, tell me if you're into it."

He showed me vintage sketches while telling me about John Willie's erotic comic strip from the 40s and 50s, how it was revolutionary for the time—how Willie had gotten away with some really dirty stuff by making it humorous, that his work had been the inspiration for Betty Page's photo shoots, and that his bondage ideas had appeared in mainstream comics like Wonder Woman (whom Mr. Green obviously had an artistic crush on, as she'd already come up a number of times).

So of course I developed a tiny crush on Mr. Green; I found his super hero references amusing, bordering on erotic. I wasn't going to act on the attraction, but he was a swoon-worthy, grown-up version of the comic book geeks I hung out with, and was one of, in high school. While he finished his tangent and got himself back on course, I smiled.

He clicked through a few more images, and one popped out that got my attention. "Ooh," I said, "I like that one! Let's try that."

"All right, to the rope . . . "

We made eye contact, both on the verge of speaking, then stopped ourselves at the last second. He seemed hesitant to touch me, or the rope. The moment was getting too weird and loaded, so I used my old friend sarcasm to cope.

"What? Are you afraid of me? I won't bite . . . much."

"Good. I'm all Top, so I won't stand for biting," he said, picking up the rope to create a basic wrist tie. With roles established, the shoot proceeded without awkwardness.

Leaving me with my hands tied together and resting behind me, he popped up off the floor to drag a fancy metal chair with curled filigrees forming the backrest into the room. He positioned this chair at the center of his lights, pausing to catch his breath.

"All right, come on over and try that pose."

After I played to the camera and pretended to be a John Willie vixen for a while, Mr. Green untied me. He swapped out the black rope for some in a gorgeous crimson shade that popped against the monochrome dress. Using this, he created the simplest chest harness possible: one line above my breasts, one below, and another crossing over one shoulder to form a *V* between the lines and travel back over my other shoulder. It did the trick, hugging my curves in interesting ways that the dress alone couldn't.

With that tied on me, he put a simple rope cuff on each wrist and ankle, strapping my hands to the arms of the chair and my feet to the chair legs. After I'd been posing for a little while and he'd gotten some good shots, he seemed to have gotten more comfortable, so I became bolder with my expressions, playing to the camera with naughty eyebrows and smiles that were making him blush.

He stopped to ask, "Can I pull your dress down?"

My eyes got big. This was not a conversation I wanted to have while unable to defend myself. "Um, what?"

"To make you look disheveled, show a little skin. Just open a couple buttons and let a nipple out."

I exhaled, relieved he wasn't hoping for something creepy. This was a reasonable question, considering the fact that we'd talked about me eventually getting naked for this shoot, so I was actually feeling weird to be keeping all my clothes on for so long. "Oh yeah, that's fine!"

There was that loaded eye contact again.

My cunt was already all wet, as it tends to be when there's a camera around. The exhibitionist in me loved the attention and the naughtiness of nudity with a stranger. This time was different: I was wet because of the photographer, because he was cute and I wasn't going to do anything about that. Essentially I'd signed up to tease myself all afternoon.

When he'd processed my grin long enough to believe it meant yes, he reached out to unbutton my dress. I willed myself not to flush and give myself away. But in looking at the photos later, I saw that I was unsuccessful. My sex glow showed in the rest of the photos.

He yanked at the edges of the opened dress to pull it under the chest ropes, tucking them away. I went ahead and giggled before he had touched me because the moment was ridiculous. He nudged my bra down and cupped my breast, pulling it into view while managing to avoid touching my nipple. Most other camera guys couldn't have gotten away with this, but I was comfortable enough with Mr. Green that I didn't need to ask to be untied in order to do it myself.

Properly exposed, I did my best to play the innocent housewife tied to a chair, which lasted until both of us were having too much fun to be serious. Now that part of me was naked, I could really enjoy the shoot. Being fully clothed in photos felt odd to me; I could never quite get in the groove unless my body could come out and play. Mr. Green and I were suddenly on the same wavelength and able to play off of one another. He turned up the music, and we dropped into that miraculous place where time and the real world fell away.

We were having so much fun making each other blush that it wasn't until we were both woozy with hunger that we realized hours had passed without us pausing. He untied me while we laughed and gibbered about movies and comics, really enjoying one another and shocked at how far we'd gotten with one outfit. The discarded strands of rope and lingerie tossed around us made for a scandalous scene. We were both sweaty and spent as we chatted a bit more, promising to shoot again soon. I hurried to the other room to put on my boring jeans and T-shirt for the trip home and took all that pent-up energy created during the shoot home to a very excited Priest.

As these things go in Portland—which is really more of a small town than a big city—now that I knew Mr. Green, I saw him everywhere. He was at the local rope group, where we partnered up. Then I saw him at a burlesque show, a book reading, on the bus, and discovered he was friends with a coworker. Total Baader-Meinhof Phenomenon stuff. So, after the second time we connected at rope practice group, we cemented a plan for another date with his camera. Since then, we've continued using our random meetings as an excuse to plan more shoots, which we haven't stopped doing all these years later. He's still on my list of photographers I'll always work with.

CHAPTER 17

THE BUTTERFLY

There was something about Mr. Hollywood that instantly made me want to break my no-mixing-work-and-pleasure rule.

He was slight and hunched in on himself as if trying to be invisible, had an accent that came and went seemingly at random, and wore cargo pants so weighed down with camera accessories that he had to continually hitch them up lest they fall down entirely. So there wasn't an obvious physical draw—rather, it was a rare instance of me being so at ease with someone that all awkwardness was short circuited. We were joking with each other as soon as he arrived, as if we'd been acquainted for years. This led to an immediate hyper creative energy that had me naked five minutes after he had walked through the door and turned my tiny apartment into a tangle of lights and cameras.

He was a traveling photographer from L.A. who mostly shot high-glamour nudes with stereotypically perfect models; many of his images bordered on porn. I was confused about his interest in working with me and assumed it had a lot to do with me offering to tie myself up for him. That was something he didn't have in his portfolio. And I didn't have any edgy sexual images in mine. So we didn't waste any time getting started.

I crawled up on the chilly stone tiles of the large kitchen counters in my apartment, naked and elated. Mr. Hollywood and I were having so much fun making sexually explicit jokes and sarcastically flirting with one another that I kept forgetting we were supposed to be working.

When he asked if the counter could hold us both so he could climb up and shoot from above, I nodded and added, "It's also a good height for . . . " I moved to the edge of the counter, spread my legs in his direction, and humped the air as if I was being fucked by an invisible partner. He looked mock scandalized, waiting for me to go on. Rather than finishing the obvious sentence, I said, "Can you hand me my rope now, please?"

He exhaled sharply, "You vixen."

I smiled and held his eye contact while I went about tying my chest into a harness. Mr. Hollywood stood by teasing me throughout this. "God, can't you tie yourself up behind your back faster than that?"

"I know, right? I'm so untalented. I suck."

"You probably do, with that filthy mouth."

"Ha!" I went back to struggling to finish off the tie in the center of my back, eventually giving up to interrupt Mr. Hollywood midsentence. "I know you're not a rope dude, but maybe you could knot this off for me?"

"Okay, I'll try." He got close but before touching me pulled back to ask, "I mean, I have permission to touch you, right?"

"Uh, yes, that's why I asked. But thanks for checking."

He ran his hands up and down his body, with a raised eyebrow. "Does this look like the hot bod of a creeper to you?"

"Kinda, now that you mention it."

Making a playful face, he turned me around to knot the rope off. When he was finished he took my chin in his hand to primp my hair, arranging my curls into some semblance of order. My heart dropped to my cunt, and I tried not to swoon at how tender this moment was. I accidently made eye contact, causing Mr. Hollywood to become serious for the first time. As we stared each other down, neither of us moved or commented. My body was telling me to lean in for a kiss, but my brain reminded me this was a photo shoot, not a date. This exact dilemma was why I worked so hard not to flirt outright with photographers; it got complicated. Now I had to wonder if his touch was foreplay or innocent primping for photos.

I made a silly face at him while backing away to end the loaded moment. "Are you going to take pictures or what?"

He sighed and licked his lips while looking me over for another beat, but once the camera was at his eye, he was all business. I was safely able to flirt with his lens in order to work off the sexual tension. And when the mood between us got steamy again, the camera drifting away from his face as he watched me pose rather than taking photos, I sat up and untied myself. This snapped him back to reality.

"What now?" I asked.

He pointed at the coffee table. "Let me see the rope. I have an idea."

"Okay, bossy, I thought you didn't know anything about rope."

"Sit."

I did, with eyes wide from being told what to do.

"Said I never do it for photos, never said a thing about my personal life." The cheeky boy had let me tie myself up for him when he could have done it himself. "You can do prettier things than I can anyway. Wanted to see what you'd get up to."

I handed him the four short pieces of rope he would need to accomplish what I assumed he had in mind. He lifted one of my hands to rest it against his chest as he bound it in a perfect cuff. I raised my eyebrows, impressed at his secret bondage skills after all his talk on the phone about not being sure about rope.

"Not bad!"

"Shush, you." He tied the next cuff a little too tight to silence me, and then pushed that limb aside and kneeled to grasp an ankle. I knew what came next.

Opening my legs, I smirked as he looked at this newly exposed flesh. My pussy was at eye level, making it impossible for him not to notice. He sighed and tied each ankle, spreading them to the corners of the table and binding them to the furniture's legs. After several false starts at making a comment, he twisted up his face. It was obvious he had something on his mind that he was having a tough time sharing.

Finally he managed, "Can I see some butterfly?"

At first I thought my not understanding was an English-as-a-second-language issue. But as I ran it through my head again, I was positive that I'd heard him say "butterfly."

He put his hands at crotch level and spread his fingers in a baffling gesture I didn't comprehend. I shook my head at him. "I don't get it."

It then became a legitimate guessing game as I learned that the words for female genitalia weren't part of his English vocabulary. I was getting more confused as he continued in dueling languages to express what he wanted. "Open butterfly. Closed is everywhere. Guys want to see the inside."

After seeing the spread fingers gesture enough times, it finally occurred to me that he wanted me to open my pussy lips suggestively. Then I laughed outright. "Guys want that? Or you?"

He shrugged coyly, refusing to answer.

This was so specific it had to be a personal turn on. Every photographer had one, just like every model had a go-to pose. These photos were likely a gift to himself to keep him warm in the long line of hotel rooms he would visit before returning home. Spread-leg—let alone spread-pussy—photos were not usually in my repertoire, but I was feeling inspired to explore the concept with Mr. Hollywood. It would be amusing to be added to his spank bank, as he was certainly going in mine. So I rolled my eyes and laughed, entertained that this was something I'd agreed to.

Though he was obsessed with my butterfly, Mr. Hollywood didn't try to arrange it himself, much to my relief, even when my hands were tied. So this went on all evening; he would snap a few shots then emerge from behind the camera to nod toward me silently. It was baffling until I realized this was his signal to fondle myself open again, at which point I would laughingly comply.

After awkwardly rearranging my genitalia to Mr. Hollywood's rigorous standards, we were ready to shoot again. He grabbed the wrist ropes and pulled me down to lie on the table. "Ready?"

I wavered, giving him an unsure expression. The problem was, I had a friend coming over at any moment and it would be difficult to answer the door if I was tied down. I also wasn't sure how she would react to walking into this debauchery. I'd only met Sock Girl a couple times before, having run into each other at her friend the Vandal's monthly rope parties. We'd bonded over our love of being silly at super serious fetish events, giggling in the corner and having a great time while everyone else was grim, seemingly determined to compete for title of Domliest Dom. After casually meeting enough times, both of us lamenting our lack of a rope partner, we decided to take the next step and have a drink while I practiced tying her up.

I'd made these plans with her thinking that Mr. Hollywood would be long gone by now. But he had been running late and we were having a lot more fun shooting than we had imagined we would; one set had become several, and we were nowhere near having exhausted our ideas. So I was now double-booked.

Should I call it quits, or hope my new friend would walk in and be amused? I didn't have the heart to kick him out, so I made Mr. Hollywood promise to make himself useful while I was otherwise occupied. "If the doorbell rings, you have to answer it, but only let the person in if it's a lady with bright-red hair."

"I think even I can handle that. Now lie down."

When we were finished at the table, Sock Girl still hadn't appeared, so I put on a frumpy gray sweater to stay warm while we took a break and waited for her. Suddenly Mr. Hollywood got excited, longing to combine the shabby sweater with the sexiness of a near-naked body. He asked, "Do you have a blindfold?"

"Of course." I retrieved a shiny latex eye mask, which he helped me into.

"Perfect! I'm loving this."

Doing a shoot blind with a near stranger was a nerve-wracking exercise in trust. So, noticing how tense I was, Mr. Hollywood started telling me everything he was doing. "I'm standing over you taking a picture of your breasts. Open your sweater. Now I'm kneeling and taking a photo of you. Can you spread your legs?"

This made things incredibly hot. I was being given instructions, which made me melt with arousal, and yet I knew someone was going to ring the doorbell at any moment. This meant there was no room for us to get carried away and wander outside of photo-shoot territory.

The idea was tempting; I was enjoying Mr. Hollywood's attention more than I did that of other photographers.

"Make a pretty butterfly for me. Now pretend to touch yourself. Put your head back. Touch one of your nipples. Put a finger in, if you're comfortable."

Ordinarily, nothing in the taking of photos was as sexy as it looked in the final product; mostly photography was a lot of holding uncomfortable poses and doing the same thing a million times at slightly different angles. But once he made this suggestion, the fingering I did was the real thing. I couldn't help myself; the temptation was too great to ignore once he put the idea in my head. He'd given me permission to do exactly what I was longing to.

I ditched the sweater and got into the moment so deeply that Mr. Hollywood stopped giving directions. When I was on my hands and knees with my crotch in his direction, three fingers inside myself, I realized the camera wasn't snapping anymore. Mr. Hollywood was just watching. This had officially become more than a photo shoot.

Before I could decide if I should stop what I was doing, the doorbell rang. I leaped off the couch, snatched off the blindfold, grabbed the sweater, and peeked out into the winter night. Sock Girl looked down at my lack of pants with amusement. "Um, we're still kind of sort of shooting," I said. "Do you want to come in? You can watch while we finish up, if that isn't too weird."

"Just weird enough!" She grinned from ear to ear and bounded in the door armed with a great bottle of wine and her loveable, overly excited energy.

Sock Girl and Mr. Hollywood hit it off right away. Handing me a glass of wine, she whispered, "Damn, he's strangely cute!"

"I know, right?"

I worried having an observer would throw off the balance of the shoot. Instead, we enjoyed ourselves, perhaps more than three people with a camera ever had before. It didn't feel odd to be lying across the back of the couch and continuing where I had left off before she joined us. I was just a bit more conservative with the fondling of my pussy, not wanting to offend Sock Girl. This was before I knew she was a world-class pervert who would more often make me blush in our conversations than the other way around. She sat behind the lights fanning herself, enjoying her wine and making appreciative noises.

Eventually Mr. Hollywood gave me the nod that meant butterfly. I adjusted things without a second thought and we went on shooting. As this continued happening, the look on Sock Girl's face became more bemused, until she finally asked, "Okay, I can't take it anymore. What's going on with the . . . ?" She pantomimed Mr. Hollywood's give-me-the-butterfly gesture.

It was such an odd set of circumstances that I crumpled in on myself laughing hysterically. Mr. Hollywood explained the rationale behind the adjustment and the name he'd given it, which only made her look more baffled. As he continued to explain, she joined me, hunched over in laughter, causing me to laugh harder. Soon it was a chain reaction that we couldn't end. Each time I regained composure, I would look at her holding back a giggle and we would explode again.

Mr. Hollywood gave up, sitting in the kitchen to drink a glass of wine, not amused. "Between the legs is serious, come on, guys!"

This started the loop of hilarity anew. Mr. Hollywood finished with his drink, crossed the room with his camera in one hand, and grabbed my hair with the other, pulling my head back to face him. When I looked up at his serious eyes, I wasn't laughing anymore. "Ready to continue?"

I didn't need to respond. He backed up several feet and gave me the nod. This time when I reached down to adjust my labia I was so wet my lips stayed spread of their own volition. I heard an *mmm* from the kitchen that Sock Girl pretended to direct at the wine.

As we continued shooting, whenever I moved my pussy lips, a little snicker would emanate from the kitchen. To this day I can't say the word *butterfly* anywhere near Sock Girl without starting a cascade of giggling fits that one or both of us run the risk of never recovering from.

We worked on a few more ideas before it was getting late and we'd run out of concepts. Mr. Hollywood called it a night and packed his gear. It was obvious he didn't want to leave; Mr. Hollywood knew once he did I was going to tie up Sock Girl, as I'd told him all about my rope date with her. So of course he wanted to stay and watch two ladies play with rope rather than go alone into the cold night.

If I had known Sock Girl well enough then, I would have asked Mr. Hollywood to stay and likely have a much different story to tell. Instead, I hugged him good-bye and told him once again that I had the greatest time ever shooting with him.

The moment I closed the door, fanning myself and trying to recover from the hotness of the last several hours, Sock Girl squealed, "You should have let him stay. He was so cute!" My face must have fell instantly because she ran over to hug me. "Aw, honey."

"No, it's okay. I don't need to start fucking hot photographers. Though if I was going to start . . . "

We watched him through the slats in the blinds while he loaded his van and I battled internally with the urge to ask him to come back in. But I ultimately decided it wasn't a good idea. Instead, I ended a very erotic evening of photography by tying up the goofiest girl I've ever made the acquaintance of. It seemed like a fitting contrast.

CHAPTER 18
THE MAN AND HIS MUSTANG

Ordinarily cars didn't interest me, but when the Sergeant arrived for our first date in his glossy, black Mustang, it was a strangely visceral turn on. There was something about his passion for that car, and the nostalgia of remembering my father's cherry-red Mustang, that got my attention. But at the base of its appeal were the leather seats, their smell and supple texture on my bare thighs as the horsepower vibrated through the car.

By the time we were regular play partners, the Sergeant knew to use the Mustang to his advantage as a foreplay machine. Especially the evening he blindfolded me, put me in the passenger's seat, and drove the long way back to his place.

I knew the roads that led from my house to his by heart, knew what they felt like without looking, so even in my blindness I could feel that he was taking strange turns, not traveling anywhere directly. I didn't know where we were or if other people could see us clearly enough to notice my blindfolded face. Occasionally his hands wandered when we were stopped, pulling aside my flimsy dress. I had to trust he wouldn't get us caught, that I was only being exposed in gentle ways. Yet his evil giggles kept me on edge, wondering what he was capable of.

Once we were on the highway, he slid a hand between my legs, forcing them open. The velocity of the new speed pushed me against the seat back, taking my breath away while he pushed fingers toward my cunt. He quickly noticed I wasn't wearing any panties under my short dress; this hadn't been part of his instructions for dressing. I was off script and asking to be punished.

"My. You are in a mood tonight, aren't you? This is going to be fun."

I shrugged and leaned back to press myself closer to his fingers. He was driving stick, so his hand just as quickly disappeared to shift gears. Each time he stopped touching me, I would melt into the lush seat as the engine picked up and thrummed through the entire vehicle. When he changed gears, it was like sitting inside an industrial vibrator.

When we arrived in his driveway at last, the Sergeant walked to my side of the car, opened the door, and took my hand to guide me to the front stoop. Inside the house, he didn't wait to close the door before putting hands on my shoulders and forcing me to kneel on a pillow. His motorcycle boots clicked across his newly varnished hardwood floors. I felt off balance and lost in a huge, empty world, unsure of what would occur or what was around me. Logically, I knew his living room well, but because he had all the power, the situation felt startling and unreal.

My hands weren't bound, but I felt enough deference for him and trepidation about his plans that I stayed still, enduring his lingering. My other senses were alight as I waited, no longer sensing the Sergeant in the room. So I startled to hear his boots clicking on the floor again. He paced, opening drawers, pulling bags out of closets and from under the bed. These noises filled me with dread; we'd been playing long enough now for me to have a general idea of what he had in mind.

When he neared, I jumped at his touch. But instead of being threatening, he ran rope along my shoulder. It was calming, and my muscles went slack and pliable so he could pin my hands behind me and tie them together. He secured them by running rope over my arms and chest several times, then over my shoulders in a primitive chest harness. He didn't have fancy rope, but I'd never cared—clothesline got the job done. For me, it had always been more about being restricted and helpless than masterful rigging. Besides, thin rope bit painfully into the skin if I struggled, so I had to be doubly sure to keep relatively still.

"That will do. Should hold you for a while."

It would indeed. The tie was so tight on my chest that it restricted my breathing. Moving my hands pulled the knots too tight on my wrists, so I had to be careful not to wiggle so much that I cut off circulation. I inhaled meditatively, trying to stay calm during the initial effort to let go and relax into being restrained, especially by someone I knew had plans to hurt me.

The Sergeant removed the blindfold so I could see the evil things he'd retrieved. With his particular DIY topping style, this was more confusing than enlightening. I saw what I thought were bamboo skewers, rubber bands, licorice whips, and a floor sander, but no traditional objects like floggers or sex toys. He was a bizarre and inventive man, so I was no closer to understanding what was about to happen.

While I was distracted by contemplating my fate, he surprised me by pulling my hair with one hand and forcing the front of my dress down to expose my breasts with the other. His leering face was so close to mine it was all I could see. I gasped, my neck stretched tight enough that I momentarily couldn't breathe as we eyed one another. Soon he pushed me away so that I was tottering to find my center again; kneeling in high heels was difficult. Eventually I righted myself and looked up at him, his hand on his hips in his tight jeans and black, muscle-hugging T-shirt.

"Now make yourself useful. Take off my pants."

My first instinct was to stand up, turn around, and go at the buttons with my hands behind my back. But when I tried to stand, he pushed me back down. "Use your mouth!" He was rarely stern when we played; mostly we laughed at one another and took turns tying the other up. So his raised voice was shocking.

His cold facial expression as he glared down at me indicated that he was serious. Still, I had no clue how it would be possible to undo the fly of his tight jeans with my teeth. It proved as difficult as I had imagined, as the first button refused to budge until I used the weight of my head to pull the button open instead of the force of my teeth. The remaining buttons opened fairly easily from there. I sat back on my knees feeling pretty happy with myself, smiling up at him.

"All the way off."

This game didn't seem fair, but I was so close to freeing his cock that I was motivated to get these pants out of the way. He moved his hips to assist with the process as I grabbed fabric in my teeth to pull one side and then the other down, one agonizing inch at a time. A torturous several minutes later, there was a pantsless man with a hard on standing in front of me.

As soon as I tried to line my mouth up with him, however, he moved away, pressing down on my head whenever I was tempted to move. I pouted at him. After all that work I was hoping for a reward.

"You can only have it if your nose stays right here." He pointed to an area an inch above his cock.

I wet the tip of him with my tongue, taking him in slowly, lubricating him with my drool as I went along. This method was apparently too leisurely for him, so the Sergeant took handfuls of my hair and forced himself down my throat. I made very unladylike sounds as he shoved himself in as far as possible and held me there despite my reflexive gurgling noises and watering eyes. It was hard to breathe with his cock taking up all the room in my throat, but my nose was pressed to the spot he'd indicated, so I'd held up my end of the deal.

We played this game for a while, me bobbing my head back and forth to suck on him while keeping my nose in place, him periodically pulling my head closer. When he got bored of listening to me gag and gurgle around his cock, the Sergeant forced me back down to the floor. When I could see through the haze of tears and drool again, he was putting his pants back on, which seemed cruel, considering the work I'd put into removing them.

There was an evil glint in his eyes as he approached me with a black fabric bag and a squishy red toy ball. I dreaded what he might have in mind.

"Let's see how long you can hold your breath." I didn't like the sound of that at all. "Open your mouth. Wide!" Being the compliant slut I was when rope was involved and my pussy was making the decisions, I did just that.

He pressed the foam ball into a small blob in his fist and promptly forced it between my teeth. This was unremarkable at first, but as the foam expanded to its original size, the ball filled much of the empty space in my mouth. This ball was much larger than the standard ball gag but squishy, so it didn't force my jaw open uncomfortably, but then again, I also couldn't force it out of my mouth. This meant my ability to swallow and breathe was restricted. Not being able to breathe was the one thing that really frightened me; I started to panic, giving him a desperate pleading look.

Next he returned the blindfold to my face, removing another of my senses. I thrashed around when he approached again, knowing the black bag was still in his hand. I gurgled pathetically and inched away, hoping to convince him not to use it. I was terrified but not enough to safeword. It was sexy and scary at the same time to have him stretching my comfort levels, but he hadn't crossed any lines.

He slapped my thigh, hard. The echo reverberated through the house. It took me a moment to process that much pain, and while it washed over me, I doubled up and grunted. Above me, I heard him say, "Hold still, damn it!"

While I was preoccupied, he forced the bag over my head. Using the drawstring at the bottom, he cinched it tight. The fabric was thin, so I could breathe through it better than I would have imagined, but it was rather claustrophobic nonetheless. I was concentrating on not hyperventilating while convincing myself I wasn't going to die from choking on the ball. By now it had expanded fully, so there wasn't a way to make a sound, and my labored breathing was making the bag so warm I was sweating.

"Okay, take a deep breath." My blood ran cold with panic but I obeyed.

He held my nose, taking my remaining source of oxygen. There was still air in my lungs; it wasn't an emergency yet, but the fear of getting to that point made me struggle against him. He chuckled as I squirmed, quite obviously in no position to get away. Just before I legitimately panicked, he released me.

I sucked in a desperate breath around the drool-covered ball and tried to compose myself, thinking the game was over. So I was unprepared when he wrapped an arm around me and cut off my air supply again. This time I kicked and pulled against him instantly. He released me for a shorter gasp of air and repeated the process. When he tired of my whining, he tossed me to the ground.

There was silence as he moved away from me where I slumped on the floor and waited. I heard the metallic snap of him removing the leather band he wore around his wrist, and I preemptively curled into a ball, hoping to give him less surface area to aim for. We had played this game before; I knew what happened next, and that tiny piece of leather hurt. It worked as a tiny, stingy belt, and if he was feeling particularly cruel, he would use the end with the raised metal snap closures.

Ordinarily he wasn't much for hitting me with things, but when he got in the mood, this was his favorite instrument. I knew it well. The precise sound of it meeting my flesh, how hard he'd hit, how long it would take him to get bored, and how much it would sting to sit on those marks for a week. The deep bruises from the snaps and the shallow ones from the leather, contrasting one another.

It was easy for him to drag me around and find places to slap. He held me down as the leather made contact with my chest, thighs, and ass. The Sergeant took the opportunity to whack anything that got exposed to him as I struggled, leaving me plenty of welts to remember him by.

When he finished, the Sergeant tucked the flowy part of my dress into the rope wrapped around me and explored between my legs. "Oh wow, someone is having some fun."

Finding my pussy to his liking, he spent awhile fingering it, tormenting me by stopping just when I would start to ride a peak of pleasure. He got me to the verge of coming a couple times from a combination of light-headedness and overstimulation. Using a handful of my hair in one hand and the fingers inside of me, he pushed and pulled me, signaling he wanted me to sit upright.

Finally, he decided to remove the bag from my head. My hair and face were a red and sweaty mess in the aftermath. He laughed and pulled me closer to rub the front of his jeans on my face, teasing me with the bulge there.

The blindfold was the next to go. Then I could plead with him to remove the ball using sad puppy-dog eyes. He made me suffer a bit longer but did eventually grab the drooly ball, gradually wiggling it out with a pop that released a humiliating amount of saliva down the front of my chest and dress. But I was rewarded with my first full breath in what felt like an eternity. My jaw ached, and I hated him for being so cruel, yet my cunt longed for him. It was a strange feeling to know that the crueler he was, the more turned on I got.

Then it was time to untie me. I waited patiently while he tugged at the knots, undoing the mess bit by bit. As each layer of rope was untangled, my circulation gradually came back, causing me to sigh and groan in delight. When he finally got around to my wrists, my hands were wobbly and unfamiliar. However, I was determined to unbutton his pants. He didn't stop me or comment this time, so his cock was soon back in my mouth where it belonged. I bobbed eagerly on it like a maniac, not caring if I gagged or gurgled.

Soon my dress was being pulled over my head, requiring me to remove him from my mouth long enough to be undressed. He used that moment of weakness to get away. The next thing I knew I was being half dragged, half carried to his bed. He was strong enough to lift me but chose not to, adding carpet burn to my list of humiliations.

I landed facedown on the mattress with one arm still tangled in rope, wearing nothing but stockings and heels. The Sergeant dutifully put on a condom and began fucking me from behind before I could lift myself fully into the bed. I encouraged him by bucking my hips back to meet his.

Having sex with him was more like a battle than anything else, as we both clawed at each other and fucked as hard as we could without one of us actually breaking. It was combative, full-contact-sport fucking. This time was like all the others, highly intense but exhausting. He banged the head of his cock against the sweet spot deep inside me until I was a mess of orgasmic thrashing, causing him to come inside of me not long after.

We fell asleep curled up on one another only to wake and start the animal lust cycle all over again. This usually went on as long as he could handle it, because as long as I was enjoying myself, I could be tricked into coming until I went comatose. And he had spent many the evening testing the limits of this particular talent only to drive me home mindless and babbling, just conscious enough to unlock the front door, crawl into bed, and make myself come one more time while grinning about the sexy Sergeant. I would email him the next morning and ask, "When can we do that again?"

CHAPTER 19
THE GUERILLA SHOOT

The Southern Gent was a photographer I'd met on a modeling site who happened to be in town for business. His hope was to do some guerrilla rope shots in the evenings during his free time. This would entail finding a location, getting me tied up and rigged to something, taking a few shots, and leaving before anyone noticed.

Recently he had conquered a landmark in his hometown by tying a ballet dancer to a statue in the city's capital. He wanted to capture equally daring photos of women in rope in recognizable locations around the country during his travels. So I was excited to help him test the boundaries of Portland's infamously open-ended nudity laws to create similar photos.

We met downtown to scope out locations. As we walked around the various pieces of public art in the parks trying to find something that inspired us, the weather was getting progressively more miserable and rainy. Our motivation and creative energy were flagging. As we circled back to his car, I was expecting one of us to call things off at any minute. But if we were going to shoot, we agreed, we needed to wait for it to get darker, when the lighting would be consistent enough to get a decent image. So we grabbed dinner and waited, hoping the rain would let up in the meantime as well.

He watched out the window at how continuously busy the streets were, even at nine at night, feeling a bit less daring than when we were talking hypothetical concepts over email. It was hard for him to believe that Portland would be as open-minded as I'd described.

"Why would I fib about something like that? I'll be the one suspended from a pole, so it's not like I can run away and leave you to get arrested."

"I'm from the South, where everything is illegal; give me some time to adjust."

I laughed, understanding where he was coming from. It had taken me a while to come to terms with the unbelievable weirdness of Portland. Now, after most of a year here, I almost took it for granted. But the first couple of times a photographer had suggested I disrobe in semipublic, I had looked at him like he was insane.

It took getting caught by the police during a shoot for me to believe in the notion of nudity being legal. That night I was sure the photographer and I were about to be arrested—instead, the officers ignored my nakedness and said, "Please don't stand in the street." After that I got a lot bolder. After all, a huge part of why I'd moved to Portland was to take advantage of the creative culture.

So, with full bellies, we drove to the Southern Gent's hotel room. If we chickened out on the guerilla rope idea, we could always shoot something there. He charged his camera battery and tied me into the basic chest and hip harnesses that would be required to suspend me later. The tying was so much easier to do in the warmth and privacy of the indoors than it would have been at the location. I would hide the rope under my coat until the last minute to cut down on the attention we attracted. Now all we had to worry about once we got to the location was rigging the suspension ring to whatever I would hang from.

Back in his car, he drummed his fingers on the steering wheel as I waited for him to decide if he was up for tying me to a Portland landmark. He turned to me suddenly. "Okay, if you're up for it, I am."

"Definitely!"

He drove toward the water, scoping out the place I had in mind. My brain was constantly on the lookout for photo ideas, so I'd been looking at it from the bus window each day during the commute to my most recent temp job. This place had cemented itself as something I wanted in my portfolio if I could find a photographer willing to shoot there.

In the narrow, grassy area between the river that divides Portland's east and west sides and the busy parkway running north and south was the giant cylindrical metal mast of a battleship. It seemed to grow incongruously out of the park and was one of the remaining pieces from a vessel built in the late 1800s. Tucked behind tall evergreens and not well lit, it was easy to miss, which made it somehow both showy and invisible.

We stayed in the shadows so as to not draw attention. Circling the mast as it towered over us, the Southern Gent decided on the section of the ladders on the mast that faced the road. It looked most secure and would provide numerous attachment points. Even as he was tossing a climbing sling over the iron railing, I could sense he was second-guessing himself.

"You still up for this?"

"Yeah?" He said it as a question.

"I don't believe you." I nudged him playfully in the hopes of getting him out of his head. "Let's not let this go to waste." I opened my coat to flash him the rope.

He shook his head at my silliness but seemed in better spirits as he revealed the small silver ring he would suspend me from and connected it to the mast via the climbing ropes and carabineers wrapped around one of the sturdy metal protrusions six feet in the air. This whole process had taken about a half hour. I didn't understand the mechanics of the rigging part of suspensions, so I could only observe. I danced in place to keep my bare legs warm while keeping watch; no one seemed to have taken notice of us.

Finished with everything else, the Southern Gent beckoned for me to come closer. "It's time. Lose the coat and let's go."

I tossed it aside in the pile of his camera equipment, feeling oddly exposed as I rubbed the goose bumps from my arms. Ordinarily, I had little concern during situations like this one where—though nudity wasn't a problem—we could conceivably be ticketed for trespassing or criminal mischief if we were caught. But feeling his nervous energy had me on edge as well. Trusting the photographer to have my back if anything went wrong was a large part of what made doing shoots like this seem relatively safe. In that bubble of confidence, I felt invincible when undressed. That was missing with the Southern Gent, and I worried that if we got caught, it wouldn't go well.

Pushing those thoughts out of my mind, I stood under the ring as he connected the harnesses on my body to the up-line ropes that would lift me off the ground. First he attached my chest and hips to the ring, lifting me only to tiptoe height in preparation for the next step. Next were my thighs, which he lifted above my head, one at a time, until I was nearly upside down, my legs in the air, my head tipped back.

"You good?"

I grinned like a fool and nodded. I was in rope and off the ground; of course I was good.

Next he lifted my hips, accentuating this arch of my body so that I looked like a kid on a swing leaning back into the rush of air, hair dangling, legs akimbo. He stepped back to take in the scene and liked it. I closed my eyes as all the blood rushed to my head, waiting for him to give me instructions. Sensing flashes of light, I assumed he was testing his setup.

I opened my eyes when he came closer. "Okay," he said, "all set. I'll get you down in a sec. Just gonna put away my light so it doesn't blow away. You all right for another minute?"

"That's it?"

"Yeah, got what I need. Be right back."

I was surprised; the shoot was over so quick I hadn't realized what was happening. As I was dangling there, swinging against the echoing metal to amuse myself, I saw a shadow nearing slowly. It walked with the careful and hunched gait of an older individual.

Oh no, I thought. The Southern Gent didn't notice this happening, so he was startled when a smiling old man came into the light.

"I saw the flashes. Do you need help?"

Still swinging around, I grinned and said, "Aw, no, I'm fine. We're just taking pictures."

He didn't acknowledge me. Walking closer to the Southern Gent with a leer and lecherous wink, he said, "I mean, do you need help holding a light? I would love to help."

I bet you would, I thought as the Southern Gent gently brushed the stranger off. We smiled at each other with boggled faces as the man walked away.

"I told you Portland was weird!"

CHAPTER 20

THE UNEXPECTED

Photographers all had their obsessions. I'd worked with a waterfall fetishist, a guy who only shot in hotel rooms, and Mr. Hollywood with his butterfly fixation. The Law Man, however, had a thing for strain, struggle, and intense emotion conveyed in the expressions of beautiful young women. His photos were monotone and moody, but it never crossed my mind to wonder how he got his models to manifest those expressions. That was until the Law Man drove me an hour from Portland in the name of finding the perfect tree and directed me to climb it while half naked.

"Look more upset. I need wrinkles in your forehead," he yelled up the tree.

I wrinkled my forehead, but it was in confusion. This tree looked like any other we could have found closer to Portland and its surrounding parks. It seemed silly to have driven this far.

"Give me intensity," he yelled. I looked at him blankly, not understanding my motivation. We'd just gotten started; he hadn't even waited for me to get situated before calling out requests. Usually, there was a little warm up and creative foreplay before getting down to business.

"Okay, pretend you just got broken up with," he tried again. I raised an eyebrow. "That's your expression? That's all?"

"Yeah. We obviously weren't that close if he broke up with me while I was in a tree."

He laughed.

This went on for a few minutes, him tossing out a strange prompt and me attempting an expression. Acting wasn't my strong suit, so this didn't go well.

"Okay, look sleepy, then."

"That I can do." I lounged on the tree like I was midnap. He took a few mediocre photos and tried again.

"Look distressed."

I sighed; he hadn't told me I was going to have to perform for him, and it wasn't a talent of mine. Modeling was a hobby and not a paying gig, so I looked for people to collaborate with that I enjoyed the company of, people I had chemistry with, which we could play off. That was completely lacking with the Law Man. He was sweet, but there was absolutely no attraction here, creative or otherwise.

Ordinarily, even if the photographer and I weren't on the same page creatively, I could find something beautiful about them—kind eyes, strong arms, a knowing smile—to fixate on and flirt with. But the Law Man was so physically unappealing to me, I couldn't use this trick. I'd never been in this situation before and felt terrible, wanting to hold up my end by helping him get the photos we'd discussed. But that didn't seem very likely.

"If you want me in distress, you could at least jab me with a stick, tell a bad joke, insult my mom, or something. Give me something to work with! I'm not good at this."

"No way. I don't want a reputation for poking models."

I climbed out of the tree to wrap myself up and get warm while he eyed me.

We'd only been shooting for ten minutes, but it felt like we were probably done, nothing was clicking, and this was turning into a waste of time. And we still had over an hour in the car together to endure before our day would be over. He'd been so much easier to connect with over coffee; I couldn't understand what had happened between then and now.

"I know!" he said suddenly, shocking me out of my head. "You're going to like this." Grunting and *mmm*ing, he fumbled in his bag. I backed away, suddenly concerned he might be reaching for something weird, like a dildo, or something scary, like a knife—it was hard to tell what photographers had in mind. So when he finally pulled out a length of dirty, knotted-up clothesline I sighed in relief while he looked at me expectantly.

"Neat." I tried to mirror his enthusiasm, though I didn't understand what was happening.

"Well, I've seen your pictures, and how much you like rope."

I didn't have the heart to tell him that the mess in his fist barely counted as rope. "I can and often do shoot things other than bondage, you know. But yeah, we can try using that if you like."

He was now full of excitement. "We just need to find a good tree for this." The Law Man angled his head around, looking every which way. I hoped this search for another tree would not be as intensive as his search for the first tree, which we'd used for only five minutes. Luckily, he found what he was looking for almost instantly and guided me toward it. The tree he had in mind now was thin and straight. His idea was that I would lean my back against it and wrap my arms around the tree so my hands could be tied behind it.

Kneeling, the Law Man ran the rope around the tree and my body a few times, loosely, neglecting my wrists altogether so that I was simply holding them behind me. He stepped away. "Okay, I know you can do this one. Now struggle against it."

"Oh, boy. I don't usually try to escape rope. But I'll give it a try." What I didn't want to tell him was that if I struggled in the least, the lines would fall right off into a pile.

"Okay. Do that." He looked unsure, the camera only half to his face.

I sighed and swooned against the tree dramatically. This he loved. Overacting appeared to be what he wanted, so I pretended to be tightly bound to the tree and in distress. His shooting pace quickened, the camera clicking frequently.

Soon the camera noises stopped. When I looked down, he was kneeling again and pointing to my cunt. I gave him a confused look. "What?"

"There's something . . . " He gestured. "Something . . . moss." He wasn't able to create a full sentence, but I eventually caught on. There was moss on my labia from straddling the tree earlier, and it was bothering him aesthetically. "May I?"

"No!"

His fingers continued moving closer. He wouldn't throw leaves at me so I would have a reason to frown, but he was apparently going to chance the reputation of cunt-toucher to get rid of this moss.

I found my arms tangled just enough in the clothesline to not immediately be able to move away, which caused a brief bout of panic as he continued to ignore my request to not be touched. I really didn't want his hand on me; the thought turned my stomach. This was my biggest fear in doing nude modeling, and now it was being fulfilled.

At the same time, I saw two power walkers coming around the curve toward us. "People!" Without explaining, I slouched down the tree and successfully out of the ropes. He stood in front of me as a shield, trying to act casual by smiling and waving as they passed.

The moment had slipped away once they were out of sight. I got dressed and picked the nature off of me, not bothering to ask if he wanted to continue. The menace of his finger an inch from my labia had closed me off completely to the notion of any further photos. So instead of strain and anguish, he left that day with a handful of sweet photos of me tied up in nature. They were lovely enough but not what he was hoping for. Which was the theme of the day: nothing had been what I was expecting.

And that moment I'd been dreading had nearly happened: a man with a camera had come close to crossing my boundaries. Not out of any malevolent intent—I understood that he had probably just gotten overeager and not heard me—but it was still a disturbing close call. One I didn't want to repeat.

After that day I gave up on shooting for a while to focus on seeking out rope in my personal life. I didn't want getting tied up to be my main motivation to meet photographers—or my longing for rope to be the reason I said yes to getting tied to a tree by someone who didn't respect my comfort levels. All the rope for photos had been fun, but I wanted more.

CHAPTER 21
THE FUCK(ING WITH FOOD) BUDDY

Kilty and I met at rope group, where, after getting over our initial awkwardness, we hit it off and partnered up to practice together. While talking, we soon realized we both had a void of rope in our lives and made plans to meet in the real world. If it went well, I hoped, we could become regular rope practice partners. At last, I'd found someone who wanted to tie me up for something other than photos!

The Sergeant's night-shift schedule made him difficult to make plans with, and the Priest still wasn't interested in rope, so I was itching for bondage in my life. And now I'd stumbled onto the perfect opportunity. At least for practice; Kilty was so busy with his wife, kids, and girlfriend that he didn't have time for anything more serious. Nor did I want anything more from him; he was too much of a dorky dad type for my taste. But we got along well, falling instantly into a happy, goofy friendship.

Aside from rope, we were both looking for an excuse to bake, so we decided to combine our passions into one very silly evening together. It went so well the first time around that we became on-again-off-again baking and rope buddies. It became our tradition to get together for cake and rope whenever possible. I would come up with a crazy recipe to bake, and he would dream up a complicated tie he wanted to learn. While throwing together the makings of a cake, we would catch up on one another's adventures. We crossed into one another's lives with months or years passing between our dates, regular guest stars in the other's rope life but never regular partners.

Kilty would talk about his kids, his work, and the ladies in his life—all the "normal" adult stuff that I could only smile and nod in response to. His dream was the opposite of what I wanted or understood. Still, I felt silly stuck in temp jobs after almost a year in Portland with the Priest as the only constant in my life. He was my home base as I flitted from date to date, seemingly unable to find someone fun, brainy, and into rope.

I didn't have my life together, but I could teach Kilty about cake and rope, showing him a complicated recipe and then providing a body to practice a tie on. It wasn't sexy rope, but the simple, nonsexual joy of simply having rope placed on my limbs was pleasant. Though it took some time to convince him that I liked rope enough to get anything out of our arrangement; I had to explain that sometimes it was enjoyable to fool around with a tie without the pressure of a scene or sex, just rope for rope's sake.

In our rope and baking dates, there would always come a moment once the cake was in the oven where I would catch him smiling at me. "Guess you should tie me up to pass the time, huh?"

His smile would grow as he winked at me in that fatherly way he had. It might have been flirting or it might not; I was never able to tell. "Sounds like the best idea ever."

I would grab our wine and lead the way into the living room, where the floor wasn't covered in flour from our messy joint baking project. In all of our time together, Kilty was oddly reserved and timid when it came to experimenting with rope. He stood an arm's length away at all times or knelt, sidling around me awkwardly rather than wrapping his arms around my body to apply chest ropes. I knew he was simply being respectful, but after explaining multiple times that friendly touching was welcome, it didn't appear to be sinking in, which made the robotic tying feel awkward.

On one particular evening, several months and a dozen cakes into our friendship, he was creating a complicated rope corset, remaining rigid and distant but friendly. When he was done, it felt like the real thing, tight and comforting. I ran my hands up and down the ropes, which felt like armor, the rope warm from my body, shifting with my movements.

Too soon for my tastes, he reversed the process by quickly pulling the lines loose, occasionally hitting himself in the face with rope ends in his hurry. He spun me around in front of him for ease of removing the rope, freeing me of the lines bit by bit, the oven timer buzzing before I was completely free.

I started in the direction of the kitchen before remembering I was tethered to Kilty, who held the rope ends. He laughed, standing to follow me and holding the rope off the floor while I located the oven mitts to remove pans of fluffy chocolate cake from the oven. With dessert tended to, he finished untying, leaving us another half hour to occupy while the cakes cooled.

"Now what?" he asked, looking at me, a little less goofy now.

"How about this?" I showed him a chest harness with fancy double coin knots at the front.

"Yeah! But you'll have to show me that knot. If you know it."

I taught him the new knot and Kilty was able to mirror me on the first attempt. And with his confidence boosted, he was able to quickly re-create the harness from the book we were learning from, sitting back on his heels when it was complete. "Not too shabby for a first try."

I insisted on seeing it, jumping up and down after giving it a look in the mirror. "Pretty!"

"I like it. Can I do it again so I can remember it for later? Rena will love this one on her."

"Of course. Go for it."

He was so adorably invested, his brow furrowed, the gears turning in his head as he saved the steps in his head. It was odd being the other woman in his life, the one that got time with him occasionally for platonic rope experiments. As our time together wore on, this became less satisfying. We became distant friends, familiar with one another's lives and lovers, but we never went further than experimenting with rope and flour.

Though I did feel a few curious twinges listening to him talk about having put the tie we figured out together to use. On one hand, it was flattering to be part of the process of him pleasing his lady friends, but on the other, I was envious. Not because I wanted him—he was plenty attractive in his silliness, but we wouldn't have worked intimately. The times I'd taken off a layer of clothing and exposed a bruise from my latest bout of masochism, Kilty would touch it in a protective way, saying, "Aw, I'm sorry."

I would look to see what he was pouting at and smile. "Don't be. I like it."

He would look startled, or disgusted if the mark was extreme. Nothing about my desire to be beaten or bruised made any sense to him. For Kilty, rope was the pinnacle of BDSM, which was equally baffling to me since I particularly enjoyed being restrained as an appetizer for rough play. Other than rope and baking, Kilty and I weren't compatible, making our odd "date nights" perfect for us.

What I did envy was him being another person who had found exactly what he wanted: two people to share his rope and romance with. I had the latter and was deliriously happy with that, but I kept hoping for the former. I didn't want Kilty to take me on trips for rope weekends; I wanted to meet my someone to go on similar getaways with.

But on my evenings with Kilty, I wasn't thinking about such things; I was too busy enjoying his company and cake. Sitting next to a man sweaty with exertion, eating baked goods in the hazy aftermath of being bound, and marveling over my rope marks was delightful. Finally, I had met a man that understood two of my passions and found a way to combine them. Life was good.

CHAPTER 22

THE ENERGY VERSUS EXPERIENCE

Sometimes it was those who had the most experience tying who were the hardest for me to connect with. There were plenty of people whose company I enjoyed greatly but who were on a different wavelength when it came to rope. Or people whose rope I might have enjoyed being in but whose personality I didn't click with when the play was over. So though I'd been bound by some very talented rope Tops, I'd found it was nearly always more enjoyable to play with a total amateur whom I had chemistry with. This baffled people who knew I had a connection to the Satyr but would then see me choose a scene with the Sergeant. Though I was obsessed with getting tied up, it wasn't *all* about the rope.

This odd contrast between real life and rope life came into sharp focus with the Hedonist. I'd seen her around the same small rope parties where I met and spent many a Sunday afternoon with Sock Girl. The Hedonist would walk into a room and everything would pause. Not because she was loud or outgoing but because there was an instant shift in the energy of the room when she arrived. Quiet sensuality oozed off of her, perhaps because very soon after making her entrance she would disrobe completely, as casually as most folks removed a coat.

She was so intimidating that for over a year I was unable to do more than smile in her direction. As I watched her from afar, the Hedonist seemed to represent everything I wished I had the guts to be. She appeared to always be doing rope, even getting paid to tie, and she was a highly sought rope partner with a constantly full dance card, whereas I was lucky to have an opportunity to play with rope once a month.

When she did eventually notice me and introduced herself I realized how easy she was to interact with; I'd been intimidated for no reason. In fact, it was soothing to be in her presence, as if her serenity were contagious, which made her even more curious to my anxious and constantly spinning brain.

After a brief chat that afternoon, it shocked me when she said, "We should get together outside of here for rope sometime."

"Okay!" I said, not allowing myself to overthink. I was, however, more than a little nervous about going to a woman's house for rope shenanigans. It was only my second time getting tied up by a lady, which felt like a big deal because it happened so infrequently. And this wasn't just any woman; she was gorgeous and dominated people for a living. It was daunting to imagine a scene with her.

Standing on the front stoop of her tiny home, I knocked for so long I worried about having the wrong address. When the house went quiet, I realized a vacuum had been running and drowning me out. This time when I made myself known I heard a tiny dog barking, along with distant requests that the barking stop. Listening to the Hedonist bargain with her dog had me smirking before she opened the door; she was just like everyone else: doing chores and calming an overexcited pet. Seeing her everyday life went a long way toward knocking her off the pedestal of perfection I had placed her on. From there I was more at ease.

Closing the door behind us, she pulled me in for a hug, as the tiny Jack Russell at our feet barked adorably before leading the way into the living room. The little fella sat in my lap while I got to know the Hedonist.

"I can get rid of him if you want."

"Don't you dare." I cuddled him to my chest like the crazy dog lady I was and settled into her spacious, heavily pillowed couch. The Hedonist perched catlike in a plush chair and handed me a mug of fragrant tea to wrap my hands around against the chill of her house.

"The heat is fickle as of late, but this should help." The Hedonist sipped at her cup of warm liquid, looking at me in a way that made me feel like it was my turn to talk.

"You have a lot of sex and spirituality books," I said, revealing myself as a puerile nerd while gesturing to her many shelves of titles about spirit molecules and sacred kink.

This was apparently the right topic to get her talking, so I sat back, listening as the Hedonist revealed herself. She had fascinating ideas and saw the world in a different way than most people. It was all pleasure, pathways to altered forms of consciousness, and other esoterica. There were a lot of big ideas tossed around, and if the Priest had been there, he would have been riveted. They could have talked about ayahuasca and neuro-linguistic programming all night. But at the time none of this was interesting to me. I found talking about higher planes of consciousness dull in the way only a person in her late 20s who is positive she knows everything and has it all figured out can be bored.

Altered states were especially unappealing to me at the time because I thought remembering and clarity were so important. I didn't have the ability to chill out in the way the Hedonist suggested; I was too busy recalling everything that had ever happened in vivid detail. It would be years before I learned the value of forgiving and forgetting (or the absolute beauty of psychedelic vacations from reality). The me that sat with the Hedonist was so tightly wound it was impossible for her to think of letting go, which is part of why I needed to get tied up so frequently, to be forced into relinquishing control.

The Hedonist and I were very different people, so as we conversed, our walls went up in the course of defending our individual worldviews. My sober, self-reliant reality and her big, open universe full of love and connection kept rubbing up against one another until we gave up on the strange silences and miscommunications. But when the Hedonist got up to sort her rope, she looked so excited the moment she made contact with it that the feeling was infectious. I stood to watch her put a sling through the hard point in her ceiling.

As I undressed, the Hedonist fondled her gorgeous teal rope. It was the color of tropical water, so turquoise it bordered on neon, a shade I'd never seen applied to rope. The notion of seeing it against my skin was so exciting that I rushed to get naked despite the cold. Once I was undressed, she looked up at me to say, "Okay, give me your chest."

I turned away from her so she could begin a chest harness, watching in awe as she circled me, reaching up to arrange a simple tie on my breasts. Up to this point I'd largely been tied by people who had a physical intimidation factor to add to the power they displayed with rope, so it was interesting to watch her swiftly tie someone six inches taller than herself. Somehow, her persona was so powerfully confident that I hadn't realized our difference in size until just then. But it was clear that size didn't matter: it was all about how well she controlled the rope. So, though there was no power dynamic between the Hedonist and me (understandable, given our awkwardness), she was definitely in charge.

As she tied, it was clear we were simply going through the motions. She was a lovely human whose talent I admired, but we had a kind of reverse Midas touch when we interacted that caused two people in love with rope to go cold during a rope scene. Yet we seemed invested in following through with this evening in the hopes of enjoying the experience. After all, we didn't dislike one another; there was simply a lack of chemistry. So I was taken aback when she suddenly broke character and said sternly, "Spread 'em!"

When I didn't immediately realize what she was asking, she slapped my thighs until I squirmed them open. Here was the Hedonist I recognized.

Kneeling, she roughly threw a harness on each of my hips, tugging me around to get at the parts of my body she needed. Effortlessly she was able to put me in a comfortable facedown suspension in the middle of her living room. I envied her in-home hard point intensely, imagining that she probably put it to use at every opportunity.

Once she had me up and rigged about a foot off the floor, she crawled underneath to lie below me face up, swinging me around and grinning like a kid with a new toy. "I've always wanted to do this!" She giggled while twirling me. Everything she did and experienced elicited a euphoric excitement that was contagious. I squealed at being swung around and smiled back at this beautiful woman lying inches below me.

The moment the Hedonist moved away, her Jack Russell took her place, following me around to lick my face hyperactively while I was still tied to the ceiling, swinging around in slow, lazy circles. It was both soul-meltingly adorable and bizarre. I love dogs as much, if not more than, rope, but the idea of combining the two had never crossed my mind. Luckily, my hands were free, so I could push him away when the kisses got to be too much.

The Hedonist stood back to laugh at me being dominated rather effectively by a lapdog. When she tired of the show, the Hedonist took my hips out of the air so I could put my knees back on the cold ground. She wrapped the rope up leisurely as she finished with it, one piece at a time, allowing me to spend more time in her remaining lines while she worked. Finally only the chest rope held me to the hard point. When she removed this it was jarring, and an instant chill caused me to shiver. She hurried to remove this final rope so I could sit basking in the space heater and slowly getting dressed. The Hedonist sat close without touching me.

Doing rope with her was enlightening. I could see why people liked her so much: she oozed sex and smiles, truly wanting nothing more out of life than those two things. But our mojo was off when we united, leaving no sensual connection to work with. Instead, she became someone I enjoyed watching from afar, vicariously taking pleasure in her happiness, always taken in by her smile and recommending her to people who were looking to play.

It went to show that just because someone had a lot of experience, it didn't mean they would be the best rope partner for me personally. The rope sluttiness of both of us hadn't been enough to make the Hedonist and I click. And that was okay. It didn't stop me from going to watch her at events, thrilled at her happiness and intensity, waiting for the day I could catch up with her unrelenting optimism.

CHAPTER 23
THE HUMAN MOBILE

There came a moment when I had to decide whether I was the type of gal who was going to ride a fucking machine or not.

This important dilemma occurred at my first BDSM conference where I learned that kinky people were basically geeks with more intimidating toys and more leather and latex in their costumes. They dressed up, bought merch, and attended panels the way they would have at any other convention. I was attending mostly for the classes but was also there because I had literally been roped into being a part of the opening ceremony performance that served as the kickoff event for the evening's dungeon party.

When the Satyr asked me to be one of his bottoms in this performance, I was flattered. Then I was terrified. Despite all the crazy things I'd done, at my core I was an introvert. I loved taking part in daring things like photo shoots and performances, but they took a lot of energy. Eventually I decided that if I was going to continue doing these extroverted activities, I should create a gregarious persona to handle the experiences. Somewhere along the way I started calling her Miranda.

In order to handle three days of a kink conference, I decided to go to the classes and send Miranda to the performance. That way everyone would be happy.

Walking into the enormous exhibition space on the evening of the show, it was no longer the innocent brightly lit room where I had attended a literary festival a few months earlier. In its place was a massive dungeon full of cages, spanking benches, and Saint Andrew's crosses; all the furniture a kinky person could wish for, lining every available space. The only clear space was a large circle at the center of the room where an enormous metal machine lay at rest.

The human mobile consisted of three heavy steel girders that a spun on an industrial-sized axis. The beam that hung closest to the ceiling was the longest. One model would hang from the center of it, and on each side of it, shorter beams would spin, each on its own swivel. One model would hang off the end of each of the shorter girders. The three poles were equaled out to our weights so that they balanced and spun in a pleasing manner as the five of us were suspended off of them. This whole thing would be raised with a winch to the top of the ceiling in the convention center ballroom to make a human bondage mobile with tied-up ladies on it.

A lot of effort had gone into planning this performance. Five models, three riggers, two engineers, and many yards of the Rope Maker's custom-made red rope went into ensuring that everything was perfect. But the evening of the performance didn't go as smoothly as we had hoped. Several of the people involved in the performance showed up hours late, which meant that two models were frantically getting their rope finished as the curtain was going up. Somehow everything came together at the very last moment, and I breathed a sigh of relief as the mobile lifted off the ground.

The crowd was momentarily silent as they took in the scene, but soon there was thunderous applause. It was exhilarating! The music thrummed. All the models were grinning like mad as we swirled toward one another, spinning from the ceiling on our individual pivots. The result was dizzying. While dangling there I couldn't tell up from down, but I wanted to stay up for the rest of the night; this was the best view in the house, as I could see people playing on the furniture below even as I hung far above the crowds.

After the song ended, we slowly dropped closer to the floor and my heart sank. Just when the magnitude of the mobile and how amazing it must look was starting to hit us, it was time to come down. The floor was the last place I wanted to be just then.

People were in a frenzy. They were supposed to be moving away from the area we were drifting toward, but not everyone was. These stragglers were the creepy, half-dressed single guys who inevitably show up to sexy events and don't exactly follow the rules. Most of them respected the don't-touch-naked-girls-without-permission clause of kinky spaces and kept their distance. Yet there was always that handful of guys who couldn't resist the urge to be helpful.

It felt like being a piece of meat in a sea of hungry sharks as we touched down amidst these men. I rolled away from the mobile as it touched down, but I was still tethered to it, which made me an easy target while I struggled to unclip myself from the steel beam that had lifted me. When the crowd rushed in, Miranda fled to a safe place and I was left there without my protective persona, wearing nothing but lacy underpants, knee-high boots, and rope.

This was how I found myself being nonconsensually untied by Milton, the stapler guy from *Office Space*, a well-known, quiet single guy from the rope group. He was probably a fine human being, but I didn't know him and didn't want him touching me, a fact I made clear repeatedly, and yet he continued to yank the rope off my body.

The Satyr was occupied with untying and attending to his partner, the Librarian, who was the queen of the introverts, so I had no hard feelings toward him. She needed him more than I did. But while he was busy I would have been perfectly happy staying in the rope, a notion Milton refused to entertain. He also obviously didn't understand that there's a ritual to removing rope, that the way that it was removed affected the energy of what had occurred. Suddenly, all the happy feelings from flying were being torn off of me by this person whose assistance I didn't desire. Once he had stripped me of the rope and, with it, my blissful rope space, I felt painfully bare.

Now I needed to walk, nearly naked, across a crowded dungeon to retrieve my dress with strange men following me, disappointed to be ignored. I focused on getting my clothes, stopping only to collect hugs and congratulations from friends along the way.

Finally wearing my scandalously short dress, I was surrounded by hundreds of people milling round doing dirty things to one another, whereas I was unprepared to interact with strangers. I needed to figure out what to do as a single lady at a giant dungeon party. Without

Miranda, I was at a loss. So, hoping to regroup, I was drawn to the one quiet corner of the room. There stood a sexy acquaintance of mine in leather pants and a cowboy hat holding a riding crop. He watched over several interesting and elaborate machines. And even in his silly get up, he was irresistible.

I'd been flirting with Rope Crush for a while but getting nowhere. It was impossible to not be head over heels for the guy. Tall, dark, and mysterious, with soul-melting brown eyes, he made me wet with unrequited lust. I had heard he built sex machines, but as I walked toward him to admire his toys, I realized this was my first time seeing them in action.

We had first run into one another at a rope party. I thought Rope Crush was just a weird guy who had come alone to the event with the intent of lurking until he found someone to tie up. Which was exactly what he had in mind, as it turned out, but he was also exactly my kind of weird, so we hit it off.

That night when I admitted to tying myself up on a regular basis, he responded with, "Me too!" So we talked about self-bondage, power exchange, and fantasies for hours. It was hot and a little startling to jump to that level of intimacy with a stranger, but he was the same amount of socially awkward I was, so our stilted conversation and silences felt comfortable. Somewhere along the way he managed to ask if I wanted to do some rope with him.

I didn't have to think for a second before saying, "Oh yeah!"

He only had one long piece of white nylon rope and a case full of electrical toys with him that night, so playing with him could either have been amazing or boring. I held out hope that he would surprise me with his small arsenal.

Rope Crush bound my breasts then ran the remaining segment of rope between my legs to tie my hands together at the small of my back. It was surprisingly secure for so little rope. I knelt there bound, with him behind me, as we had a whispered negotiation about violet wands and pain, both of which I was curious about experiencing with him. He was so warm and welcoming, and he was barely touching me. I was smitten and wanted anything he was willing to give, any excuse for us to make contact.

As he went about the business of plugging in his device and preparing it, he held intense eye contact, which cumulated in a raised eyebrow and his asking, "Are you ready?"

Unsure what I was getting myself into, I blushed and nodded. Grounding the electricity to himself, Rope Crush was able to use his own body to release energy from the wand. Starting at a low level of intensity, he touched my thighs then moved higher, to my belly through my dress, then on to my bound arms. The sensation was like a thousand hot pinpricks, the concentration of the tingling heat changing as he moved over the different fabrics on my skin. And the rope transmitted it most intensely; the electricity radiating through the length of nylon made the rope feel warm.

Soon he was kneeling behind me, our legs woven together so I could fall against his chest while he raised the intensity of the current. He continued to roam the front of my body, using his hand to electrify my skin. It was like being drunk, every sensation, every nerve ending both dulled and heightened simultaneously. Everything went fuzzy and warm around the edges. He hadn't once touched me sexually, but I was vibrating with lust.

Everything else at the rope party melted away, until he was the only person in the room and the hot sparks from his fingers that danced over me were all-consuming. His face was so close to mine I could feel him smile, his lips moving against my neck as he asked, "Are you enjoying yourself?"

Nodding, I rolled my head to rest on his shoulder. He danced his fingers along my arm, over my neck, and onto my face, making me go as still as a statue, my head swimming. I was so under his spell I couldn't find the power to open my eyes.

"Do you know what happens when electricity touches something wet, like lips?" he murmured in his deep voice.

I trusted him not to cause harm but didn't know what to expect, so I stayed absolutely still. He ran one finger along my lower lip, and

I couldn't help parting them under his touch. It was similar to the radiating smolder on the lips after eating something spicy; it throbbed and raced through my skin. I gasped and again felt him smile. He put down the violet wand as I leaned against his body, fanning my hands where they were trapped between us to feel the muscles of his stomach through his shirt.

When he finished, I was a puddle, barely able to hold myself upright as he untied me. It took a minute for me to find the ability to say, "Thank you. In case you're wondering, this dopey expression and messed-up hair means I had a very good time."

His only response was a wry smile.

Since then he'd had me intrigued. So when I saw the Rope Crush at the conference standing alone next to his infamous machines, I approached and watched his sly grin widen. His masterpiece was a device much like a black leather saddle mounted on a power source that made it buck around like a mechanical bull in a country and western bar—except the center of this saddle had been hollowed out. In that space two black silicone dildos gyrated up and down, out of sync with one another. At the swell of the saddle, a Hitachi had been mounted so that the person riding it would be constantly thrown against the vibrator while getting penetrated. Even with no one riding the thing, it looked scandalous.

It seemed exciting, but the notion of riding it in a room full of people was beyond my level of comfort. This seemed to be the same problem everyone was having. They would walk by *ooh*ing and *ahh*ing, but no one would ride it. Everyone was too intimidated.

I must have looked at the saddle one too many times while chatting with Rope Crush, because he asked, with a glint in his eye, "You want to ride it, don't you?"

Shrugging, I blushed. "Yes but no. I'm still recovering from being up in the air."

We watched people mill about, expressing interest in the machine but not wanting to be the first victim. After looking at it sidelong a few more times, secretly interested but refusing to ask, I realized that

Rope Crush could read my body language.

"Okay, Emily. What would it take to get you to ride this? What can I do for you to make it appealing?" My name on his lips sent a shiver through me.

What I wanted to say was, "You're what I want." But I knew he was unattainable, because it was common knowledge he seemed more interested in machines than women; I was far from the first person to develop an unrequited crush on him. I'd never have him, but if I was going it ride this machine in public, I wanted to get something out of the deal.

Across the room I noticed the Pirate. She had long, flowing black hair and the kind of smile that's sweet and naughty at the same time. I fell a little in love with that grin the first time we met and had never recovered. That combined with her wide, chocolate-colored eyes and plush lips made her irresistible. Suddenly I wanted nothing more than to be tied to her, so I tried something revolutionary for me at the time and asked for just that.

"You could tie her to me." I pointed the Pirate out to Rope Crush, thinking I was calling his bluff, that there was no way he could lure her over.

"Hey, stay here for a second and watch my machines. I'll be right back," he said, surprising me. Before I could stop him, Rope Crush was approaching her; I watched their conversation which culminated in him turning to me and pointing. She flashed that saucy smile while gazing at me over the top of her glasses. Soon they were walking my way as my heart beat nervously.

This is how I came to be tied to the most gorgeous girl in the room by the guy in the cowboy hat as his fucking machine watched.

The Pirate and I wrapped our arms around each other, resting our heads on the other's shoulder as Rope Crush snugged his line around us until we were trapped in an inescapable hug. Her chest was pressed tightly against mine as I breathed in the scent of her long, luscious hair. The music transitioned into something tribal and drum heavy as

Rope Crush used his crop, first on my ass and then on the Pirate's, to the rhythm of the music. When he hit her I could feel the reverberations run through her body into mine. It was sexy and overwhelming, and it was only a short time before he untied us.

Once we were free, the three of us grinned and giggled as if we'd just gotten away with something. In the quiet of recovering from the moment, it didn't take us long to come back around to the machine. Rope Crush and Pirate both looked at me as if I was the obvious solution to this problem, which made me turn a million shades of red.

"What? Why are you looking at me?"

"If you think it's so interesting, then why don't you give it a try?" the Pirate asked sweetly, which only made me redder.

"Okay, okay. So I *am* curious. But there's no way I can take something that big up the ass, so the point is kinda moot."

Thinking I was safe from the threat of riding this monster, I flirted with the Pirate, but I eventually noticed her looking over at Rope Crush. It's then I realized that she'd been the bait all along, distracting me while Rope Crush was busy behind my back. When I turned, the rear dildo had been removed and he was grinning. I had no more excuses.

"You should do it," the Pirate said with a look that oozed sex and could have convinced me of anything.

"Okay, let's do this," I said, resigning myself to the inevitable.

Rope Crush was suddenly animated, springing into action to prep the machine, putting condoms on the dildo that remained and the Hitachi. This was jumping a million steps up the intimacy scale very quickly with two people with whom I had no previous sexual relationship. Especially jarring was the fact that until this moment I'd drawn the line at sex in public, always keeping my underwear on at parties. That was about to change.

I slipped my panties off under my dress and tossed them in my purse. The Pirate flashed me that spectacular smile, which comforted me enough that I jumped onto the machine before I could change my mind. The dildo slipped in, and I took a moment to absorb the sensation of being penetrated by something that sizable with no warm up. Rope Crush guided my feet into the stirrups of the saddle and signaled that he was about to ramp up the power to the machine.

With the motor humming, I held on to the fork of the saddle as I got my brains scrambled by the machine. The dildo moved in and out of me at an odd pace, never quite hitting a really great spot in my pussy, but I twisted the weirdness into pleasure as the machine threw me against the vibrator each time it bucked forward. This probably would have taken me over the edge if I hadn't made the mistake of opening my eyes.

A crowd of people stood in front of me, watching. These were mostly the same creepy single guys from before, except now they were wearing even less clothing while licking their lips like I was dinner. I snapped my eyes closed, hoping that if I couldn't see them, they couldn't see me.

The Pirate must have noticed my discomfort; she pet my hair to put me in a better headspace, which lulled me into the sensation of being bucked around on the saddle. The penetration was enjoyable, but the unpredictable tempo of the machine's movement was chaotic and difficult to get accustomed to, so I was thankful for her touch. Rope Crush knelt in front of me with a boyish glint in his dark eyes. He seemed to be enjoying himself, watching with anticipation as he stroked my leg. As much as I was enjoying oscillating back and forth in front of him, I felt serious performance anxiety. I would never be able to get off under so many watchful eyes, but I would feel like a failure if I didn't. So, in one of the least proud moments of my life, I decided to fake an orgasm for a robot.

I thrashed and moaned, putting on a show that must have been convincing, because Rope Crush eventually turned off the motors and took my hand to help me stand on shaky legs. At the last second I realized there was still a giant black cock inside of me and no subtle way to dismount it. I closed my eyes and jumped off with a sickening wet pop that left behind a dildo covered in girl goo and lube. Pretending to be unfazed by this, I hugged and thanked both Rope Crush and the Pirate for a lovely time and walked away to enjoy the party.

The rest of the weekend I kept hearing, "Aren't you the girl that was . . . " And I would hope the sentence would end with, "part of the opening ceremonies mobile?" But it was always, "Aren't you the girl that was riding the fucking machine? That was hot!" Not exactly what I wanted to be recognized for, but I was amused to be notorious for something.

CHAPTER 24
THE SOUND AND THE FLURRY

Mr. Old School and I had been tiptoeing around one another at events for months, sharing small talk and friendly banter but unsure what to make of each other. We both often showed up to parties alone, but neither of us appeared willing to make the first move. So I was curious enough to say yes when I saw him at the kink conference and he finally asked, "Want to find me for a bit of rope when you're done here?"

He had chosen the darkest corner of the room and a vintage medical examination chair, an untraditional choice for a rope bondage scene. Busy spreading open a plethora of bags that displayed an assortment of rope in every fiber, diameter, color, and length imaginable, it took him a few beats to realize I was in his space. This gave me time to observe him tinkering and plotting the upcoming interaction in his head. Mr. Old School gave off a calm and focused aura that was missing from much of the room. He was devoid of the aggressive or narcissistic air of many Tops, which made him difficult for many of the women in the community to understand. Only in this scene would a man who wasn't forceful and demanding of immediate sexual favors be thought of as odd or creepy. I, however, knew better.

He began by showing off the newest addition to his collection, a handful of bright-red hemp. "The Rope Maker spun it just for this weekend," Mr. Old School explained, "the convention special."

I grinned, "Did you see the opening ceremonies?"

"Why yes, I did, peeking from behind the curtains while wrangling the sound, as I do. It was quite the whirlwind of poetic rope artistry. A flash of skin and metal to get the blood pumping."

"That's the rope he made for us to use in the mobile. For all we know, it could have been on my body while I hung up there."

Mr. Old School's face lit up like I'd told him he'd won the lottery. "Is that so now?"

"Uh huh."

He clutched the tangled rope to his chest, stroking the ends of it. "Well, if that's the case, he far undervalues the worth of these ropes. I paid far too little. Miss Emily, I will treasure this length of natural-fiber lines that journeyed from the fingers of the Rope Maker to the curvature of your body, keeping it pristine and close to my thoughts. A jewel in a bag full of plebian buttons in comparison."

The riddles he spoke in took time to unpack, so I filled the silence by saying, "It does seem a sweet bit of synchronicity that you'll use the same rope on me now."

"Said so simply. Leave it to a writer to phrase something so poetically with so few words."

He began another tangent, but I knew that claiming a piece of furniture to play on was often a battle at a party of this size, so it seemed rude to make people wait even longer as he wooed me. We could talk anytime; besides, I was ready to get on with rope. To let him know we could wrap up the verbal foreplay, I asked, "How naked do you want me for this?"

His seemed unsure where to begin. "Ah well, I'm rarely asked such a loaded question. The scoundrel in me, that boy with greased-back hair cruising around for beauties and driven by lust, wants you bare. But the gentleman who runs the show these days thinks it's wise to keep you in skivvies. A specimen such as yourself shouldn't place her delicate nethers on a rough blue chair like the one I was able to secure for our encounter. Especially seeing as how I don't have a proper blanket to lay upon it."

I took off my dress, and he continued to spin riddle-like prose while binding my hands behind me. He was in no great rush, sure of himself but considering his every move. We had been in many of the same rope classes over the weekend, and I sensed him using a technique we had learned together hours earlier. Smiling over my shoulder, I mentioned knowing what he was up to. "Ah, the cat's paw from

Lee Harrington's class?"

He was stunned. "How could you tell?"

"We just learned it in a class together a couple hours ago, silly. But even though I know what you're doing, I promise not to escape."

"Well, no, you would never, and not because you're well mannered—quite the contrary, you are as devious as the best or worst of them. No, because you find your bliss in rope and wouldn't anger the deities that have brought you into their grasp by wiggling away. That would be Shibari blasphemy of the highest order. My passion for tying rope seems parallel to yours for living in it. At least that's the stream of feeling I've subscribed to, seeing you in rope."

I nodded in agreement as he guided me to sit in the chair. He looped lines around the leather arms and metal footrests, weaving a pattern over my body and the chair that left no wiggle room. Not that I had any desire to escape—instead, I relaxed into the slippery seat, enjoying the feel of the hemp cinching me tighter. I felt centered for the first time since dangling from the ceiling the night before. It was almost as if the happiness I'd left in this same rope yesterday was finally returning as the lines were placed around me with tenderness instead of in a moment of panic.

Time got fuzzy as soon as I lay back in the chair. My clammy skin was soothed by the firm neoprene of the old chair, the coolness soaking in. It was the first time all weekend that I'd felt calm and as if I could finally stop wandering. The biggest problem with attending an event like this solo was constantly searching for a place that felt comfortable; finally, I was with someone I could relax with. Mr. Old School genuinely wanted my time, my attention, my body, and to share an experience together. He wasn't just using me to pass the time.

When he ran out of red hemp, Mr. Old School moved on to something else from his vast collection (and each rope had a story, which he shared with me afterward while I watched him re-coil his lines). He wasn't creating anything fancy or artistic, just wrapping rope arbitrarily, almost as if he were going to mummify me with the miles of cord in his possession. The three enormous bags he was well known for bringing everywhere with him certainly contained enough rope to cover several people from head to toe.

I lost track of what he was doing and saying, none of which was essential for me to understand while he was in control; I could lay back with nothing expected of me other than that I react to what Mr. Old School had to offer.

When he blindfolded me, his voice became a pleasant hum, gravelly and comforting, just above the roar of the thumping music. I felt him finish with the rope, so much of it that I couldn't move anything but my toes, as everything else was cradled in hemp, jute, and nylon. The mechanics of the furniture jerked ominously as Mr. Old School lowered the chair to a horizontal position. Once I was reclining he came near, his mouth so close to my ear that I could feel his exhalations. For quite some time he merely exhaled on my skin while listening to me breathe.

Soon he began whispering. Not the vulgarities of body parts or actions, but rather something akin to poetry in story form, as if I had been bound by Rumi. He painted scenes of tranquility and longing with his words, his face never moving more than an inch from mine. To give in to his deep, soothing voice was like being hypnotized. His words overpowered the loud bass beat of the music, which faded away into ambient vibrations somewhere in the distance. All the while his ear was at my lips and his at mine, creating an endless feedback loop.

His hands floated over me, not touching but providing the heat I longed for, the tease of physical contact, which he portioned out in tiny doses, almost as if he feared touching me, though he was welcome to. I was too far away to tell him, "Touch me, take me, hurt me." Occasionally his hand would wander innocently to my arms and chest, supplying gentle sensations that would elicit a sigh or cause the breath to catch in my throat. This in turn caused him to exhale deeply, the warmth of his breath spreading across my body.

Relaxing deeper into the chair, sweat pooled at my back where my arms were tied. They started to tingle under my weight, but I pushed that sensation out of my head as Mr. Old School put a hand to my face. Cradling my cheek tenderly, he became bolder, traveling to my ear for a tiny tickle, then tracing the edge of the blindfold.

His fingers, suddenly around my neck, were a shock. Exerting no pressure, he wrapped his digits around the vital veins in my throat until his pulse became my pulse; our blood moving in sync. He increased the pressure for a moment, a threat, before removing the hand altogether. He said, "This hasn't ended, and I already want to bind you again, pull the tension lines to tease and release the nerves you've wound so tight. I crave the sounds you make, though it's hard to focus in this din."

I wasn't aware of making noise; the music was so loud I couldn't hear myself, the thump of bass so intense I felt the pound of it in my chest. In order to elicit a deeper response, he reached for a rope that until then I hadn't realized ran between my legs. He'd applied so much rope—so many ties woven together, like he was trying to assemble a puzzle of all the techniques he'd learned that weekend—that I'd lost track of them all. With him tugging on this rope, I arched against the sensation as much out of surprise as pleasure.

"The sounds you produce are magic. It's nearly making me drunk with self-indulgence, listening to you take this journey that no one can share but I'm witnessing. That moaning and breathing under my domain, delicious."

One hand on the rope at my cunt, the other hand at my throat, he stroked, pet, and teased. "Holding your chin, feeling you crave that touch and able to withdraw it at my whim is a heady game."

He moved one hand to my mouth, which I opened to allow his thumb trespass. Salty and earthy from the rope's oils, it probed my mouth. In the intimate wetness between my lips he held my tongue, and then he released it as he pulled the crotch rope again. This pattern of tugging and grazing my lip with his thumb seemed to go on forever. Eventually, when he pulled his finger away, I came back to earth long enough to feel my body and whispered, "My hands."

He raised the chair upright. First went the blindfold. Newly able to see the frenzy of the dungeon from afar, I was glad to be in that calm corner with him. A feeling of well-being came over me as the ropes were removed and my body gradually came under my control again. All my worries and anxieties were left in the hemp, to be coiled up and shut away in the dark of his bag.

When the lines no longer held my torso down Mr. Old School pushed me forward to remove the ropes from my wrists, where the tie we learned earlier had cinched down on itself uncomfortably. "I won't do that again. A fine cuff for a takedown but not worthy of an angelic moment like this that should have lasted much longer, perhaps into infinity. I apologize."

I sat up and used my newfound freedom to touch his arm, hoping to put an end to an unnecessary apology. He smiled wanly while returning to the long unwrapping, kneeling at my bound feet to fight at the ropes that had tightened during my movement. I was dizzy with rope drunkenness and pleasure, unencumbered by the emotional pain that had brought me to his chair.

When the lines were a tangle on the floor, he returned my dress to me as if I should cover up. Instead I stood, not caring to return to the banal world of clothing and responsibilities until it was an absolute requirement. I watched as he put away his ropes, and he seemed surprised to find me near. "Miss Emily, you're free to go. I know your dance card is full and you have many admirers. You've already given me more of your time than I ever thought I could wish for. It's been a dream come true to put my ropes on your skin."

"Let a girl come back to earth before sending her away. Besides, a polite rope slut knows the scene isn't over until the rope is put away. The least I can do is stand by and keep you entertained until you're finished." To me, this was part of the deal; our connection ended not when the rope came off but when both of us were ready. But it was true I had another play date; Mr. Zen was standing in my periphery, trying to get my attention. I flashed him a palm in a gesture indicating I needed five more minutes. He nodded and disappeared to secure a place for us to play.

"Thank you for the ropey comfort. I needed to get past the awkwardness of this weekend. And you provided that and more."

"Oh, you are most welcome. It's the least I can do, especially knowing now that you're the type of lass who will stay during the dull parts of the rope, the putting everything in its place. The others I wrap in my hemp skip away the second it's all over." It saddened me to think of the people who usually took up residence in his ropes, using him but not giving anything to the moment in return. He deserved better.

"Let's do this again, Mr. Old School. Now I must away." I hugged him tight. It was my turn to be there, to provide the space for him to return to reality. Smiling, I walked away knowing that as long as we were both in Portland, Mr. Old School would never be far away from my rope adventures. We were equally and hopelessly addicted to rope, our shared drug of choice.

CHAPTER 25

THE BUDDHA ON THE ROAD

Leaving Mr. Old School, I walked across the dungeon to Mr. Zen. That late into the evening the room was sparsely populated, making him easy to spot sitting atop a leather bench smirking as I approached. He pulled me into his arms, which acted as an instant comfort, my body already alight and longing for him.

From the start I couldn't have explained why this man affected me the way he did. And at that moment, months into our dalliance, I still couldn't understand. He was a mystery. All I knew was that he felt right, that our bodies aligned to create mind-altering amounts of pleasure, a passion I'd very rarely experienced before.

After meeting at a group photo shoot, I invited him out for drinks so we could get acquainted outside of the charged atmosphere of a room full of camera equipment. Mr. Zen and I chatted that night until we were hooked on each other, reveling in how much we had in common. Soon we were on-again-off-again fuck buddies.

He became a means for me to explore my kinky side and relieve my unrelenting sex drive, which the Priest was unable to satisfy alone. But it was when Mr. Zen and I tried to do anything besides fuck that things became ugly for anyone involved. If we could have kept our interactions contained to the bedroom, all would have been well, but we weren't that self-aware in the moment. We were so in love with each others' bodies that we seemed to wish for something more, hoping that same passion would appear in our real-life interactions if we just kept trying.

It was hot when he would strap me to the bed, demanding that I call him Sir. I wasn't interested in D/s (in which one person is always in control and that power exchange often extends outside of sex), but something about him made me willing to give it a try. While spread eagle with him between my legs, a breath away from being penetrated by him, he would look at me like a wild animal, declaring, "Say it and I'll give it to you."

I would whimper, pretending to not hear him. When I looked over my shoulder into his eyes, he would grab my throat, this time insisting, his words sounding more like a roar than anything human. "Say it."

Eventually, my body's need would lure me into acquiescing. I would say or do anything to have him inside me at times like these. "Please . . ." He would look at me expectantly, both of us trying to be more stubborn. "Please . . . Sir." The last word a whisper.

"Good girl," he would say as he dived in, fucking me so hard it hurt in the best possible way.

The problems started when he would attempt the same exertion of control when we were fully clothed, when I had no interest in being told what to do. So it left me cold and angry when, over dinner, he would demand. "Go get me a glass of water. Now!"

I would look at him like he was deranged. "Save it for later."

The next time it would be a whispered request: "Meet me in the bathroom so I can fuck you."

"Sorry, that doesn't do anything for me."

He would sigh, annoyed. I'd tried to explain that this fantasy was only hot in the bedroom, that orders given to me in real life made me see red. Now I can understand his confusion; sometimes when he pushed my boundaries, the payoff was increasingly intimate and hot sex, but other times it led to arguments and my not answering his calls. I was inconsistent because even I didn't understand what was bothering me. Deep inside, I secretly longed for what he was offering, a life with kink subtly sewn throughout it; the problem was the way he went about implementing his power. If we could have communicated outside of the bedroom, perhaps we could have found a middle ground where we both got our needs met and I didn't feel controlled in an uncomfortable way.

My ability to admit how much I needed BDSM in my real life as well as in bed hadn't developed yet. Nor had my ability to chill out and forgive Mr. Zen his mistakes. Instead, every time he tried to force a power exchange on me, I would take it personally, responding passive-aggressively. Often I would immaturely play with someone he didn't like at a party I knew he would attend, trying to show Mr. Zen that he didn't own me. It would lead to an argument, then to us hooking up for animalistic sex, clawing at one another's flesh until all was forgiven. The emotional bruises we doled out couldn't compare to those one or both of us would end up with after the resulting tussle in the bedroom.

By the time the conference rolled around, we were at a prickly truce that I could sense was the true beginning of the end of our relationship. Seeing each other frequently all weekend while in close quarters had put us on our best behavior. The uncharacteristic sweetness of our interactions—and his putting rope on me for the first time while using me as a bottom in classes—had me forgetting my better judgment and falling in lust with him all over again. The body I was fixated on was using the fetish I was addicted to, drawing me desperately closer to Mr. Zen all over again. So regardless of how unhealthy our relationship, I was hooked and wanted him one last time.

Normally he was interested in quick bondage, so rope had never come up in our play before; leather cuffs had been all he'd bound me with previously. So I was both ecstatic and frustrated as he reached into my rope bag to tie me to the cross we stood in front of that night in the dungeon. I'd asked him for this so many times and it was finally happening. But it was too late; I wished he could have stepped up to fulfill my desires earlier in our time together, or that I could have been clearer in asking for what I needed. But as he bound each wrist into a simple cuff and secured me to the hard points, I was too busy enjoying myself to think.

This tie left my arms spread and lifted above my head, my back to him. As he tied the rope off, Mr. Zen pressed his body against mine, roughly tossing me against the frame of the cross, forcing the air out of my lungs and making me gasp under his weight. Using my hair, he twisted my head back to him so we could tangle tongues. And at the simple touch of our mouths, the uncontrollable need I had for him coursed through my body. His goatee and glasses rubbed my face harshly, but I didn't mind; I wanted as much of him against me as possible. All of him touching me, taking me, and filling me.

He liked my simple black dress so much that he left it on, tucking it out of the way into my garter belt. Soon his hands were all over, caressing my thighs, pinching my nipples, and slapping my ass. He would move on to a new bit of skin before I could fully process or enjoy what he had just doled out, thus keeping me on edge.

Then he was rummaging around in my bag of tricks again, leaving me to wonder what his devious mind would decide to do with whatever he might discover. Before rising from his crouched position he slapped at my ankles as a silent order for me to open them, and I did. As he stood, Mr. Zen pulled my panties down my spread legs and tossed them aside, leaving me exposed. The rough texture of his dress pants chaffing my bare ass as he leaned into me was a comfort, a reminder he was near.

He teased with a small vibrator, pressing it against my clit, then moving it away, forcing me to buck my hips in order to make contact with it again. This game went on until I was moaning in frustration, clawing at the ropes that bound me and wishing he would keep the device in one place long enough for me to get off.

Finally he inserted it, and I sighed, clenching my pussy around it. He rubbed himself against my ass so I could feel the bulge in his pants as he growled in my ear. This sound would ordinarily have been followed by biting and hair pulling, but this time he fucked with my expectations by forcing a bright-red ball gag between my teeth and cinching it tightly behind my head. The moment something was placed between my teeth I would become pliant and full of deference, the fight pulled out of me with that small gesture. So I leaned into the cross and enjoyed the thrum of the vibrator inside me, waiting for Mr. Zen's next move.

He stepped away, leaving me waiting and exposed to the chill of the air. His next touch was a palm against my ass, the loud and sudden skin-to-skin contact echoing in the room. He fondled, clawed, and spanked me at length. All the while I rested compliantly against the wooden frame holding us up, trying to balance with my legs spread wide and occasionally bucking my hips to manipulate the vibrator into a more enjoyable angle inside me.

Before I knew what was on his mind, Mr. Zen was removing the vibrator and replacing it with his fingers, ramming hard into the center of me. He touched my cunt expertly, rubbing my clit until I was moaning around the gag, so distracted I was no longer worrying about being overexposed. This was only the second time I'd played sexually in public, and as we continued, a small crowd of observers gathered. I knew better than to look up or fully take notice of them.

Mr. Zen pulled the front of my dress open to pinch at my nipples with his other hand until I cried out and danced in place in a fruitless attempt at escaping the pain. "Poor sweet thing." He nibbled my ear as I whimpered and leaned into him. The teasing only lasting until he slapped my cunt to elicit a loud whine, and then he returned to my ear with teeth and tongue. "Can I fuck you?"

It took me a minute to puzzle out if this was an opportune moment to allow him to relieve me of my public-sex cherry, but I nodded in the affirmative, apparently willing to continue my weekend experiment in exhibitionism.

"Mmm." Knowing my usual stance on sex in public, he growled in my ear, excited to have swayed me into finally agreeing to it. That was another boundary he had been able to nudge me toward destroying.

Before I knew he had even grabbed a condom, he had it on. His pants fell to his feet as he rubbed his sheathed cock on my ass. I bent forward at the waist as best I could to allow a better angle for him to enter me, and he grabbed ahold of my hips and drove himself in. It was exactly what our bodies were calling out for, as the only way the two of us actually knew how to connect was when joined this way. Mr. Zen rammed himself into me in a frenzy as I moaned around the ball gag, keeping my eyes firmly closed so I wouldn't accidentally make eye contact with anyone watching.

As Mr. Zen continued, I reminded myself that this was our final evening of bliss; no matter how hot he was, I needed to cut the cord. So it was out of a desperate need for catharsis that I was fucking him where others could watch. This was so necessary to our farewell that I gave myself over to it, on the verge of tears. Not because he was hurting me—or that, in the greater scheme of things, I was terribly upset about ending my intimacy with him—but because this was one more experiment that had failed. This farewell fuck contained all the sadness and frustration we had doled out to each other combined with the ecstasy of the moment, all for anyone to watch. I had never felt as vulnerable as I did tied to that cross. I breathed in time with him and forced away the tears. It felt like being forced in two by him delving so deeply to the center of me, emotionally and physically.

Soon he finished inside me with a grunt and disentangled himself, leaving me for several endless minutes, exposed, empty, and clinging to the cross, longing for more of his touch. Standing there waiting, I was a sweaty, emotional mess and wished for nothing more than to be invisible, to skip ahead and already be home in bed with my dog friend.

When Mr. Zen ran his hands up my body to remove the ball gag, the trail his fingers had traveled left me cold. Mr. Zen then untied my arms and I rubbed them back to life as he helped me crumple to a pile on the ground while I attempted to collect myself. He held me as we came back to earth together; I was quivering as much from emotional confusion as pleasure.

Curled up in his strong arms, I wondered if I could ever be satisfied. I had everything I had ever wanted but still was searching for more. Always wandering, waiting, wanting, wishing. Kindness and rope would never be enough. If they were, my search would be over. I had people like Kilty and Sock Girl for that. And cruelty in rope wasn't enough either, or the Sergeant would have filled the need. What I was missing was some intensity of connection, someone cruel and calculating in beautiful ways, someone to keep me on my toes and keep to their word.

Love and sex weren't lacking in my life. All that was lacking was this mysterious, nameless spark I'd yet to find in anyone I enjoyed enough to have a deeper relationship with. A spark that I kept confusing with the lust I felt for men that had a glint of debauchery in their eye. Something I had to hope was out there waiting for me. I'd found the Priest, so I figured I should be able to find my ropey other half somewhere as well.

But that person wasn't here in this room, so I walked out into the night alone, watching Mr. Zen walk in the opposite direction after a passionate kiss good-bye. I was through with settling. I wanted the real thing; a rope soul mate, whatever that might look like.

CHAPTER 26
THE ONE THAT GOT AWAY

One day the Nomad appeared in Portland, and suddenly he was everywhere, walking silently into every fetish event clad in his Matrix-style, long, black coat and carrying a dark leather satchel. He seemed to be cloaked in a shield of invisibility due to his preternatural quietness and slightness of frame. As a fellow terminally quiet person, I found him endlessly interesting, but our shared shyness also made it difficult for us to find an excuse to speak. However, my inner introvert's detective agency was able to conclude, over a few weeks of finding myself in the same room with him, that he was British and in town for a matter of months on his way to Asia, where a job awaited him. He was a switch and a tightrope walker; the Nomad got more fascinating each time I learned more about him.

As time went on I circled closer to him, thinking about talking to him then scampering away anytime he would look in my direction. I didn't believe he had any interest in conversing with me, because each time we were introduced he would say hello and nothing else. I found out later that the Nomad had been intimidated into silence by what he thought was my obviously outgoing personality after seeing my modeling portfolio and noticing me easily chatting with people I was well acquainted with. So he was waiting for me, the supposed extrovert, to initiate a conversation. He didn't reveal this until months later, when we realized that talking via email was the obvious solution to our problem.

One weekend the Nomad and I ended up doing some very hot scenes next to each other at one of the Vandal's rope events, concentrating on what we were doing with our partners but continuing to make sidelong appreciative eye contact. Afterward, we stammered around trying to give one another kudos, only to succumb to sitting in frustrated silence. The woman the Nomad was staying with, the Potter, noticed us side by side, not speaking, and said, "Hey, do you know one another?"

"Um, yeah, but kinda, no . . . " We both sputtered.

The Potter laughed and facilitated a brief exchange of pleasantries between us that culminated in the exchange of email addresses, a revolutionary notion neither of us had considered before. Free from the burden of trying to talk face to face, emailing enabled us to send long, rambling messages about the delight of watching one another tie. We also shared our rope journey with each other, reveling in the similarities of our learning processes despite coming from very different places. It was like writing love letters to rope as much as we were wooing one another.

It became obvious we wanted to throw rope around together. The Nomad was only in town briefly, so it seemed as if the built-in expiration date would motivate us into interacting. I'd done so many other crazy things, I thought surely I could overcome our joint shyness to make a rope scene happen. And yet it never quite did.

During his stay in Portland we would stumble through the token five minutes of stilted small talk at every rope event possible but were never able to actually converse. The following morning we would do the introvert ritual of writing long, eloquent emails to each other detailing how much we enjoyed watching the other's public scenes and promising to communicate better next time, only to repeat the process at the next event. For a while it was endearing to only carry on virtually. At a certain point, though, I gave up on him, thinking that if our rope date was meant to be, it would happen. If it didn't happen, he would just be the one that got away.

Finally, at his last outing before heading off on his next adventure, we found ourselves in the same corner of a rope group, without partners. Miraculously, he broke the ice and asked if I wanted to do some tying together. Two people who swing both ways trying to negotiate who's going to take control is both adorable and maddening, especially when both people are trying not to be pushy. I eventually ended the battle of who could be nicer by turning away from him, crossing my arms in the small of my back for the start of the box tie that was being taught and saying, "You go first."

He faltered with the rope for a moment before centering himself. As he ran the soft, perfectly conditioned jute over my chest and arms to cinch me in, I smiled, imagining the stories his rope must have to tell. If I closed my eyes, I could almost hear the journey it had taken, traveling from Japan, where it was made, to Britain and over the ocean again to arrive in this florescent-lit basement dungeon; if only it could talk. The man behind the rope and I would obviously never sit down long enough to share those sort of stories, but now I would be added to the tales this length of jute had to tell, a teeny part of me going along on his next trip.

Once the Nomad relaxed into the moment, he was remarkably skilled, making me even more excited that we could connect, even if briefly. The room was the typical murmur of learning and giggling that made up the monthly rope group. But something about our collective quietness made the space that the Nomad and I shared feel silent. Nervousness tickled through me as I enjoyed his touch, memorizing the sensation, since this would be my only opportunity.

When we were close our energy felt magnetic, as if our poles had been aligned incorrectly these months, forcing us apart as the matching poles of our shyness continually bumped together. Now that we were lined up complimentarily, we sunk into one another. He kneeled behind me as I sat sidesaddle between his parted legs, head bowed and meditative in order to fully experience what he had to offer as he used me to experiment upon.

His body was small but he felt large, a looming presence that overshadowed his physical self, a quiet assertiveness that filled him with Hulk-like strength when rope was in his hands. I'd watched his sadism from afar at parties, wondering at how it was possible the Potter could be in so much distress under the fingers of this slight man. Now I sensed it up close—how he, like so many people who truly loved rope, was changed by it and was granted superpowers in its presence.

He was intimidating in a different way now.

Our magnetic attraction pulled us so close that I couldn't fall away from him as he drew me into the orbit of his rope. I sunk into his jute, listening to the ship-mast creaking of it as he pulled it deftly over itself, laying the lines straight across my curves. I enjoyed the small grunt of force when he cinched something down to tuck my body in harder and closer with his lines. It was such a simple tie, one I'd been in a million times before, but coming from his fingers, it meant so much, and the brush of his fingers over my clothed chest made me dizzy.

When he was finished I refused to open my eyes, having no interest in the real world. He sat with his head on my shoulder so that we were embracing in the way only a rope Top and a bound bottom can—in a way that meant so much to us both. Our breathing fell into sync and my body sang, every inch of my skin goose bumped and thrumming. My head had gone silent, trying to hear his thoughts and wishing we could hook our brains together, our bodies being well-versed in a language our mouths couldn't speak.

I don't know how long we sat there absorbed in each other, looking to the outside world as if we were doing nothing. It felt like forever and also no time at all, the way time only passes in bondage.

Suddenly someone noticed the Nomad and, recognizing that this was his last event, burst into our space to say hello. We crash-landed back in the unexpectedly bright basement with someone gracelessly attempting a conversation. Ever polite, the Nomad said farewell while I sat patiently until he could untie me. Once the rope was removed, the awkwardness flooded back into our interaction. Suddenly neither one of us knew how to use our limbs, as they had been short circuited by the shared experience. He kept floundering as he unknotted the rope. I gently smiled at him, saying over my shoulder, "Thank you."

"My turn?" he asked and we traded roles. I tied him so clumsily that the ropes were too loose. Lacking tension, my tie continually fell down his arms, causing me to nervously retrace my steps until there was a semblance of order. He smiled, but I wasn't sure whether in amusement or alarm at my ineptitude. I knew this tie, but I couldn't locate the files in my brain to create it properly, so the finished product had the neatness of a kindergartener writing her name for the first time. It was a disaster and I untied it immediately.

"Thank you that was . . . something."

"Shush," I said winking at him while untying, enjoying the sight of his arms crossed together behind him so that his tattoos, which read *courage* and *future*, touched. His flesh was something I could read, a swoon-worthy graphic gift. I let that image sink in before releasing his hands into a hug.

After that, we were both woozy with the experience, unable to speak to each other for an entirely different reason now. I offered him a ride home so we could share more time together, but the trip to his place was as silent and awkward as our other interactions. As I dropped him off we said our good-byes and mourned never getting around to a proper rope scene now that it was too late to change that.

After the Nomad, I became determined not to let interesting opportunities pass me by. Realizing how much of a shame it was to almost miss out on him altogether changed me. I became more obvious about my intentions with people, having learned to stop sitting back and waiting for things to happen or hoping for the perfect moment. I only regret not having grasped this concept before the Nomad left.

Now I'm left to wait, hoping that life will bring him back to Portland and I'll have the courage to ensure that I have a proper rope moment with him next time around. Even if I have to intimidate him into topping me, I'm determined not to let him slip away a second time.

CHAPTER 27
THE DISGRACE

"You belong to me," the Vandal grunted in my ear, sending a shiver of fear and arousal through me.

This had started as him demonstrating a tie while we sat on the wide-open floor space of his studio but suddenly transitioned into an exchange of power, and the transformation had occurred as fast as the flip of a switch.

The Vandal quickly forced me facedown onto the hard floor. Swimmy with pleasurable pain, I lay there yielding and waiting, keeping my eyes closed to the crowd that I could hear filing in closer to watch the impromptu show. I was suddenly glad for the dress I was still wearing, which protected me from their gaze, but not from his, as the Vandal's eyes burned into me from above while he considered his next move.

Slipping his toe under my hip, he angled me so that when he stepped on my rump with his other foot, this digit dug deep into a pressure point. He prodded this collection of nerves so thoroughly that I couldn't remain stoic; my instinct was to wiggle away from the sharp pain that made me jump and grunt until he finally stopped. While I was still recovering, he grabbed my arms and tucked them in the crook of my back, clasping them there with one surprisingly strong hand. Straddling my legs so I couldn't thrash away, he reached for a skein of rope and shook it open with a loud thump. Yanking roughly, he pulled a length of jute under my joined wrists, tugging the loops of rope into a cuff that he tied perfectly taut.

Taking a handful of my hair, he suggested I kneel, assisting when I couldn't fully lift myself. Once I was upright he slid behind me, mirroring my position and pulling me against his body to wrap his arms around my chest. He dug fingers into the soft flesh of my upper arms at points of painful pressure, holding me so tightly that I bucked back into him, inhaling sharply to process the sensation. He had stole all the day-to-day discomfort from my muscles with this brutal form of massage, making me relaxed and pliable, so that when he doled this out, all I felt was the pain he created. This made everything sting in a more immediate way as he strummed my body for his amusement.

He seamlessly pulled the rough rope across my chest with one hand while forcing me to stay near him with the other. The ropes were pulled over my upper arms and chest, then back to the start of the tie and tugged tight, almost too tight, to create a box tie. When I was bound to his liking, he used the harness to tug me around, holding me at an arm's length and jerking me in a half circle in front of him to show me off to our crowd, displaying me like a trophy.

Before tugging me in another slow half circle, he pulled open the front of my dress, tucking it under the ropes that hugged above and below my breasts, to expose me. I felt hot with shame; it prickled through my blood until I bowed my head, hiding my face from the eyes of the crowd. These were my friends, so they'd all seen me naked, but this was somehow different; the Vandal was using my exhibitionist nature against me.

He yanked my head back by the hair again, tangling his fingers in my curls, forcing me to face their attention. "What's the matter? I thought you liked attention, princess."

To defy him, I opened my eyes, looking at the crowd of people who worshipped this man who had chosen me to toy with that day. Everyone in his rope clique either wanted to be him or to be tied by him. I would have felt sorry for their blind reverence if I hadn't been one of them, or if I hadn't been so flattered to have been selected for this special attention.

Rope Crush sat directly in front of me, smoldering with a smirk. His chest heaved, near panting as he took in the show. It was so vulnerable to be dangled under his watchful gaze that I wished I could disappear. We locked eyes for a moment and his grin widened, hungrily. My sight was glazed over, and I was only barely able to recognize him; I was already drugged on my own brain chemicals, which made my body limp with deference.

"Stay. Don't go anywhere." The Vandal had seen my moment with Rope Crush. In response, he jealously pushed me to the floor near the other man's feet. I felt him creating an up line so he could drag me off the floor by running a rope through the handle at the back of my harness. He grasped that rope while I heard the clank and click of him running it through the shiny silver ring just above his head. As he suddenly pulled me up, the jerk of being lifted was a shock, the air knocked out of me through what little rope was on my body.

He pulled until I was just above where it would have been comfortable to kneel, causing me to hover off center, letting me endure this uneasiness with gravity. The Vandal had no interest in allowing me to float away on a happy cloud of pleasure or endorphins; it was more attractive to him to keep me present and suffering. So everything he tied was slightly awkward and uncomfortable rather than blissful.

With my body arched at a crazy angle, I scrabbled up on knees and toes as best I could to meet his tugs against gravity. Sometimes I lost balance completely and careened in circles, spinning until I could gain purchase on the ground again. It was nauseating.

Soon he stopped me by holding out a length of bamboo pole that worked as a brake. He ran it along my body, teasing, until finally he decided on tormenting the curve of my calf where it was stretched and tense to hold my weight. Tucking the smooth, cold pole against my tight leg muscles caused a noise like a gurgled cry to jump from my lips. He snickered and repeated this contortion of body and bamboo until I forced myself into a spin to escape.

I opened my eyes to examine the space for a form of egress, my body gone into fight or flight even as my brain understood this as consensual. At this angle I saw the Nomad and the Potter cuddled up together, mouths agape, holding one another as if they were witnessing a horror movie. He would later add watching me play this hard with the Vandal to the list of reasons he found me intimidating.

The Vandal prodded my other calf while I was distracted, and I spun away again, protectively holding up my leg and wrinkling my forehead in annoyance. This was real, sharp pain to get my attention, and it worked; I was very aware of where the Vandal was in relationship to me at all times. I was hyperfocused, so my breath caught when he uncinched the up lines that connected me to the hard point and let them go. There was a group gasp.

At the last possible second, just before I hit the floor, he caught the ropes and retied them so I was touching the ground but not free to move away.

Again, he used that sadistic toe, this time moving between my legs, forcing a thigh to the side as I dangled, my chest and head bowed submissively. His other foot, on the opposite side of my leg, pinned me in. When the toe between my legs angled up to my very inner thigh, tormenting my femoral nerve, I could only groan, as there was no wiggling away.

My head shot up, and again I was looking for escape. In my frame of view was Mr. Zen, arms crossed over his chest, watching over the rim of his glasses. This was a posture that once would have driven me wild with lust, but we'd broken up for good just days before this experience. It was baffling to learn he was there, having crept in late while I was otherwise occupied. A new wave of shame washed through me; it couldn't feel good for him to have to see my tits hanging out, playing with his rope mentor.

Grabbing the rope harness, the Vandal pulled me closer, farther onto his foot. I gasped, my eyes snapping shut as my focus returned to him. That toe moved from thigh to cunt, and his ankle rubbed at my clit in a strange way I didn't want to admit was sexy. I was quietly moaning while at odds with my body.

I didn't want to give in to the sensation, but the Vandal knew my desires, where to touch and tease to make me powerless. The arousal I was feeling was out of my control and made more powerful by knowing he could feel how wet I was through my thin panties. He explored with his toe, grazing my labia and utilizing the rope handle to steer me onto the bones of his foot, wiggling it to make me crazy. His goal wasn't to get me off so much as hold the maximum amount of my focus, to own as much of my body as possible. He was hypnotizing me with his ability to dish out pleasure and pain, ensuring I'd keep returning for more. In this ropey game of spin-the-bottle, he was twirling me as an offer to our friends, declaring his momentary ownership as much to them as to me. There were only two pieces of rope on my body, but I was totally helpless.

He tugged me back onto him roughly one last time before dropping me to a slump again. This time when he released me from the ring he brought me closer to the floor gently, teasing by lowering me then steering me back and forth, so that it felt like riding a wave, being tossed in the swelling tide. I drifted an inch lower, swinging in invisible water, fluid and floating. And lower, lost on the wave of his power, until I was back to earth physically with my mind still soaring.

He walked around me and finally came to stop at my side, dropping down beside me with his sadistic stick in hand. I didn't bother to squirm away now, so far gone that all I wanted was his touch. As a vessel for his cruelty, I'd take anything he had to give.

He used the rope that had recently connected me to the sky to messily wrap my leg so my heel was frogged up toward my ass. He sat on my other leg, straddling it, his knee at my cunt as he spread my thighs for the crowd. When he lifted my dress, I felt the chill of exposure. He then utilized the length of bamboo pole to alternately massage deeply at my gluteal muscles and, using the rough edge, poke at pressure points. Never knowing what to expect, I alternated between purrs of delight as he worked at often overlooked muscles and sighs of surprised pain. I couldn't float away; he was keeping me present and constantly reacting.

When all I knew to anticipate from him was cruelty, the Vandal shocked me by bucking his knee into my cunt, putting me perpetually on the edge of orgasm. And just when I trusted his capacity to be kind, he stopped, quickly standing to walk away.

I knew without opening my eyes that the crowd was behind me, with Rope Crush sitting closest. Though I could near their breathing, no one said a word as everyone followed proper kinky protocol by not approaching me midscene though my Top had left. In this state of loopiness it never occurred to me to close my legs or wiggle into a less vulnerable position. So I was left there alone, listening for any clue to what would happen next, open to the crowd's gaze. At first I couldn't believe the Vandal had left me, but as the minutes went on, my exposure and helplessness made me more aroused; he had known exactly what he was doing.

Returning to my side, he set down a glass of water, well outside of my grasp. I looked at it with great longing, not having realized how thirsty I was from the panting and thrashing until he placed the liquid just out of my reach. Now it tormented me, bringing attention to how dry my mouth was; I was desperate to be untied so I could drink.

He pressed at sensitive bits of my body with his toe while leaning in to unbind my leg, massaging it roughly as it was released. This simultaneously restored circulation and was a torment as he pressed at the pins and needles of blood rushing into the limb. I squirmed, trying to rebel, but he pressed my face into the floor with one hand as a reminder of who was still in control. He then dragged that same hand down my back, bringing a chill to my spine that made me curl into his touch.

Lifting me by the rope again, he pulled me against him. Once I was in his lap I lolled against his chest and shoulder, a tenderness he rewarded by squeezing my nipples until I cried out. He then pushed me forward to begin untying. This was a blur of tugs at rope while my body was tossed around. The Vandal moved me sharply, keeping me under his sway until the last cuff on my wrists was all that bound me. This he snapped open, dramatically freeing my arms.

He pulled me to him until our heads were close, and I mumbled, "Thank you."

His face stretched into a smile before he said, "I think you should go get some divine intervention now. Your priest wants you."

I looked to the far corner of the room and saw the Priest. Though he had been the one to prod me into having the courage to finally ask for this experience, I had almost forgotten he was there. When he sensed my looking in his direction, a huge smile crossed his face.

"How was it?" he asked, arms wide to welcome me as I stumbled toward to him. Though we'd come a long way together, the Priest still didn't understand this portion of my life, so he'd never seen me this far gone after a rough scene, loopy and full of happy chemicals.

"Awesome!" I said, popping up out of his arms and smiling at him long enough to fully express my joy before falling back against his comforting chest.

"Good." He pet my head until I felt him look up. Soon Sock Girl was prancing over to us. (I wasn't looking, but I would have recognized her giggles and bubbly voice anywhere). He whispered over my head, "Join us."

"Rope, is . . . so good. The Vandal. Yum," I said, sounding drunk, repeatedly tripping over my words.

"Wait, you played with him . . . finally! And I missed it?" I nodded, all excitement and smiles. She giggled again and stroked my head. "Oh, honey. You're adorable and so freaking rope high. It was good?" I nodded.

More giggling from Sock Girl. She'd been the most enthusiastic in suggesting I ask him to tie me up, emphasizing how much of a positive experience a scene with him could be. She'd played with him a number of times and had nothing but great things to say, which seemed to be the consensus among those who had experienced his rope.

Leaning into my ear, where the Priest couldn't hear, she said, "I told you!"

I smiled gently, managing to grab her arm and pull her to the couch next to us for a celebratory group cuddle. After that day, I couldn't stop talking about being in the Vandal's ropes. It really had been the transformative experience that others had described. I'd learned so much about rope and pain from being tied by him just once. And if that was what he had to offer in public, while I was fully clothed, I was excited to find out what else was possible with him.

• • •

Months later I was in the Vandal's kitchen while he dithered in the shower. I didn't know my way around his space but was making due. After all that he'd done for me—connecting me with talented folks I wouldn't otherwise have met, offering me acupuncture free of charge, rope lessons—I felt as if I owed him this meal.

We'd progressed quickly from two people who passed each other by without talking to weekly dinner and rope dates in his high-ceilinged rope dojo. I would cook while we caught up. After the meal he would give me a brutal massage or acupuncture session, manipulating my body until it was without pain before he would put rope on it. First he'd make my body worship him by healing every ache, then he would tie me sadistically. His touch was the equivalent of taking off uncomfortable shoes after a long day, a full-body sigh of relief at the miracle of being entirely without bodily discomfort. It was dreamy, and yet many of the most intense rope scenes I'd ever experienced also came at the hands of the Vandal.

After the rope was removed, he would place my hands on his body, showing me how to massage or masturbate him, teaching me about his body as he had learned about mine. Sometimes when the mood hit, he would languidly lap at my cunt and I would return the oral favors until we were satiated. But that was as far as things went, as neither of us had an interest just then in exploring a further emotional or sexual connection.

Sitting on the couch, enjoying the warm buzz of alcohol washing through me as I watched the sun set through his west-facing, floor-to-ceiling windows that night, I felt a peace and hope for the future that I'd lost sight of in the preceding months. Without my having shared the specifics, he seemed to intuitively grasp my struggle with depression and food allergies, insisting on curing those ills with an irresistible combination of rope and acupuncture needles.

Though he wasn't talented at interacting with people, the Vandal was gifted with the skill of healing them. He often knew people's bodies better than they did. His ability to effortlessly end whatever suffering a person was enduring, using only his hands, made it easy to fall under his spell. But as much as he got off on healing people, the Vandal enjoyed hurting many of those same bodies with rope as well. This made his particular brand of sadistic play amazing to watch, even more so now that I was experiencing it on a regular basis for myself. It felt like perhaps I'd finally found the ropemance I'd been longing for.

The Vandal was also what people would politely refer to as "a character." He looked and dressed like a cross between a Zen master stereotype and a stoned hippie and spoke in sarcastic riddles. During our first moment alone together, he said, "Don't worry, I have no interest in fucking you. You wouldn't be able to handle my chi anyway." I laughed it off, thinking, *That's just the Vandal; sarcastic and strange.*

More frequent were the moments when we connected and I felt blessed with seeing something very few people witnessed: the human side under his cynicism. So I took every opportunity to attend his classes and go to his Sunday rope parties, especially as we became closer in the whirlwind of his wife leaving him. I assumed that he, though momentarily prickly with stress, was harmless. His eccentricities were well-known and seemed to be part of what made him the guru of the rope community and a respected rope instructor. It was the perfect situation for my overwhelming desire to get tied up to subdue my logic and reason, allowing me to fall for him very quickly.

So we sat this particular evening watching the sun set in his warm loft, the remains of our dinner in front of us, each holding a nearly empty glass of wine as our arms slowly drifted closer. This was the beginning of his glacial pace of seduction. Though we had a spark, it was a heat that we could only unlock after a glass of wine and a long conversation.

Just as I thought he'd drifted off in his head, the Vandal reached for my glass, setting it aside and pulling me to the floor. He was on top before I knew what to expect, working at my muscles as he lay above me to dig elbows into the pain, using discomfort to make what was there before disappear. He stole my stress away before turning me over, our mouths on one another in a flurry of tongues. As this moment lingered, it felt so normal and vanilla that I was confused. We'd both voiced distaste for sexuality without a hint of power exchange, and yet here we were touching and tangling bodies as equals.

Where was the rope? It had been weeks since he'd tied me up, and I was missing that connection. I wondered if he'd lost interest in me, but as I pulled away to ask, he slid down my body to pull off my underwear, leaving my skirt in place. His hand drifted toward my cunt, fingering me under my clothes and drawing me back into the moment. I tried to return the favor, reaching for his crotch, but he pulled me away, tugging at me until I was straddling him.

"Come here," he said guiding me up his body to slip his head between my legs where he could lap at me, his tongue delving into my cunt. He ran hands up my body, working them under my shirt to caress and fondle my nipples until they were hard and at attention.

This would have been delightful if I enjoyed gentle sexual contact. Instead I was longing for a pinch, slap, or bite; anything that would have asserted his dominance. I could have gotten this tenderness from anyone, being treated gently wasn't why I spent time with the Vandal, and it was so unlike him to be tender that it was startling. I tried to roll off of him and transition into something else, but he held my hips, keeping me on top while redoubling the efforts of his tongue. This was utterly unexciting to me, so again I tried to stand, but he held me still, looking up at me with a suggestion that I accept the sensation he was providing.

Realizing that he wasn't going to let me go until I'd climaxed, I moaned and groaned as if I'd come in order to put an end to this moment. As soon as I completed this performance, he pushed me off of his face, wiped his beard and grinned at me. Maybe he didn't read bodies as perfectly as I'd imagined.

Sitting up, he asked, "Want to do something for me?"

Since we had drawn the line at becoming play partners who often ended our time together with mutual oral favors I thought it would be rope or blow-job related, and said, "Of course."

"Come with me."

I took the Vandal's hand to follow him to his bedroom, a place I'd never been invited before, seeing as we weren't lovers. We were fully clothed and he had been considerate of my boundaries up to this point so I wrote him off as harmless, thinking I would simply put him to bed and head home.

He explained that all he wanted was some physical contact and warmth to lull him to sleep. So I crawled into his bed with him, tucked the blankets around him and lay alongside his body, hoping he would fall asleep soon so I could drive home. Just as I heard his breathing shift toward what I thought was him drifting off, he suddenly dislodged himself from the cocoon. We kissed again, this time with him tugging at my hair so that he eventually got me on my stomach so he could sit on my rump. This was pretty standard form for him to begin tying my arms behind my back, so I didn't think anything of it. I made myself pliable, relaxed my face into the pillows, and waited.

There were no rumblings of rope being located, however, and I felt my skirt being lifted. He was into dishevelment as a preamble to a scene, though, so I still wasn't concerned. I waited to see what he was up to, wondering where he kept the jute rope in his bedroom. It was so cozy in that moment that I moaned at the weight of him. The heaviness and proximity of him was making me almost uncomfortably hot, but I was at ease and curious about what was happening, near purring in anticipation.

His penis was inside me before I had time to register what was happening.

He sat atop me, unmoving, and the moment dragged on until he did finally move his hips, making his penetration that much more obvious and sickening. The violation of trust was so great that I was in shock. Time slowed down and everything became very quiet. I traveled outside of my body to overanalyze every sensation and detail, in this cliché unending moment. Soon I realized he wasn't wearing a condom, and fight or flight kicked in.

Too shocked to speak, I lifted one of my arms behind me to press against his belly, hoping to either communicate that he should stop or push him off. Instead, he continued penetrating me while twisting that arm into the small of my back and holding it there, his thumb pressed into the squishy veins of my inner wrist so I wouldn't pull it away from him. I winced.

This was many levels of not okay. The lack of protection in addition to the total lack of consent spoke to how very little he cared about or respected me.

I was struck dumb by the ordeal, unable to believe any of this. That he had tricked me into feeling tenderness for him only to violate me. That I would need to attempt an explanation of what had happened to the love of my life. That I had no idea what filth he was passing on to me.

My next plan was to try to lift myself up off the bed with my remaining arm to disentangle myself from him. Then a firework of clarity went off in my head, allowing me to realize the ultimate way to quickly end this. He was a woo-woo sex and energy guy, so if I went limp and stopped giving off any vibes he could misconstrue as arousal, he wouldn't be interested anymore. But I didn't realize how difficult it would be to not fight back while an unwelcome man forced himself upon me, to simply lay there and let it happen, never crying, whimpering, or groaning.

I turned off the part of my brain that thought of my vagina as a sexual organ because if I thought about him using the same part of my body as my lovers, I couldn't imagine ever having sex again. So I tried to think of him as something as inconvenient but benevolent as the gynecologist, closing my eyes and breathing while otherwise holding perfectly still.

Lying there with a man holding me down, I realized how shockingly quiet violence is and the silence a moment like this is ensconced in. Because this was not okay: this was not consensual, this was not sex. It was violence. He was taking something that wasn't his, something I had never planned to give him, something that was never discussed. There was no thunder or clamor or shouting, just the blood pounding through my ears. Everything else was far away and muffled.

He was extremely warm, almost clammy, but I couldn't feel anything other than his genitals making contact with my bare skin, so I assumed he had snuck his penis out of his fly rather than dropping his pants. Likely to lessen the chance I would figure out what he was planning as he rested behind me.

The whole event only lasted thirty seconds, but felt like a lifetime.

He rolled off of me without climaxing; that had obviously not been the purpose of this act. It was about control, not pleasure, not even for him. Adjusting himself back into his pants, he laid facing away from me, and I stayed still. My plan had worked—he had lost interest when I stopped moving—but I hadn't yet regained motor control. So I lay staring at the ceiling, wondering how to get out of his loft now.

Eventually he reached around to grab my arm, physically demanding I move closer. I snatched my hand away, feeling sick at the contact between our bodies. I was baffled at how he could behave as if nothing had happened, and at how I could endure lying there in his filth. It seemed like eons passed as I looked blankly at the back of his neck, oddly numb and knowing I needed to leave. As I stirred, he rose to walk me to the door for a hug. I cringed, feeling infected by his touch but allowing it.

Neither of us had said a word since the incident, as if all the language had been sucked out of the space. Out of habit I kissed him good-bye, walked to the car, and sat inside staring at the steering wheel. *What's wrong with me? Who kisses someone good-bye who did this to them? Was I just raped?*

Driving home, I was on slow-motion autopilot, dreading telling the love of my life what had happened. That evening the Priest had his new girlfriend over for the first time. I didn't want to ruin that moment with my bad news, but I also couldn't keep this to myself. It had to be said, no matter how much it would hurt him to know or that saying the words would suddenly make it all real.

I didn't realize then that this evening would be the beginning of the end for the Priest and me, the evening that would break us apart while bonding him to his new lady friend, the woman he's now deliriously happy with. We would never be able to get beyond this trauma, though we tried to convince ourselves that we were an exception to the rule, that our bond was so strong we would make it through. Unfortunately that wasn't possible, not even for us.

When I was finally able to walk from the car and open the door to the kitchen, where the Priest was cleaning up after dinner, he knew instantly something was going on but allowed me to lead the conversation.

"How was your night?" I asked.

I could see how happy he was, but I was barely able to listen to the fun he'd had, knowing I was on the verge of ruining his night when he asked, "How was yours?"

I began my story by saying, "I think the Vandal just raped me . . ."

He looked as if I'd punched him. "I'm so sorry. Do you want to come here?" He held out his arms, but I couldn't bear to be touched yet. "Do you want me to go beat the shit out of him?"

I shook my head and slumped in on myself. In the silence that ensued, I watched the Priest process how violated he also felt. He'd trusted the Vandal, attending his parties even though he didn't particularly enjoy rope, giving the Vandal glowing recommendations and openly supporting our burgeoning relationship.

He fumed, screaming into a sky that couldn't respond. This is what broke me open as I began to spew forth every tiny detail, thought, and emotion until I was empty. I paced the apartment, threw small unbreakable things, and swore, a lot. Our dog friend tried to calm us, inserting herself into the room to lick at our legs, but neither of us could be brought back to earth just then. When she lay down next to me with a sigh, that's when I cried. Curled into a ball in the Priest's arms like a baby, I wept while he held me.

Once it was all out, I was back to numb and strangely okay, all things considered. Empty of tears, I spent most of an hour in the shower, went to bed, and slept like the dead for most of the next day.

In an attempt to understand how my journey in rope had brought me to the Vandal, I wrote wildly that day, unpacking how I had believed the beautiful things everyone had to say about him, thinking that getting close to him was a good idea, and realizing that my desperation for rope had helped to blind me to his true nature. It was tempting to say I would never have sex or explore rope again because they had played a part in bringing me to something as ugly as the Vandal. So I wrote about the best of my experiences, along with the worst, until my love for rope made sense again. I still loved it. He didn't get to take that away from me.

Those words became the first draft of this book. It was my way of healing, allowing me to travel back in time to smile over twenty-six rope adventures, good and bad, and one rope disaster. The writing also kept my mind from spiraling into hopelessness as I reflected on all the people I'd met who shared their time, rope, and energy to make me the person and rope bottom I was now.

This just happened to be about thirty days before my thirtieth birthday. Needing something to occupy my mind, an excuse not to get too lost in sadness, I decided that getting my number of rope partners up to a round thirty individuals before my birthday would be a fitting project. It might even help me to learn to trust someone to tie me up again. The Vandal had bumped me momentarily off course, but I was going to take that pain and turn it into inspiration.

There were dark moments as those weeks went by and I waited for my test results from Planned Parenthood. I was terrified, making deals with a deity I didn't believe in while begging to come out of this sane and free of disease. So when I finally got the call from the clinic that all was well, I crumpled with relief.

Now that I knew I was safe, the reality truly hit me that I had to tell this story, with the hopes of keeping it from happening to anyone else. Soon I would find out that telling the world about the Vandal would be the most painful part of the entire ordeal, leaving me second-guessing everything that had happened between us and questioning if I wanted to continue being a part of the Portland kink scene, a community that had been protecting this monster for years.

CHAPTER 28
THE DIVE

The only thing I knew to do now was to continue making art.

I trusted the Aesthete—I'd stood in the middle of a covered bridge while naked, dodged traffic, and explored a condemned building that was falling down around us in the course of our numerous crazy photo adventures. He was one of the few people I was willing to model for at the moment. He was the most respectful photographer I'd ever shot with and was quickly becoming one of my favorite folks in Portland.

We had first worked together with the Satyr on a group photo shoot and fell into an instant camaraderie. I found it so easy and enjoyable to work with him that everyone assumed we already knew one another, so we just kept acting as if we did. He began inviting me to events around town and drawing me into his large social circle until I truly felt at home in Portland. I was glad to have been inducted into his band of brainy outlaws.

After discovering we were both from the same part of Wisconsin and shared similar sensibilities that were rare to Oregon, I wanted to keep him around and was glad he returned the sentiment. We fell into an easy banter full of sarcasm and flirtation that made producing photos with him comfortable and effortless. Then I saw the photos he took and fell a little deeper into our dalliance. The Aesthete knew what he was doing behind the camera. Not only that, he was able to capture the spark between us, an energy that somehow only seemed to appear when a camera was in the room.

With this in mind, we became muses for one another while utilizing as many amazing locations as possible. It was like a whirlwind tour of the best the Pacific Northwest had to offer, feeling at times like a vacation with a new lover: the romance of beautiful places, cavorting about playfully, and having adventures. Except we never followed through with the flirtation because the reality could never live up to the fantasies we played out in his camera while rolling around on a pristine, sandy beach together.

With that odd, distant sexual tension in mind, it took a long time for him to suggest tying me up for photos. When he showed me a picture of a waterfall with a wooden platform in front of it like an altar to the gods of water, we knew it was begging for someone to be tied to it. He didn't have to ask me twice if I wanted to take the long drive there and bring rope.

The weight of my troubles started lifting as we left town. I relaxed into the soft leather seats of his car, gladly talking with someone who didn't know what I was going through in the wake of the Vandal. The Aesthete felt no need to handle me gently. He treated me like he always had, which was exactly what I needed just then.

My relief soared as we crossed into the Columbia River Gorge where everything was lush and hilly. Sinking farther into the seat, I listened to his music, the thrum of the wheels on the well-worn road, feeling alive and well again. It was as if I'd left behind the negativity that had consumed the last month of my existence in Portland and was getting away from real life for a while.

Fidgety with coffee and drunk on sunlight, we turned off the main road and followed the seemingly random directions to this secret location he'd received from a fellow photographer. When his GPS chimed that we'd reached the waterfall, we were on a remote abandoned road, but all we saw were trees. We parked precariously off the road and could hear the distant rumble of water falling the moment we stepped out of the car. Nothing was visible through the foliage, but we could smell that the water was close. Giddy, we grabbed our gear and trekked down the hill in search of the falls.

Halfway down the trail, thick pine trees gave way to a grassy clearing that led to another, steeper hill with a waterfall running near it. Everything was wet and rainbowed with moisture catching the sun. I was in awe, reminding myself to watch my step instead of staring off into nature.

At the wooden platform we leaned over the belly-high rail to gaze down the cliff at where the water terminated dramatically in a swirling pool of water that overflowed to create another, much smaller waterfall at the ground. I was already looking at all of this through the filter the Aesthete favored in his photos; the greens a little greener, the water a crisp, high-definition white, the reds leaning toward magenta.

I got naked and knelt on the wooden overlook while the Aesthete set up his camera and pulled out the rope in which he'd recently invested. He put a very simple rope cuff on each of my wrists while I talked him through it. Spreading my arms wide, he tied off the remaining, long ends of the rope to the far rails of the deck. I looked and felt like a sacrifice to the water rumbling powerfully behind me.

I struggled in the ropes a bit while he shot from different angles, but after we got the one perfect shot, we were essentially finished in that location. While he untied me, I could see his brain spinning; the Aesthete was already plotting the next concept.

"Want to misbehave and crawl underneath here for a photo of the water without the railing in the way?" He pointed at a small, unofficial path under the deck.

"Yeah!" I fearlessly clambered down to this small rocky outcropping. Heights didn't affect me, so I crawled there naked without hesitation.

"One second—I need a reflector!" I heard him yell from above.

I was left with the summer air on my naked body, crouching on a mossy rock with the water ten feet across the gap, the mist of it hitting me. If I looked up, the tendrils of water rushing or trickling over the green rocks filled my view, leaving only a sliver of blue and clouds above my head. Prisms of rainbow light bounced off everything, and even near the thunderous volume of water, it was sublimely peaceful.

Grasping a small tree, I leaned over the edge, craning to see the bottom of the waterfall, the rocks gorgeous and lined in ferns. From there I could watch the entire journey of the water traveling from the top of the falls to the river below; it was hypnotic and perhaps the most beautiful thing I'd ever seen. The added bonus was that I had the opportunity to observe it all while naked.

While admiring this, a voice in my head said, *This would be a great place to die. It's perfect. How great would it be if this was the last thing you saw? No more pain, fighting, recovering. You could give up.*

I shook off the devil on my shoulder, but that cruel inner voice was tempting. This entire period of my life had been about sewing up the wounds left behind by being raped by someone I had trusted, as well as reporting my rape to the police and outing the Vandal to the kink community. Each time I thought I'd made progress, I was back to hiding under the covers, unable to be touched by the Priest, a man I loved and trusted implicitly. The victim-shaming and cruel words of people I shared my story with in an attempt to keep the Vandal from hurting other women were more painful than the rape itself. And now that I'd put my experience out in the world, these hurtful words seemed endless.

You should totally jump; there's no better place for your body to rest. And you'll die naked after a lovely day.

As I got drawn into the water again, thinking about how little it would take to let go of the tree, I heard, "You ready? I'm gonna stay up here and shoot. Just pose for me there." The Aesthete shocked me out of my reverie, and I posed like nothing had happened.

It's called Stendhal's syndrome, being so maddened by beauty that it makes a person lose track of reality. And I lost myself in it for a moment. Though logically I had no desire to jump, the swirls of blue almost fooled me. As hard as life was, I didn't actually want to die. Going through what I had actually made me more passionate about life. And there was no way the Vandal was going to have the satisfaction of hearing about my death. Instead, I'd be around for a long time, keeping an eye on him and doing everything I could to prevent him from hurting anyone else.

With that in mind, I stood up tall and posed for the Aesthete's camera as we explored all around the waterfall that day. By the time we were driving home, I felt more able to face another day after having created something beautiful.

CHAPTER 29
THE CARRYING ON

The Surfer and I listened to the far-off roar of skateboards and dirt bikes on impromptu ramps and teenage voices calling out from the other side of trees, their owners unaware that we were camouflaged amidst the graffiti-covered rocks. The oddness of this place was why we'd chosen it for our photography-as-foreplay. I'd suggested he bring his camera on our date even though I normally didn't mix cameras and lovers. But my norm had gotten me where I was, so why not try something new? I'd decided to branch out and see what happened.

At first we were shy, though we usually weren't during rope practice or over drinks when his travels brought him into town. But that afternoon was different: we were taking a calculated jump beyond the casual, and I was weighing the wisdom of letting him in and whether to venture into his bed.

So we sat side by side looking at the tagged rocks, listening to the cheers of children on the verge of not being children anymore, just as we were friends on the verge of being something more than friends. When our arms finally touched, the angle at which we were perched on the uneven rocks leaned us into one another, the force field that had kept us apart broke, and we were free to be ourselves.

Emboldened, I angled an eyebrow at the Surfer and stood up, hurrying out of my shirt. I was quickly rewarded with a view of his gap-toothed smile. Camera in hand, he looked over the rim of his hipster glasses with sweet brown eyes. I giggled and folded in half with genuine delight, disbelieving that I was disrobing for my friend. Of course I'd thought about him flirtatiously, but he was always traveling and had a woman in every city. So I'd never found what little time he had to offer romantically appealing. But just his friendly hug that day had awakened something in my body I hadn't felt since before the Vandal.

And I so desperately wanted to feel something good, even if just for a moment, that I was seeing him with new eyes.

Hearing the shutter click, I was startled into straightening up, so that he caught me midmovement. Squinting into the image, he declared, "That's perfect."

I gave him a dubious look and demanded a do over. The Surfer refused; instead, his hand dived into his bag. Out came a utilitarian bit of rope—not the finished hemp he'd used in class when we'd practiced together, this was nylon line for the outdoors. The sort of rope he used on his adventures in rock climbing, surfing, and camping. Soon that rope was on my skin, two lines above my breasts and two below to create a decoration for the girl who adored rope. The tie was simple and clean, an excuse to touch me. His fingers grazed my chest politely, but they made me smirk. He backed away to sit down, catching me off guard by choosing this moment to take the next photo before I could pose.

Wrinkling my nose, I asked, "Really? Again?"

His diastemic smile charmed me into goose bumps. He didn't respond, but gravity and attraction pulled us together on those rocks, kissing until we were lost, bumping teeth in an effort to get closer while laughing at ourselves. Before we could get carried away, he removed the rope, shoving the mess in his bag as I dressed. We didn't have to talk about what came next.

I followed the Surfer through the steep trails up the butte, through trees and rocks as we hiked the long way out. We stopped at the top to look down over the city, wrapping arms around each other while taking in the view and each other. The second half of the walk was littered with pauses as we leaned against trees, walls, and rocks to drift into kisses.

At his truck, we relaxed in its cool shade, sweat evaporating off our bodies. I took in the living collage on his dash, which was covered in reminders of his travels in the form of collected feathers, rocks, or paper. I added a tiny twist of metal we'd found during the hike, and he nodded approvingly. Hand in hand, we drove to his place, where we clambered down to his basement room. The Surfer only broke the kiss long enough to ask, "Do you want rope?"

"No, I want you. Just you. All of you." He tossed the skeins of hemp to his mattress on the floor, keeping it close as a reminder that desire was our only motivation.

He threw me onto the bed on top of the coiled rope, and we lost ourselves. And it was the size of him as we undressed one another that first time that struck me. His long, sun-brightened limbs. The broad and welcoming expanse of his chest. The way our bodies tangled perfectly. The general scale of him in comparison to me, especially his hands and their tender largeness. They were the perfect size to cradle my entire head in his palm or cover my whole face in the heat and sex-scented beauty of his long fingers. I wanted them all over and inside of me.

As soon as our bodies met, it was as if a door had been opened. After months of near misses and near flirtations at rope events, once we touched lips, I couldn't stop; the desire to feel his skin against mine consumed me. I wanted to feel his chest pressed against me more than anything, desperately longing for our flesh to touch.

Touching heart to heart, we threw our heads back and sighed. It was something so simple and yet so intensely right that we lay there embracing for minutes on end, soaking in the feel of one another before moving on to more vital flesh. Soon our hands traveled lower to discard further clothing, leaving us thigh to thigh.

He felt warm and right, and something about the beat of his heart near mine made me light-headed. Some people are an instant comfort; there was no other explanation for the lack of awkwardness or indecision. Our bodies knew each other instinctively. It was as if he were something I had experienced before and had been missing without knowing it. Something I was unsure how I had lived so long without having. Something I knew but had forgotten and needed to be reminded of.

He smelled like sunlight and filled me with light. I was nothing but the thrum of pleasure around him; all joy and no pain. I felt like a person without a past or future in his arms as I truly lost myself to him. I had no flaws or worries or doubts. He looked straight through me to the filthy, gorgeous core where I was perfect and whole as he stroked me at the exact frequency to fill me with nothing but lust and beauty for a few glorious moments.

When I was with him, nothing was ever enough—no matter how hard or deep or wet or intense, we both wanted more. There was something addictive about him, and like any good addict I gave myself over to him with no thoughts or regrets. I was lost in the sea of his fingers, tongue, and cock. Every inch of him was lovely and I couldn't keep my hands to myself. I wanted to experience all of him, to touch and taste and take in everything he had and then beg for more.

Please. Yes. Thank you. Again. Oh fuck.

I would have given anything for one more breathless mind- and body-quaking orgasm, which he elicited easily. Like magic, one lap of his tongue and a well-placed finger was all it took. I became another version of myself in his presence, one that gave and took without shame or a second thought, able to tell him exactly what I wanted and where I longed to be touched.

My mouth seemed to exist only to take him deep inside, to lick and taste every inch of him—that firm, slick flesh gliding between my lips and over my tongue to press against my throat. I wanted to consume him but settled for the taste of his come on my lips, dripping down my body onto his. The heat of this salt tide mingled with the sweat on our skin as we embraced and fell into an unbreakable seal of lips and tongue.

Later, lying on his chest with my cheek resting in the hollow of his body, I reveled in the rapture that followed our exploration of one another. I was coming back to the world, believing in beauty again. He had cracked open my shell and let me free. Suddenly what would come next was a blessing, something to be looked forward to, anything possible instead of everything to dread.

Before him I had thought to give up on rope, on men, on

humanity; I was ready to reduce myself to a life of writerly hermitude. Then the universe offered him up like a gift, a reward for having survived. And who was I to argue.

I couldn't have asked for a better present, one that tricked my troubled mind into being in the moment. I needed someone who knew little about me and had no preconceived notions. The Surfer was comforting in his newness, a place to start over, a reminder that there was good and pleasure in the world. He was someone I could let it all go with. Someone who fit my new mantra: "Would you like him if he didn't do rope?"

He didn't know he was repairing me because he didn't know I was broken. Feeling no need to be tender or therapeutic, he was simply his genuine, openhearted self. I lost two afternoons to him, and just as suddenly he was gone, moving on to the next city and his next adventure. He was like a dream or hallucination, something I could never be sure had happened.

It was perfect, as there was no chance for the brightness and pleasure to fade; I only had fond memories of him. I needed that: one person whose memory had no rough or sad edges. I loved his body intensely and without reserve twice, and that was enough.

He was the one I didn't let get away, the one whose body won out over rope.

CHAPTER 30
THE BRIDGE FETISH

Mr. High Jinks was the only person who jumped into this project on purpose, knowing that he would be written about by volunteering to be my thirtieth rope partner just before my self-imposed deadline. He was brave enough to email about shooting together knowing that I had resolved to openly record my rope experiences. It didn't bother him for a second.

We sat down for coffee on a strangely cold and rainy summer morning to discuss location possibilities for our shoot, both of us tired and feeling a bit uninspired by the weather. But we carried on, deciding to drive to check out a bridge I'd been obsessed with for a while. The other photographers I'd taken there hadn't been impressed, but I knew Mr. High Jinks had a predilection for bridges and would likely be game. And since Portland is a city of bridges, we had a few to choose from.

Once we'd climbed under the small bridge on an out-of-the way bike path, his wide eyes let me know he was inspired. Mr. High Jinks wasted no time whipping out his rope to create a sexy open-air suspension point on the shore of the stream. We had hushed negotiations about rope work and the angles he wanted to shoot from while we listened for any overhead thumping that would signal someone was passing overhead. While he tied, I stayed vigilant for the possible sound of someone coming toward us to avoid the awkwardness of being caught. Each time the bushes rustled, we fell silent and looked at each other intensely until the noise stopped, only to then carry on with our open-air bondage as if it was the most natural thing in the world.

Mr. High Jinks's signature was to tie extremely detailed body harnesses that were nevertheless utilitarian. Whereas most rope Tops tended to make either a pretty harness or one that would be great for sustainable suspensions, he created both in one. And he'd brought along new gray synthetic rope that he was excited to use. I smiled as I watched him painstakingly weave together a beautiful and totally symmetrical harness with it. The tiny diameter of the rope made the weave of diamonds and triangles in the harness intensely tight where it wrapped around my chest and torso. This rope was so narrow that it was possible to create very elaborate patterns, designs that wouldn't have been noticeable had they been tied with larger rope.

Once he had finished the harness and tied some of his lovely self-dyed hemp around my wrists and ankles, we were ready to go. At this point I realized that getting tied up outside was becoming almost commonplace in my life—it certainly didn't have the edge of danger I'd experienced the first time. But after twenty-eight years of not giving myself permission to love my body, I still enjoyed any excuse to disrobe, especially in the outdoors. I never seemed to get tired of showing nature my boobs.

As Mr. High Jinks lifted me, I realized it had been some time since I'd been suspended facedown, and I had forgotten how quickly it wore me out. The position compressed the chest and made breathing difficult, so, though I'm usually the girl who begs to stay up in the air forever, I knew I wouldn't last long with only the chest and ankle ropes to hold me. While I was up, Mr. High Jinks beautifully captured the lushness of nature under this rusty and graffiti-tagged bridge, working quickly. The backdrop provided such vibrant images that my bound body was almost an afterthought. Meanwhile, I had a blast swinging around and playing up to his camera.

Even when I knew it was for the best, it was always disappointing to ask to be untied. Though logically I knew that it was silly and the rigger cared about me more than the rope, it always felt like I was letting the rigger down or wasn't tough enough. My safety was most important but . . . rope!

Afterward I got to revel in the deep rope marks the thin rope had left behind. Sometimes this was my favorite part of being bound: the marks were like a souvenir I got to keep as a reminder of the experience, causing me to smile slyly to myself for days afterward about how they got there.

Since Mr. High Jinks and I had such a great time, we repeated the experience again the next weekend. Same photographer, rope, and model, but with a different bridge. This time we conquered a gorgeous red steel bridge in the north half of Portland. It was busy with bikes, pedestrians, and cars, but no one bothered us as I posed while bound in another of his geometrical harnesses. When he realized the true openness of Portland's nudity laws, Mr. High Jinks beamed. "Wow, no bridge in Portland will be safe from me now!"

And with that shoot, I had finished my project and inspired him to start his own.

EPILOGUE

There's a common misunderstanding that I'm so open with my body and stories because I'm an exhibitionist. What most people don't understand is that this couldn't be farther from the truth. In fact, I'm painfully shy and awkward, preferring to stay home alone with a dog friend than to be social. Instead, I tell my stories as loud as possible as an act of service. Because I can. Because I don't have a family or kids to worry about. Because I'm unafraid and can risk drawing attention to myself. This attention is simply a side effect of telling my story for those who can't.

I realized how important it was to share my rope stories as soon as I started putting them online. The messages flooded in: "Me too!" And, "Thanks for sharing. I thought it was only me." Or, "You're so brave for talking about your misadventures in kink—we usually only talk about the good stuff."

Then I posted the story about my rape and the messages turned into, "Oh my god, that happened to me too." Or, "I think I know who you're talking about and I've always suspected." And, "That's **** isn't it? He did that to my girlfriend." Or, "Thank you for speaking up about him; I've been too scared to say it myself."

As I read the words of those women whom the Vandal had also raped, manipulated, or abused, I was in shock. I couldn't stop crying as the many messages hit my in-box. I wasn't alone and I was furious—it was bad enough that this had happened once, but now I knew it had been going on for some time and no one had said a word.

At first I was livid at my community for not looking out for others, as this had been happening again and again with no consequences for the Vandal. Then I realized it would be so much more valuable if I directed my energy toward yelling louder, to a wider audience, about this terrible thing the Vandal had done to me and these other women.

In speaking louder for everyone who couldn't, it was my hope that

I would lessen the chances that he'd have an opportunity to do this again. I wasn't intimidated by his childish threats, which he and his posse tossed at me hourly, trying to shame or intimidate me. It hurt but it didn't shut me up.

Even as the police bungled the report of my rape. Even when the rope community largely turned against me. Even when those other women who outed him were shamed or ignored. Even when the district attorney said, "Maybe if you could get five more women to come forward, we could get a jury to understand that rape is possible in BDSM."

People only got serious about taking action when community members with big names—famous rope instructors, fetish models, photographers, pro-Dommes—got pissed when the Vandal violated consent at a famous conference years later. Finally, people realized it might be important to choose sides, though it would mean losing a teacher and a play space in shunning the Vandal. And though I'm furious for all the pain he caused and saddened it took so long for the community to catch up, I'm so thankful my rope heroes stood with me. That even belatedly I was believed. That isn't an opportunity everyone is afforded.

Though it cost me many friends and gained me a reputation as a loudmouth, I'm never sorry I spoke up.

And this is why I play in public: Because I'm that girl who talks about her rape, and everyone's heard about it. Because I hope that people, especially survivors, can see me enjoying myself, being vulnerable in rope and carrying on after everything that happened, and know the Vandal never gets to win. Here I am not merely surviving but thriving. I'll keep telling my story and you can tell me yours.

This isn't a book about rape. It's about my adventure in rope... only one tiny letter different and yet worlds away. It's about the mistakes I've made and the bliss I've found. I wouldn't change a thing, because all the people I met, all the rope I've experienced, brought me here. I'm blessed to have met lovely individuals and been a part of their lives and rope. And this is just the beginning.

EPILOGUE

    I've come so far from that timid girl in cow-town Wisconsin, and in that time I've learned a lot about life and rope, especially this: If you can tell your story, you should. You'll be surprised at how much it heals you, and it just might save someone else's life. Don't let anyone keep you silent. Silence kills. Don't let anyone tell you you're weird for liking what you like. Ask for it and let your freak flag fly.

    And no, I still haven't found my ropemance, my happily ever after. Instead, I found something so much more important: myself.

ACKNOWLEDGMENTS

This book is for anyone who has ever felt lost, alone, weird, or fucked up. Especially those who found healing from those things by visiting this strange land called kink.

These stories are dedicated to anyone who has ever been a part of my rope journey. There's a spark of you each time I touch rope, and the experiences and passions you've shared with me has coalesced in these pages. Thank you all for so openly sharing your bodies, dreams, and knowledge with me over the years.

Thank you also to those who contributed to my crowdfunding campaign; this book wouldn't be possible without you! I appreciate you believing in me enough to help me turn these stories into something you can now hold in your hands. Thank you also to the large and always warm Portland writing community that welcomed me warmly and reminded me not to give up, even when the journey toward publishing this book became complicated.

A special thanks to JSV and otto phökuz for contributing their photos to my book covers and P. D. Miller for the author photo. You all are my favorite fellas to shoot with! To HardestWalk for turning those images into very sexy cover art and contributing his services to the lovely page layout. To Susan DeFreitas, editing rock star, who turned my tense-jumping manuscript into the book you see before you.

To Vee at The Office for her endless willingness to provide space and warmth for my rope ventures. To Mo Daviau, Sarah Marshall, and Lora, who were game to be tied to statues for crowdfunding shenanigans, giggling all the way. To Chris Ginter, my longtime friend, editor, and sounding board for weird ideas. And to everyone who helped with my Indiegogo video or generously provided perks.

To Shay Tiziano, for writing a foreword that gets to the heart of my journey; thank you for understanding and being a part of this. And to all the other women out there holding one another up with words and support, you're the reason I'm still alive and able to swim through the darkness. Well, you and puppies.

Finally, to the other woman who stood with me and said "this is not okay" when no one else believed, I'm so sorry we shared such a shitty experience, but I'm so glad I met you.

EMILY BINGHAM has enjoyed being tied up since she was four years old and she has been writing for almost as long. It all started with jump ropes on the playground and progressed to a full-on rope obsession. She lives in Portland, Oregon, where she writes, teaches rope bondage, commits random acts of nudity for photography, and obsessively pets strangers' dogs. Her erotica can be found in a number of Cleis Press anthologies, including *The Sexy Librarian's Big Book of Erotica,* and online at www.emilyerotica.com.

Author photo by P. D. Miller.

www.ingramcontent.com/pod-product-compliance
Lightning Source LLC
Chambersburg PA
CBHW070559300426
44113CB00010B/1321